At the end of the Second World War, the Polish Allied Forces under British Command refused to stand down when America, the Soviet Union and Britain decided that Poland would be part of Russia's new sphere of interest in Europe. This defiant gesture became known as the 'Polish problem' and was extremely symbolic, since it threatened to embarrass Britain's entry into the war on behalf of Polish independence. To resolve the issue, Britain established the Polish Resettlement Corps under the country's first ever mass immigration legislation. The initiative was just as much a face-saving exercise as it was a noble act of one ally on behalf of another.

This book describes the methods and the legacy of the resettlement programme, which not only required the support of Trade Unions, Professional Associations and the Departments of Employment, Health and Pensions amongst others, but also the lobbying of the Vatican City and the Governments of Argentina, Brazil and Southern Africa, as well as the Commonwealth countries.

Britain's solution to the Polish problem eventually became a heroic as well as a tragic act, often referred to, but rarely explained.

Wiesław Rogalski was born in Britain. During the Second World War his parents served in the Polish Allied Forces under British operational command and were invited to settle in Britain after the War. They arrived in 1947 and were demobilised by British authorities. They eventually settled in London. Wiesław studied the history of Curriculum Development Projects at London University, where he was awarded a higher degree. He is currently the Vice Chairman of the Third Carpathian Infantry Division Ex Servicemen Association and is a museum trustee at the Rural Life Centre, Tilford near Farnham. The photograph shows Wiesław visiting London whilst researching the book.

THE POLISH RESETTLEMENT CORPS
1946 to 1949

BRITAIN'S POLISH FORCES

Wiesław Rogalski

Helion & Company Ltd

To Alexandra

Helion & Company Limited
Unit 8 Amherst Business Centre
Budbrooke Road
Warwick CV34 5WE
 England
Tel. 01926 499 619
Email: info@helion.co.uk
Website: www.helion.co.uk
Twitter: @helionbooks
Visit our blog http://blog.helion.co.uk/

Published by Helion & Company 2019
Designed and typeset by Farr out Publications, Wokingham, Berkshire
Cover designed by Paul Hewitt, Battlefield Design (www.battlefield-design.co.uk)
Printed via Jellyfish Solutions (www.jellyfishsolutions.co.uk)

Text © Wiesław Rogalski 2019
Photographs © Wiesław Rogalski unless otherwise noted

Every reasonable effort has been made to trace copyright holders and to obtain their permission for the use of copyright material. The author and publisher apologize for any errors or omissions in this work, and would be grateful if notified of any corrections that should be incorporated in future reprints or editions of this book.

ISBN 978-1-912390-89-2

British Library Cataloguing-in-Publication Data
A catalogue record for this book is available from the British Library

All rights reserved. No part of this publication may be reproduced, stored in a retrieval system, or transmitted, in any form, or by any means, electronic, mechanical, photocopying, recording or otherwise, without the express written consent of Helion & Company Limited.

We always welcome receiving book proposals from prospective authors.

Contents

List of Images	vi
List of Tables	x
Preface	xii
Introduction	xiv

Part I The Dismantling of Polish Military Authority under British Command

1	The Eastern Ally	19
2	The Defeat of Poland	25
3	Pragmatism versus Idealism	33
4	Trouble in the House (the Crimea Conference Debate)	38
5	On the Question of Repatriation	42
6	On the Question of Emigration	49
7	Nascence of the Polish Resettlement Corps	54
8	Further Consultation and Clarification	58
9	The Polish Resettlement Bill	62
10	The Polish Resettlement Act 1947	66
11	Conditions of Service – Polish Land Forces	69
12	Conditions of Service – Polish Air Force	73
13	Conditions of Service – Polish Naval Wing	75
14	Conditions of Service – Female Personnel and Members of the Home Army (AK)	77
15	Accommodation – The Camp System	80

Part II The Resettlement Programme

16	The Transfer of Polish Land Forces to Britain	93
17	Procedure for Enlistment into the Polish Resettlement Corps	101
18	The Rundown of the Polish Forces	112
19	The Command Structure	115
20	Health Services	121
21	Vocational Training	124
22	Employment	128
23	British Protests	137
24	Security Concerns	144
25	Special Needs	149

Part III The Rundown of the Polish Resettlement Corps and its Legacy

26	Termination of Service	157
27	Rundown – Personnel	162
28	Rundown – Records and Archives	166
29	Rundown – The Resettlement Corps	169
30	Polish Resettlement Corps – Final Report	172
31	Life in Families' Camps	181
32	Triumph and Tragedy	188

Epilogue	197
Bibliography	204
Index	208

List of Images

Figures

Figure 1: Destiny of Polish forces in the Second World War.	30
Figure 2: Gender breakdown of dependants brought to Britain.	86
Figure 3: Age profile (in years) of dependants brought to Britain.	86
Figure 4: Jasper Camp, Surrey – later used in the Polish Resettlement Programme.	87
Figure 5: Algonquin Camp (Canadian base in Surrey) – used in the Polish Resettlement Programme. Note the water treatment works top left.	88
Figure 6: Laurentide Camp (Canadian base in Surrey) – used in the Resettlement Programme. Note the parade ground.	88
Figure 7: The camp system as used in the Resettlement Programme.	89
Figure 8: Transfer of Polish Allied forces to Britain (1946–1949).	98
Figure 9: Protocol for filling in the War Office questionnaire.	104
Figure 10: Polish Authorisation Passes.	106
Figure 11: Total numbers enlisting, 1946–1947.	108
Figure 12: Age profile of Members of the Polish Resettlement Corps.	108
Figure 13: The distribution of Polish Resettlement Corps units into Home Commands.	109
Figure 14: Paper trail for PRC enlistment documents.	110
Figure 15: Command structure of the PRC Land forces.	118
Figure 16a: The command structure of the Polish Resettlement Corps.	119
Figure 16b: Location of Polish Naval units.	119
Figure 17: The Polish Air Force was embedded within the Royal Air Force and therefore in its command structure.	120
Figure 18: Diagram showing how the health care of Members of the Polish Resettlement Corps and dependants was integrated into national health services.	123
Figure 19: Breakdown of PRC personnel versus reasons for discharge. (Global figures adapted from War Office data for February 1951.)	163

Photographs

(All photographs from author's own private collection, unless stated otherwise.)

A travel pass issued to a Polish soldier by the Hungarian State Railway for a single journey in a third class carriage of a non-express train. The ticket was issued on 24 July 1940 for a soldier escaping to the West.	26
Polish men and women of fighting age, having reached the West, enrolled in the Polish Armed Forces abroad. This is an enrolment document for enlistment into 2nd Carpathian Artillery Brigade dated 9 December 1942 (issued in the French protectorate of Syria).	29
Throughout the Resettlement Programme, Polish personnel were given the option to repatriate. For members of the Polish Resettlement Corps this required an application to be made to terminate service. This form was used for the purpose.	44

LIST OF IMAGES   vii

If a member of the Resettlement Corps decided to emigrate to a country other than Britain, an Application Form for Emigration had to be filled in.	50
Cover of the Polish Resettlement Act, 1947. The Polish Resettlement Act provided the legislative framework for the Resettlement Programme. The Act provided social welfare rights in Britain for all Poles who had arrived as part of the Resettlement Programme. (Crown copyright)	67
Model of a barracks block: Polish Resettlement Camps, where barracks were the predominant building, were sometimes called 'Hutted Camps'.	81
Information leaflet issued by the Ministry of National Insurance describing benefit rights for dependants of the Polish Resettlement Corps.	82
Certificate of Registration: Polish dependants in Britain were issued with this document under the Aliens Order 1920. Demobilised personnel were also issued with this document on becoming civilians.	83
Polish 100 Złoty banknote.	99
Polish 100 Złoty banknote, reverse.	99
Egyptian five Piastres banknote.	100
Italian 10 Lire banknote.	100
German 50 Pfennig banknote issued by Nazi Germany.	100
Currency of the British Military Authority 10 Shillings.	100
Egyptian five Piastres banknote, reverse.	100
Italian 10 Lire banknote, reverse.	100
A British Military Authority two Lire currency note.	100
Currency of the British Military Authority 10 Shillings, reverse.	100
It was important for the War Office to keep records of enlistments into Polish Resettlement Corps for statistical purposes. This form was used to record the nominal roll of men who had agreed to enrol.	102
Form for enlisting into the Polish Resettlement Corps dated January 1947.	110
Before a Polish soldier could enlist in the PRC he would first need to leave the Polish Forces. This is a Polish Demobilisation Certificate which incidentally carries the same date as on the form used for enrolment into the PRC. This signifies that joining the PRC does not mean a break in service.	110
Discharge papers from the Polish Armed Forces in Britain – issued on enrolment into the Polish Resettlement Corps.	113
Members of the Polish Resettlement Corps were entitled to receive British service medals and awards. Individuals were presented with Notification of Awards cards.	114
Lieutenant General Stanisław Kopański – Inspector General of the Polish Resettlement Corps. (Courtesy of the Polish Library, POSK, London)	116
38 Egerton Gardens, London. Headquarters of the Polish Resettlement Corps.	116
Officers in the PRC were encouraged to find training on their own. This letter from the London School of Foreign Trade informs an applicant of the examination he would need to sit before his application could be considered.	126
Letter from the School of Foreign Trade regarding examination results.	127
Once a member of the PRC accepted employment in the private sector, he was notified that his army pay would be withdrawn.	129

A Certificate of Registration was issued to members of the PRC on demobilisation. At this stage he/she would be considered a civilian.	131
The Polish workforce was made up of ex-members of the Polish Resettlement Corps. Employment offered to Poles was as unskilled labour, irrespective of their Polish qualifications.	134
An advertisement placed in the Polish Press in Britain on behalf of the National Coal Board. The caption reads 'BECOME A MINER'.	135
Note on alleged clandestine political activity of Poles resettled in Britain.	145
Endorsements and remarks recorded by the Police on the employment and movements of Poles in Britain.	146
A letter from the Security Services concerning alleged clandestine Polish broadcasts from Britain.	147
Polish Institute and Sikorski Museum, Prince's Gate, London.	154
Discharge Certificate from the Polish Resettlement Corps.	159
Application for Discharge from the Polish Resettlement Corps.	160
Discharge from the Polish Resettlement Corps took place when a member of the Corps accepted employment in the private sector, or a PRC Contract of Service had lapsed, whichever was the sooner. This document was issued when the contract with the PRC had been completed.	164
Home Office letter regarding British naturalisation.	183
Character reference for naturalisation applicant.	184
Naturalisation Certificate: naturalisation was sought when travel abroad was contemplated and a British passport was required.	185
Travel Documents were issued by the Home Office for 'Alien' individuals who had not yet obtained naturalisation, but needed to travel abroad. The holders could travel to countries other than Poland, although without the protection of British diplomatic or consular services.	186
Ex-member of the Polish Resettlement Corps settles down to family life in Britain.	189
As the Poles grew in confidence in their new homes, and resources were accumulating, they started their own institutions and cultural centres. This is the front of Polish Cultural Institute in London. It was built using donations, bequeaths, and gifts.	191
Plaque at 51 New Cavendish Road, London.	198
Sign outside the Polish Social and Cultural Association, Hammersmith, London.	198
Monument to the Polish Airforce, London.	199
Part of the remembrance Wall in London dedicated to the Polish Airmen who fought in the Battle of Britain.	200
Plaque on the Rubens Hotel, London.	200
Rubens Hotel, London Headquarters of General Sikorski during the Second World War.	201
They did not return to Poland even when their country had finally obtained independence and freedom in the late 1980s, some forty years after the end of the War. For many of them it was too late to return, since their personal identity had grown to be deeply rooted and reshaped by Britain's culture. Many of these veterans had lived in Britain for much longer than in Poland; nevertheless, they continued to consider themselves as Poles in exile rather than British citizens of Polish extraction. This is a general	

view of the cemetery at Gunnersbury showing the graves of ex-Polish Resettlement Corps personnel. 202

Cartoons

Cartoon 1: General Anders leads the Polish Army out of Russia to the British protectorate of Palestine. 31
Cartoon 2: The Polish Army is transferred to Britain for resettlement. 36
Cartoon 3: Making the decision to join the Polish Resettlement Corps. 95
Cartoon 4: Integration started with learning the English language. 111

List of Tables

Table 1: Daily Rate of Pay Resettlement Corps (Polish Land Forces) shillings/pence	70
Table 2: Approximate number of men in Polish units eligible to join the PRC	72
Table 3: Approximate number of men in Polish Air Force Squadrons	74
Table 4: The Admiralty published the daily rates of pay as follows	76
Table 5: Approximate number of men in Naval units	76
Table 6: Approximate number of personnel in these units	78
Table 7: Pay for members of the ATS/PRS	79
Table 8: Aims of the Liquidation Mission in France	96
Table 9: Unit Name	96
Table 10: Forces Entertainment Groups	99
Table 11: Collated Data for Enlistment	107
Table 12: Recruitment into the Polish Resettlement Corps/Section by Home Command (February 1947)	109
Table 13: Breakdown of Personnel and numbers in the service of the PRC Headquarters and the War Office in London	117
Table 14: Registration for Employment by the Ministry of Labour up to 17 May 1947	130
Table 15: Fluency in English of Poles Registered in the PRC	130
Table 16: Distribution in industries which had absorbed more than 400 PRC Members	132
Table 17: The Trust's Statement of Investments for 1953	151
Table 18: Names of Polish causes receiving money from the Polish Resettlement Trust	152
Table 19: Clothing issued or retained by PRC Personnel on Relegation to Reserve	160
Table 20: Scale of Military Clothing retained by PRC Personnel on Discharge	161
Table 21: Global Numbers – 30.09.1949	174
Table 22: Number of Emigrants PRC, Polish Forces, Civilians – 11 June 1949	174
Table 23: Number of Emigrants PRC, Polish Forces, Civilians – 3 September 1949	174
Table 24: Strength and Distribution PRC – 11 June 1949	175
Table 25: Strength and distribution PRC – 3 September 1949	176
Table 26: Provisional number of personnel due to complete their period of service during 1949–1950	177
Table 27: Number of discharges affected by expiry of service	178
Table 28: Poles in Great Britain in groups according to source of income*	178
Table 29: Distribution in industries in which more than 400 Poles had been placed	179
Tables 30–1: SPK Branches in 2000	192

	POLISH MILITARY ACTION IN THE SECOND WORLD WAR	
LAND ARMY	1939 September Campaign, Battle for Poland P	
	Tobruk B	
	Monte Cassino B	
	Ancona B	
	Bologna B	
	Falaise B	
	Nancy B	
	Arnhem B	
	Wilhelmshaven B	
	Lenino S	
	Warsaw S	
	Stettin S	
	Berlin S	
	Kołobrzek S	
POLISH AIRFORCE	1939 September Campaign, Battle for Poland P	
	Hamburg B *Bomber Command*	
	Wilhelmshaven B *Bomber Command*	
	Kassel B *Bomber Command*	
	Frankfurt B *Bomber Command*	
	Cologne B *Bomber Command*	
	Munich B *Bomber Command*	
	Genoa B *Bomber Command*	
	Battle of Britain B *fighter squadrons*	
	Northern France B *fighter squadrons*	
	Berlin B *fighter squadrons*	
	Toulouse B *fighter squadrons*	
	Warsaw B *transport squadrons*	
	Arnhem B *transport squadrons*	
	Athens B *transport squadrons*	
	Tunis B *transport squadrons*	
POLISH NAVY	Mediterranean B *submarines*	
	North Sea B *submarines*	
	Adriatic B *submarines*	
	Arctic Convoys B *submarines*	
	North Sea B *surface vessels*	
	Arctic Convoys B *surface vessels*	
	Atlantic Ocean B *surface vessels*	
	B – Under British Operational Command S – Under Soviet Command P – Under Polish Operational Command	

Preface

After the Second World War, Britain needed to honour her treaty obligations to Poland if her reputation as an ally was to remain untarnished. At the Yalta Conference held in the Crimea,[1] Stalin[2] declared that, on account of her huge exertions during the conflict, the Soviet Union had earned the right to continue stationing the Red Army in Poland and to impose communist rule in Warsaw. This meant that His Majesty's Government could not stand idly by. Even the pleading of Winston Churchill, who was negotiating on behalf of the Poles, failed to convince the Soviet leader that such an occupation would be problematic for Britain, and would complicate relations with the Polish military and political authorities exiled in London.[3] Churchill's prediction was not far off target for, on 13 February, the Poles rejected the Yalta accord and accused the British Prime Minister of surrendering their country to Stalin and betraying a loyal ally. Churchill attempted to explain to the Polish Government in exile why he had failed to secure its return to Poland, something that was expected by both sides in the light of the Anglo-Polish Alliance signed in 1939. The dismayed Poles also wanted to know why Britain, with America's agreement, had allowed approximately 50 percent of Poland's pre-war territory to be ceded to the Soviet Union without as much as a word of consultation. The issue grew to be more serious when the Polish Forces under British Operational Command refused to stand down, protesting that it was Yalta, not the war, which was preventing their country's coming of age.

Benefiting from the alleged unpopularity of the Conservatives in 1945, though not of Churchill, Clement Attlee won the first post-war election by a landslide and it was he, who then had to resolve the Polish problem.[4] His initial response was to echo Churchill's view, that the Poles should accept the fact that circumstances in Europe had changed significantly since 1939, and that they would do well to embrace the realities of the new order and return home to rebuild their country. This hardly pacified the protesting Polish authorities. They believed that if they followed such advice, their primary war aim to reinstate a free and independent country would have to be set aside, despite having made a significant contribution to the victory over Nazi Germany. London feared that the problem would spin out of control and thus derail the euphoria that had erupted spontaneously in Britain over the capitulation of Germany. There was also concern that the issue would precipitate disobedience, or even result in mutiny in the Polish Forces – something that would reflect badly on the British. It was clear that Polish protests had to be rebuffed and, if possible, neutralised. As far as political dissent was concerned, this was blocked relatively simply for the British Government merely removed its recognition of the exiled Polish Government.[5] This surprising decision was then followed by an audacious resolution – to transfer Britain's allegiance to that of the communist regime imposed on Warsaw by Moscow. In order to counteract the expected protests, the Polish elite in Britain were offered continued exile

---

1 February 1945.
2 Joseph Stalin, Leader of the Soviet Union.
3 Victor Sebestyen, *1946: The Making of the Modern World* (London: Macmillan, 2014), p.172.
4 Giles Radice (ed.), *What Needs to Change, New Visions for Britain* (London: Harper Collins, 1996), p.251.
5 1945.

under favourable terms. However, the removal of the military objections – namely the protestations of the Polish Allied High Command – was far more complex and required a degree of creative planning, radical thinking and financial resourcing. Not only was it a matter of what to do with approximately 118,000 disgruntled service personnel, who had fought alongside the British throughout the War, but how to maintain Britain's reputation as a country taking her international obligations seriously.

This work outlines the history behind the eventual and unprecedented decision to transfer the Polish Allied Forces to Britain, where they would be demobilised; the first time this had been attempted with a foreign sovereign army. London realised that such a policy would be expensive and politically sensitive, for the British public had not as yet understood why the resettlement of so many foreign troops of one nationality was necessary, and why they were apparently being given favourable treatment under British law. Consequently, Attlee worked covertly with the War Office, the Cabinet, and the Ministries of Labour, Health and Pensions – only discussing the resettlement plans when challenged to explain his government's decisions. Although the plan to settle a foreign army on British soil was unique in the country's history, the decision to do so was probably the best resolution to the impasse that had developed between the two allies – short of starting a war against the Soviet Army in order to remove it from Polish territory.[6]

My thanks go to the staff at The National Archives of the UK (TNA), Kew, Surrey, to the Polish Institute and Sikorski Museum in London, and to the Imperial War Museum. I would also like to thank the many Polish veterans and ex-servicemen and women who shared their wartime experiences, as well their recollections from the Polish Resettlement Corps in Britain. I would also like to thank the members of the 3rd Carpathian Infantry Division ex-Servicemen Association, who provided materials and pictures for this project with enthusiasm; and last, but not least, special thanks to my wife, Alexandra.

---

6   See Operation Unthinkable.

Introduction

'What next?' was the question on everyone's lips. A young Captain of the Polish Allied Forces sat in his base in Italy contemplating what the end of the Second World War would mean for the Poles under British command. Knowing that Poland had been placed firmly behind the Iron Curtain a few months earlier, he concluded that the end of the war for him and his country had ended in tragedy. Not only was Poland lost to a foreign power, but half her territory had been ceded to the new occupiers of his country. He lamented the fact that, after six years of hard slog, he and his comrades were unable to return to a free, independent homeland and wondered what the future held. He feared that they would be disarmed prematurely, before true Polish independence had been achieved. This would constitute an unforgivable betrayal of his wartime exertion.

Eryk, an officer in the Polish 2nd Corps, was in a reflective mood. In his book, *The Price of Being Different*, he wrote,

> I cannot not accept the fact that, despite my wartime odyssey during which I left my home, served for years in the army, coped with unrelenting hardship and risked my life on the battlefield, I am still unable to return to my birthplace, Cieszyn, to my family whom I have not seen for such a long time. After all, it was for this that I escaped internment and chose to take up arms. I could, of course, have stayed put and sat out the war, but I chose to fight and live in exile, but to no avail. I just cannot accept this.[1]

He tried to understand why the War had come to such an unsatisfactory end for the Poles and attempted to predict what the future would hold; nevertheless, one thing seemed clear, he and his men would not return to a Poland under Soviet domination. This had been the very regime that in 1939–1941 had rounded them up and tormented them in concentration camps.[2] In his speculation he guessed that his men could be resettled in the United States, be deployed to a remote territory such as Madagascar where they would be demobilised and left to fend for themselves, or disbanded and sent to God knows where. All these hypotheses were possible, but time eventually showed that what had transpired was their unceremonious demobilisation by the British and encouragement to start a new life in Western Europe, Canada, Australia, Africa, South America or North America. However, for Eryk and his men it was the order to hand in their weapons that caused them the most concern as they knew that, once this happened, their fight for a free homeland was over. The feelings of betrayal were so strong that they planned disobedience and even contemplated mutiny for this, they believed, would alert the world to the grave injustice that had befallen their country. They knew, of course, that such action would be futile, if not impossible, given that the British had their hand on the Polish Forces' 'windpipe'. In the event, Clement Attlee, managed to disarm and dispose of the Polish Forces without a drop of blood being spilled, a most notable personal achievement.

---

1 Eryk Nanke, *Cena Bycia Innym* (Kraków: Biblioteka Centrum Dokumentacji Czynu Niepodległościowego, 2000), p.146. (translation).
2 Gulags.

This work attempts to answer the following questions:

1. What were the reasons for the sentiments expressed by the Polish Forces under British Command in 1945?
2. Why did the Polish exiled government and the Poles under British Command refuse to accept the agreements reached at the Teheran, Yalta and the Potsdam Conferences?
3. Why did the Poles, who had fought alongside the British, feel betrayed and why were they brought to Britain in 1946?
4. What was the policy of the Attlee Government towards the Polish Allied Army in the West?
5. What was the legacy of this policy?

It is divided into three sections:

Part I   The Dismantling of Polish Military Authority under British Command
Part II   The Resettlement Programme
Part III   The Rundown of the Polish Resettlement Corps and its Legacy

Part I

The Dismantling of Polish Military Authority under British Command

*No man has a right to lead such a life of contemplation as to
forget in his ease the service due to his neighbour.*
(Augustine, City of God, XIX, 19)

1

The Eastern Ally

Britain's and Poland's destiny in the Second World War became intimately intertwined during the early months of 1939. By this time, Britain's policy of appeasing Hitler, so energetically championed by Neville Chamberlain,[1] was known to have failed. The German Fuhrer's casual approach to the Munich Agreement (signed in September 1938 and sometimes considered to be the high point of the appeasement policy), had demonstrated that it would be unlikely to bring 'peace in our time' as expected. The iconic picture of a relieved, but tense Chamberlain, brandishing Hitler's note above his head,[2] soon turned into an image of sad betrayal when the German Fuhrer returned to his old ways of challenging the status quo in Europe, demanding the return of the 'Polish Corridor'[3] and the transfer of the Free City of Gdańsk (Danzig) to the Third Reich. The realisation in London that a new approach was required regarding the German Chancellor was not long in coming.

During the early months of 1939, the policy of appeasement was quietly replaced with a new strategy, sometimes referred to as the 'Encirclement Plan'. The rationale behind this idea, which was Britain's last throw of the dice to avoid war, was deceptively simple and involved establishing a ring of allied countries around Germany in order to corral her ambitions and bellicosity. However, if the policy was to succeed, an ally in the east would have to be found to complete the 'circle' around the country – the two most obvious candidates being the Soviet Union and Poland. Winston Churchill[4] argued for the Soviets, for he not only coveted the immense military potential of the Red Army, but was informed by Vyacheslav Molotov[5] that if Britain approached the Soviet Government with an offer of an alliance, she would receive a very favourable response. Churchill was soon overlooking his fervent anti-communist feelings and pressed the British Government to make the formal approach. However, he lost the argument when Chamberlain rejected this advice, arguing that the Red Army was incapable of waging effective warfare at the time, on account of Stalin's recent purges of the Soviet High Command, which saw the removal of experienced front line officers whom he deemed to be politically unreliable. Józef Beck[6] hurried to London in order to beat the drum for Poland and, to reinforce his message, made it clear that his Government would not allow the Red Army to cross Polish territory in order to reach Germany's eastern border. His message was clear; the Polish Army, some 1,000,000 strong, would be more than adequate at fulfilling the role of Britain's eastern ally. Despite the country's outdated military equipment, Chamberlain settled for the Poles and in March 1939 announced to the House of Commons,

---

1 British Prime Minister, May 1937–May 1940.
2 Taken on the 30 September 1938 at Heston Aerodrome on his return from Germany.
3 A strip of Polish territory through Germany connecting Poland and the Baltic Sea.
4 British First Sea Lord, 1939–1940.
5 Soviet Foreign Minister, 1939–1949.
6 Polish Foreign Minister, November 1932–September 1939.

In the event of any action which clearly threatened Polish independence and which the Polish Government accordingly considered it vital to resist with their national forces, His Majesty's Government would feel themselves bound at once to lend the Polish Government all support in its power. May I add that the French Government have authorised me to make it plain that they stand in the same position in the matter, as do His Majesty's Government.

In the light of the British Prime Minister's decision, secret meetings were arranged between military planners from the two countries whilst the Soviet Union, not wishing to be left isolated, looked to others for friendship. In May, British General Staff met with their Polish counterparts in Warsaw. The British were represented by General Clayton, Naval Commander Rawlings and Lieutenant Davidson of the RAF.[7] The Poles were represented by General Wacław Stachiewicz, Chief of the General Polish Staff. The result of the meeting was a defence plan which eventually formed the basis of a formal agreement. In order to assist its success, the plan was kept as simple as possible. If it was the case that German forces would be thrown westward, that is towards France and the Low Countries, the French and British would move to confront them, leaving the Polish forces to open up a front on Germany's eastern border. If, on the other hand, German forces were to attack Poland (which was the more likely scenario according to incoming secret information from Berlin), Polish forces would resist, leaving France and Britain to open up a front on Germany's western border. The rationale was quite clear; whichever direction German forces were sent, they would be split by the existence of two fronts. The plan sounded logical and feasible, but much work was needed to be done in order to work out the details. In subsequent meetings the Poles were keen to learn about the kind of help they could expect from their allies. For example, would it include army, naval and air operations and what was meant by the phrase 'immediate British help'? General Clayton informed the Poles that the use of Britain's land army would depend on French permission, since intervention would require operations being launched from French territory. Commander Rawlings explained that naval assistance would be limited, as the priority would be the protection of Atlantic shipping lanes and British interests in the Mediterranean. General Stachiewicz, therefore, presumed that what the British really meant by 'help' was RAF bombing of German targets. This did not worry the Poles unduly, for it was RAF help that they coveted most. General Stachiewicz pressed the British to clarify what types of targets the RAF would attack. Lieutenant Davidson said that all military targets would be considered, if it was decided that their destruction would help the war effort. General Stachiewicz enquired about civilian targets. The answer was that the RAF did not bomb civilians but, if it was known that the Polish population was being targeted by the Luftwaffe, then civilian targets in Germany would be considered as legitimate. Regarding what was meant by the phrase 'immediate response', Davidson explained that the RAF would respond just as soon as the British Government declared war on Germany, after having received an alarm message by radio communication from Warsaw. He also added that this would be done, even if British territory was not being threatened directly. He then proceeded to give the Poles a breakdown of the aircraft prepared for action: 524 bombers, 500 fighters, 96 support planes and 184 reconnaissance aircraft.

In the plenary session, General Stachiewicz confirmed that it was the policy of the

---

7   Royal Air Force.

Polish Government to resist German aggression against Polish territory, but went out of his way to remind London (and Paris) that Poland could not fight on her own for long – an estimate in terms of weeks rather than months – without the military assistance of Britain and France. The resulting formal guarantee made to Poland also reassured London that Poland would not ally with Germany and that there would be no Polish equivalent to the 'English Right Club' in Warsaw. The understanding between Britain and Poland was the last piece of the jigsaw required for the policy of encirclement. The British contingent left Warsaw with General Clayton wishing the Poles good fortune. The meetings between London and Warsaw were peculiar in that one side was attempting to gain as much as possible from the agreement, whilst the other was endeavouring to give as little as it could. The Polish Foreign Minister was buoyed by the arrangements and felt emboldened to address the Polish Parliament saying,

> Peace is a precious and desirable thing. Our generation, bloodied by war, certainly deserves peace. But peace, like almost all things in this life, has its price, a high but measurable one. We in Poland do not know the concept of peace at any price. There is only one thing in the lives of men, nations and countries that is without price and that thing is honour.[8]

The document between London and Warsaw was signed by the Right Honourable Viscount Halifax on behalf of the British and by His Excellency Count Edward Raczyński[9] on behalf of the Poles.

The significant elements of the document read as follows:

Article 1
Should one of the contracting parties become engaged in hostilities with a European power, in consequence of aggression by the latter against that contracting party, the contracting party will at once give the contracting power engaged in hostilities all the support and assistance in its power.

Article 2
1) The provision of Article 1 will also apply to the event of any action by a European Power which clearly threatens, directly or indirectly, the independence of one of the contracting powers and is of such a nature that the party in question considers it vital to resist it with armed force.
2) Should one of the contracting powers become engaged in hostilities with a European power in consequence of action by that power which threatened the independence or neutrality of another European state in such a way as to constitute a clear menace to the security of that contracting power, the provision of Article 1 will apply without prejudice.

---

8   *Józef Beck*, Polish Foreign Minister speaking to the Polish Parliament, May 1939.
9   Polish Ambassador to Britain.

Article 4

The method of applying the understanding of mutual assistance provided for by the competent naval, military and air authorities by the contracting powers.[10]

The existence of a formal agreement between London and Warsaw was finally announced on 25 August, when it was clear that there was no hope of persuading Hitler to settle his issues with Europe without reverting to war.

The Soviet Union, smarting from the fact that Britain and France had been less than enthusiastic in securing an understanding in 1938–9, looked for friends elsewhere and in order to avoid Soviet isolation, signed a pact with Berlin. This became known as the Molotov-Ribbentrop Agreement.[11] The pact between the two countries renewed the anti-Polish arrangements, which had bound together the Hohenzollerns and Romanovs, in imperial times and had precipitated the destruction of Poland. The understanding between Germany and Russia meant that neither of them would interfere with the other's expansionist plans. Article One of the agreement stated,

'The two Contracting Parties bind themselves to refrain from any act of force, any aggressive action and any attack on one another, both singly and also jointly with other Powers.'[12]

Following the German-Soviet agreement, Hitler knew that Stalin would not oppose Germany's operations in Poland; whilst Stalin was reassured that Hitler would refrain from interfering in Soviet operations in eastern Poland, Latvia, Lithuania, Estonia and Finland. The two leaders also compromised on the terms governing the occupation of Poland, agreeing to share the territory between themselves. Stalin, however, was deeply troubled by the existence of the Anglo-Polish Agreement, which threatened allied retaliation if Poland was attacked. Hitler reassured Stalin that it was highly unlikely that Britain and France would go to war over Poland and the pact that they had signed was no more than a hollow threat. In August 1939, Hitler called Britain's bluff and made a final demand on the Polish government. The headlines in the *Daily Express* proclaimed, 'Hitler rejects peace offer and makes a clear demand. "I must have Danzig and the Corridor".[13] Poland resisted and refused to cede any of her territory to Nazi Germany with the words, 'We value peace, but not at any price'. Hitler responded by ordering his troops to cross the Polish border on 1 September,[14] without officially declaring war. A shrill headline appeared in the *Star* newspaper, 'Poland invaded. Warsaw and other towns bombed'.[15] The article continued saying that the Polish ambassador in London had called on Lord Halifax to invoke the treaty.

The first shots of the Second World War were fired by the German battle cruiser, *Schleswig-Holstein*, which had previously entered Danzig Harbour (*Port Gdański*) on what Berlin had called a 'courtesy visit'. Despite the harbour being a demilitarised zone, the ship's turrets were silently turned onto a small Polish garrison (protecting Polish interests in the region) on the Westerplatte peninsula, at the tip of the Polish corridor. Following a disingenuous

---

10 The Anglo-Polish Mutual Assistance Agreement, 1939.
11 Signed in Moscow, August 1939.
12 Non-Aggression Pact between Germany and the Union of Soviet Socialist Republics, 1939.
13 The Polish Corridor was Polish territory located in the region of Pomerania, formerly East Prussia, which provided Poland with access to the Baltic Sea via a land corridor. Approved at the Versailles Conference after the First World War.
14 Case White.
15 *The Star Newspaper Publishers*, 1 September 1939.

accusation that Polish Forces had crossed the German border, Hitler unleashed 'Case White', the code name for the invasion of Poland. He justified the attack by arguing that all he was doing was defending his country from Polish aggression. A comprehensive land invasion ensued, with armour pouring into Poland from the west, the north and the south. The Poles rushed to meet the German advance, but soon made a costly, tactical error by deciding to protect the full length of the country's border with Germany, thereby stretching her defence line into a narrow corridor. This tactic was no answer to Blitzkrieg and soon saw German mechanised armour break through and wreak havoc behind the Polish lines. Following the rejection of a final demand for the removal of German troops from Polish territory, Britain and France declared war on 4 September. Polish jubilation erupted in Warsaw. The *Daily Telegraph* published an article describing the euphoria in the Polish capital on the news;

> News of Britain's declaration caused a tremendous outburst of joy in Warsaw. A crowd numbering tens of thousands marched to the British Embassy on Nowy Świat Street, shouting, 'long live King George' and 'long live England'. Colonel Beck appeared on the balcony of the embassy building with the British ambassador Sir Howard Kennard. Raising his hand to hush the crowd Colonel Beck said, 'We never doubted that England would fight alongside Poland'. There were moving scenes outside the French Embassy too. The crowd sang patriotic songs with two fingers of the right hand raised, 'Never shall the German foe tread on our soil'. A French military attaché, who appeared, was lifted into the air by cheering students.[16]

Meanwhile, Stalin stood fast trying to gauge whether the British and French forces would come to Poland's aid. Just as soon it was clear that they would not[17] and that Hitler had been correct in predicting that neither would open up a front on Germany's western border, he sent the Red Army into eastern Poland, as had been secretly agreed in the Molotov-Ribbentrop Agreement. This Russian move on 17 September disorientated the Polish High Command, as it was unsure whether Russia had entered Polish territory as an ally,[18] or as the country's next occupier. The confusion was further exacerbated when Moscow signalled that the Red Army had entered Polish territory 'simply' to protect fellow Slavs from German aggression. However, as the dual invasion progressed with the Germans and the Soviets driving relentlessly towards Warsaw, it soon became obvious to the Polish authorities that the two invaders were colluding to partition the country. It was decided that further resistance from Polish territory was futile and that the fight for independence would have to continue from exile. Once it was certain that France and Britain would remain passive, the Poles opted for total withdrawal. This took them via Lithuania, Hungary and Romania to the West (France and Britain). Bucharest had had a long-standing agreement with Poland assuring safe passage for Poles responding to a national emergency.

With Polish resistance collapsing, it was only a matter of time until Poland was defeated and wiped from the European map. Using a classic pincer movement, it had taken the dual invaders one month to complete the task. Whilst the Polish Government – alongside approximately 60,000 retreating Polish servicemen – regrouped in Paris, the territory of the Second Polish Republic was bisected and shared out between the two new conquerors.

---

16 *The Daily Telegraph*, 4 September 1939.
17 See the 'Phoney War'.
18 Poland had a non-aggression pact with Russia at the time.

The order to withdraw also saw Polish airmen flying directly to Britain and France, with the Polish Navy sailing to Rosyth in Scotland. The Polish Government – now exiled in Paris – did not give itself the luxury to ponder why its defence plan had gone so horribly wrong. Preferring to return to the issue after the war, it concentrated on planning resistance from exile.

2

The Defeat of Poland

With the Germans We Risk Losing Our Liberty, but with the Russians Our Soul.[1]

Despite Great Britain and France declaring that they were inflexible in their determination to fulfil their promise to the utmost, the inactivity of the Allied Forces on Germany's western border in September 1939 was a bitter and catastrophic blow to Poland's defence plan. Warsaw had never planned to confront the Nazi Forces alone and certainly not to deal with the dual invasion, which emerged when the Soviet Union joined Germany in dismembering the country. Even today, the allied torpidity on Germany's western border, often referred to as the 'Phoney War' remains a controversial topic amongst academics. It is also unclear why Britain failed to declare war on the Soviet Union when she attacked Poland in September 1939, as the Anglo-Polish Pact had required. Were the Poles naïve about the possibility of allied help arriving in 1939 or were Poland's allies disingenuous in promising immediate help, knowing full well that the likelihood of this happening was highly improbable? The answer to this question is probably somewhere in between.

News of Poland's defeat erupted in western newspapers with a vengeance, and it finally dawned on people in Britain that the war would last far longer than had been predicted. However, the first victims of the war in Britain were not fighting men, but children who were evacuated from densely populated urban areas to the relative safety of the countryside, where life was continuing relatively unaffected by the conflict. In rural areas, children continued to attend school, farms continued to operate and churches remained open; however, those involved in the evacuation experienced social and personal trauma. Host families had to readjust to a sudden influx of 'alien' children from suburbia, whilst parents were expected to hand over their offspring to strangers. The social divide that existed between the working classes from the cities and the landed gentry is well illustrated in a 1940s cartoon, which shows child evacuees arriving at the door of a country estate with the matron saying, 'Now I want you to promise me you're all going to be really good little evacuees and not worry his Lordship'.[2]

On 23 September, *News Chronicle* published an article describing how Poland, on the other side of Europe, had been dismembered by the regimes in Berlin and Moscow. It announced alarmingly, 'Russia to control half of Poland. Stalin gets oil and Hitler gets the steel'.[3] Russia gained 96,467 square miles of Polish territory and 16,000,000 people. Germany gained a similar number of people and 52,584 square miles of territory. The demarcation line between the two zones of occupation ran along the rivers Pisa, Narew, Vistula and San. The industrial gains for Russia amounted to extensive agriculture, timber production and 27 refineries, whilst Germany received industrial plant, coal mines and the

---

1 Marshal Śmigły-Rydz, Poland's Military Leader 1939.
2 Susan Briggs, *Keep Smiling Through*, (London: Weidenfeld and Nicolson, 1975), p.19.
3 *News Chronicle*, 23 September 1939.

A travel pass issued to a Polish soldier by the Hungarian State Railway for a single journey in a third class carriage of a non-express train. The ticket was issued on 24 July 1940 for a soldier escaping to the West.

textile industry, as well as crude oil production (at that time calculated to be 141,000 tons per year). Polish timber exports were estimated to amount to 1,689,422 tons per year, with farming yield being recorded as 2,171,000 tons of wheat, 7,000,000 tons of rye, 300,000 tons of barley and 34,000,000 tons of potatoes. The principal coal mines were in Kielce and Silesia, with metallurgical factories located in Warsaw, Łódź, Bydgoszcz and Poznań. Iron and steel production amounted to 724,000 metric tons of pig iron, 1,145,000 metric tons of steel and 1,047,000 metric tons of rolled iron.

It can be argued that, following the catastrophic September Campaign,[4] Poland's wartime history fragmented into three discernible historiographies. The first of these was the escape of the Polish Government with the remnants of Poland's armed forces to the West. Approximately 60,000 men left Polish territory via Romania and Hungary alongside the nation's politicians and religious leaders, heading for France and Britain (Poland's allies). The remnants of the Airforce made their way directly to British and French airfields; the Polish Navy had already reached Scotland early on in the conflict via the Baltic and North Sea, when it had been decided not to engage the German Navy in futile operations.

In 1939, Poland's southern border with Romania and Hungary was called the 'Green Border', as it was lightly defended and relatively safe to cross. The specialist knowledge of foresters, who lived in the southern borderlands of Poland, was exploited by individuals and

---

4   Name given to the campaign to defend Poland in September 1939.

groups of Poles escaping their country on foot across the Carpathian Mountain range. This is how Kazimierz Szydło describes his escape from Poland

> Andrew was to be our guide and he expected 100 zł for his services ... He first took us to his house where his wife prepared some bread and warm milk for us. We left at midnight. He led us up into the mountains along snow-laden paths and we had to make sure we did not slip. After three hours walking we had crossed the mountains and arrived in a village called *Vyrawa* in Slovakia ... Our next objective was to reach the Polish consulate at *Uzhorod* in Hungary. It was another 30 kilometres to the Hungarian border followed by 80 kilometres to the consulate offices.[5]

Bucharest had a long-standing agreement with Warsaw which allowed for the reception of Polish citizens in times of national crisis, but this soon changed when Berlin warned the Romanians not to harbour or assist enemies of the Reich. The threat resulted in Bucharest deciding to place those who had reached Romanian territory into internment camps. Nevertheless, a blind eye was often turned, and many escaped to continue their onward journey to the West. Crossing the Hungarian border was not as straightforward, since Budapest did not have any formal agreements with Warsaw. There was only an age-old legend which told of a 'special relationship' between the Poles and the Magyars. German forces, already in Hungary when the Poles arrived, were not permitted to intervene until the signing of the Tripartite Pact had taken place in September 1940. Meanwhile the Polish Consulate in Hungary provided clandestine assistance through the provision of false names and travel documents for the onward journey.

The objective of the escaping Poles was to reach France, Poland's nearest ally, but if this was not possible, to head to Syria instead, which at that time was a French protectorate. The tens of thousands of Polish servicemen who managed to reach France, where the exiled Polish Government had reformed, were reorganised into a fresh Polish army and placed under French operational command. When France fell in 1940, they were evacuated to Britain via Dunkirk[6] and subsequently re-equipped in Scotland alongside Polish forces who had arrived there previously (for example, the Poles serving in the RAF and alongside the Royal Navy).

When the Poles decamped to London in 1940 Winston Churchill, who by now was Britain's Prime Minister, was so appreciative of the fact that the Poles wanted to fight on, that he told General Sikorski,[7]

> We are comrades in life and death. We shall conquer together, or we shall die together.[8]

Churchill's enthusiastic appreciation of the Poles during this time was a response to the scarcely veiled hysteria in London that Britain would be Hitler's next victim. General Sikorski[9] soaked up the flattery he received in the British capital; however, before Polish Forces could embark on operations from British territory, a new Anglo-Polish understanding

---

5   Paraphrased from Kazimierz Szydło, *On a Soldier's Trail*, (Self-published, 2008), pp.4–5.
6   Operation Dynamo.
7   Polish Prime Minister and Commander in Chief.
8   Churchill to Sikorski, 18 June 1940.
9   Polish Prime Minister and Commander-in-Chief 1939 to 1943.

was required based on the Allied Forces Act of 1940. This agreement committed the British to the furnishing of arms, equipment and training facilities, as well as to providing help in reorganising the Poles along British military lines. Although these forces were commanded by Polish officers, they fought under British operational command. At the same time, the Poles in the French protectorate of Syria transferred to Palestine and placed themselves under British command, rather than surrendering to German authorities on the fall of France. These men eventually saw action in Tobruk and El Alamein alongside British and Australian troops.

Amongst the escaping Poles in 1939 were the cryptologists who had broken the Enigma Code in 1932.[10] When Britain became Poland's formal ally in 1939, Warsaw had agreed to share its secret work with London; this was later instrumental in the establishment of Bletchley Park, Britain's wartime cipher bureau. The accuracy and speed of deciphering improved significantly when Tommy Flowers[11] applied basic computing techniques to the Polish methods. This allowed the British to cross-reference information from Bletchley Park with data emanating from the string of coastal radar stations and, therefore, glean the most accurate and pertinent information about German tactical intentions.

The second historiography, after the debacle of the September Campaign,[12] concerns the Poles who found themselves left behind in west Poland under German jurisdiction. The events surrounding this history are probably the most familiar today, as the German occupation of Poland became a popular topic of academic research after the war. It demonstrated that the people in this zone suffered the most brutal hardship and shameful treatment, where discipline and order was maintained through terror, public executions, mass murder, beatings and deportations to slave camps. This action would eventually contribute to the death of 6,000,000 Polish citizens, half being Jewish.

German authorities considered the Poles to be '*untermensch*' (sub-human) and therefore suitable for exploitation as slave labour. The words of *Friedrich Uebelhoer*, the German governor of *Łódź*, spoken on 11 November 1939 illustrate the German attitude towards the Poles that prevailed at the time,

> We are the masters. We must therefore behave like masters. The Pole is a servant (*Knecht*) so he must serve. We must have steel in our backbones ... and never allow Poland to be reborn. Be strong ... [13]

Millions of Poles were uprooted and transferred to Germany and Nazi-occupied Austria where they were put to work in factories, in domestic service and on the land. Some unfortunate individuals were also included in medical experiments where people were treated no better than laboratory animals. At the same time, on reaching the age of 18, numerous Poles remaining in German-occupied Poland were conscripted into the Nazi Army under pain of death. Many would later endeavour to join the Polish allied forces under British command.

The third discernible historiography after the fall of Poland in 1939 concerns the

---

10 See J. Różycki, H. Zygalski and M. Rejewski.
11 Thomas Flowers, MBE, designed and built Colossus, the world's first programmable electronic computer.
12 The name given to the failed defence of Poland in 1939.
13 *The German Occupation of Poland*, (The Ministry of Foreign Affairs, Republic of Poland), extract of note addressed to the Governments of Allied and Neutral Powers, 3 May 1941, pp.1–2.

Polish men and women of fighting age, having reached the West, enrolled in the Polish Armed Forces abroad. This is an enrolment document for enlistment into 2nd Carpathian Artillery Brigade dated 9 December 1942 (issued in the French protectorate of Syria).

population in Eastern Poland, which found itself under Soviet rule. The attitude of the Soviet regime to the Poles was significantly different to that of the Nazis. Firstly, the Soviets believed that large swathes of eastern Poland were really Russian territory which had been unjustly snatched through Polish military aggression in 1921[14] and, secondly, that the Poles were political enemies of the Soviet regime and so had to be neutralised as soon as possible. Just as with the Romanov family, some 100 years earlier, the view was that the best way to do this was to 'cut off the serpent's head', in other words to dispose of the Polish intelligentsia, including the political and military elite and community leaders. In April 1940, for example, Stalin approved the execution of 20,000 Polish nationals in the Katyn Forest region, many of whom were army officers of the Polish Eastern Command and high ranking civil servants who had been rounded up in huge operations by the Red Army.[15] Other representatives of the Polish state, those on the second tier of importance, were not killed but sent for trial and then interned in 'corrective camps', where they were indoctrinated with Marxist and Leninist ideology. However it would be wrong to think that the Soviets did not also use Poles as slave labour. On the contrary, tens of thousands of Polish nationals (many of them women and children) were rounded up and forcibly deported to regions such as Siberia and Kazakhstan, where they were placed in labour camps (*Gulags*) and forced to toil for

---

14   Sometimes described as the Polish Wars of Independence.
15   See the Katyn Murders.

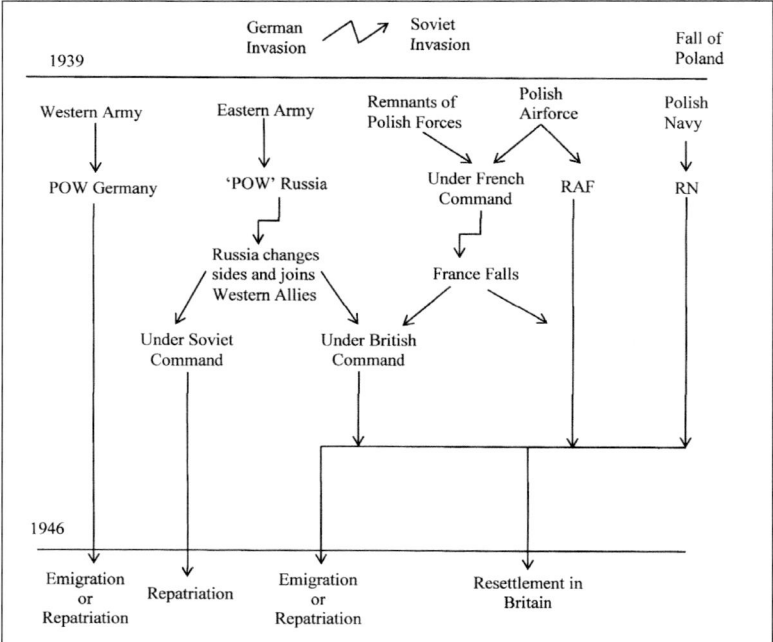

Figure 1: Destiny of Polish forces in the Second World War.

the regime.

This probably would have been the end of the story for Poles under Soviet jurisdiction if it had not been for Operation Barbarossa.[16] Secretly, Berlin had always considered the Molotov-Ribbentrop Pact a temporary arrangement which could be discarded just as soon as it was convenient. Germany decided that this could happen on 22 June 1941, and attacked her Soviet ally, starting what is sometimes called the 'war of total annihilation'. In the face of the German onslaught, Stalin turned to London seeking an alliance with Britain. Churchill, who had always coveted the military potential of the Red Army, snatched at the offer, resulting in Soviet Russia changing sides in the war. The price Britain had to pay for the 'services' of the Red Army was to conveniently forget Russia's early military exploits in the war, which included attacking the Baltic States, Finland and Britain's ally, Poland. It was obviously convenient for both London and Moscow to avoid highlighting these events, just in case they had an unfavourable influence on public opinion. Even today this history is little understood in the West and totally ignored by Russian historians who describe the start of the Second World War[17] as beginning in 1941 – the year Russia joined the Western Allies. Churchill knew that allowing the Soviet Union to join the Allies would make Britain's relationship with exiled Polish authorities in London fractious; nevertheless, he pressed the exiled Polish Government to accept the Soviets. Sikorski[18] took a huge political and personal gamble in accepting the British Prime Minister's advice for his political retinue, particularly ex-members of the pre-war Polish government, had warned him that the decision would be

---

16 See the German invasion of the Soviet Union, 22 June 1941.
17 What the Russians call the 'Great Patriotic War'.
18 General *Sikorski*, Polish Prime Minister and Polish Commander-in-Chief.

Cartoon 1: General Anders leads the Polish Army out of Russia to the British protectorate of Palestine.

a grave mistake; but perhaps Sikorski appreciated that the Soviet Union would be hugely influential in post-war Europe when the existence of Poland was going to be decided. He only accepted Churchill's recommendation on one condition – that Stalin would release all Polish citizens who had been forcibly deported from eastern Poland between 1939 and 1940.

Stalin's approval was a miraculous change of fortune for these deportees. Operation Barbarossa did not only furnish them with a new start in life, but also provided the Polish Government with a fresh reservoir of potential troops who could be conscripted into a new Polish army in the East. Tens of thousands of undernourished men and women, who saw enlistment as a route out of Russia, flocked in their tattered prison clothes to Polish recruiting stations. With them came the children, the orphans, the old and the sick, also released from captivity. When General Władysław Anders saw these wretched people he declared, with Britain's approval, that the Polish Army would take them into its care.[19]

Stalin welcomed General Anders back to the fold, declaring that brave Polish men would fight alongside the Red Army and enter Poland from the east. General Anders baulked at the idea, for why should the Poles under his command fight beside the Red Army, when they had only just recently been enslaved and tormented by the Soviets. He argued that the Polish Army should fight alongside the British and cabled the exiled government in London to inform it of his position. Following a period of toing and froing between Moscow and London, Stalin eventually agreed to the total evacuation of Polish soldiers and civilians from the Soviet Union, allegedly saying, 'Go, we only want men who want to fight!'.

19 1892–1970.

Eventually Polish forces, along with approximately 30,000 desperate civilians, left Soviet territory to fight alongside the nearest British forces. These happened to be stationed in the Middle East, where they were protecting Arabian oil fields and the Suez Canal for the Allies. The Polish civilians were placed in British safe havens in the Commonwealth, whilst the fledgling Polish army was transferred across the Caspian Sea, through Iran, Iraq and finally into the British protectorate of Palestine. After resting, they were amalgamated with Polish units[20] which had recently completed operations in Tobruk and Gazala. The merger saw the formation of the Polish 2nd Corps, under the command of General Władysław Anders. The corps spent the rest of the war as an integral part of British 8th Army in the Italian campaign.

General Sikorski addressed the men of the newly formed corps,

> Soldiers! The Polish divisions formed in the Soviet Union were transferred to the Middle East in late August. When these units are merged with those from Tobruk and the desert, a significant Polish military potential, formed on British and American power, will be created. Soon this formation will resume the fight against our enemy, Germany ... Soldiers! Such a great increase in Polish military power is occurring on the third anniversary of our taking up arms against the aggressor. Then, Poland served as an alarm for the rest of the world. Now, our very much increased potential is a signal that we are fighting for the ultimate Polish victory.[21]

In the meantime, civilians were sent to British 'safe havens' in various parts of the British Empire – countries such as Rhodesia, South Africa, India and New Zealand, pending a return to Poland after the War.

When Germany capitulated at the end of the war in May 1945, Churchill turned to the Poles, thanked them for their 'heroic' contribution to the war effort and said that they could now return home as heroes to rebuild their homeland. The exiled Polish Government in London, together with the Polish High Command, were flabbergasted. How could it be the end of the war, they protested, when Poland was now occupied by the Soviet Union? They argued that they had not fought for six hard years only to replace one occupier of their country with another. They pointed to the rubric of the 1939 agreement between Britain and the Polish Republic which stated that neither contracting party would lay down its arms until true and full independence was achieved for both countries. The occupation of Poland by the Red Army and the imposition of a communist regime in Warsaw could hardly be called 'independence'. This was an awkward and very powerful argument which His Majesty's Government had to resolve.

---

20   3rd Carpathian Infantry Division.
21   Order of the Day Number 16, General Sikorski, 27 August 1942.

3

Pragmatism versus Idealism

The age-old diplomatic adage of making friends with the country next to yours but one, seemed to have been well learnt in 1939. Both Britain and France, together with Poland, had calculated that such an arrangement would corral Germany and keep her at bay, whilst Germany and the Soviet Union had judged that their pact would allow both countries to pursue their individual expansionist policies unhindered by the other. Subsequent events showed that Germany and the Soviet Union had applied their theory successfully, for Poland was wiped off the European map within one month, and the Baltic States and Finland were invaded by the Red Army.[1] The position regarding Britain, France and Poland, on the other hand, could not have been more different, for, despite the pledges they had made to each other, France was not prepared to fight in 1939 and Britain was simply not ready. Before anything could be done, it was all over for Britain's eastern ally. In fact all that London manged to achieve at the time was to order Bomber Command to blanket Germany with propaganda leaflets, a gambit which today is known as the 'Confetti War'.[2]

France, on the other hand, tentatively sent its forces into the German borderlands, only to withdraw them rapidly on the appearance of a German response.[3] Hitler's prediction in 1939 that the Western Allies would not fight over Poland was correct.

Strategic objectives are paramount during military conflict, whilst the secondary objectives, such as the right of peoples to choose their own government (as enshrined in the Atlantic Charter),[4] or what the nature of post-war Europe should be, remain subordinate. However, in 1944 as Germany headed for defeat, these political issues rose rapidly in the agenda. Fearing the development of a power vacuum in central Europe on German capitulation, the Allies quickly turned their attention to agreeing post-war settlements and the new order which was to prevail on the continent. However, just as soon as they sat around the table to thrash out Europe's future, they were confronted with the age old conundrum: to what extent should pragmatism supersede idealism?

The Teheran, Yalta and Potsdam conferences were essentially discussions on the possibility of achieving the 'ideal' for Europe as outlined in the Atlantic Charter; however, as soon as deliberations started, they degenerated into a power struggle between Stalin and Churchill forcing the British Prime Minister, who was also negotiating on behalf of the Poles, to compromise on idealism.[5] The underlying tensions brought out what was true all along into the open – that the Allies were fighting for different political and strategic objectives – apart, that is, from the defeat of Nazi Germany. The conferences also demonstrated that

---

1 Sometimes called the Winter War.
2 Hansard, *Parliamentary Debate*, 5 September, Vol. 351, col. 582 for PM's statement on war situation, 7 September.
3 See the Phoney War.
4 Document outlining Britain's and America's war aims.
5 November–December 1943.

America and Britain had different value systems to those of the Soviet Union, as Stalin was attempting to eke out a new sphere of influence (empire) in Europe. The independence of all the countries liberated from Nazi occupation would have to be realised if the ideal was to be achieved. However, Stalin had other ideas and insisted that the Red Army should remain on the territory it had 'liberated', implying that only 'Soviet friendly' governments could be installed in Prague, Budapest, Sofia, Bucharest, Riga, Vilnius, Kiev and Warsaw.

At the Yalta Conference, Churchill confronted Stalin over his proposals, particularly those concerning Poland, and called on Roosevelt for support. The Polish nation was important to London, because the protection of the country's independence had always been portrayed as the main reason for Britain's entry into the War; however, the American President was outmanoeuvred by Stalin, who reminded the Americans that they might still need Soviet help in defeating the Japanese in the Far East, where the War was continuing apace. Consequently, Roosevelt, who was still uncertain whether the Manhattan Project[6] would succeed, was cautious about browbeating Stalin on his policies for post-war Europe. Stalin's *raison d'être* was that those who had borne the greatest burden in the war should be responsible for writing the peace. Churchill, on the other hand, was on a different page believing that the greater powers should discharge their moral responsibility and leadership, with moderation and respect for the rights of smaller nations. As far as he was concerned, the rights of smaller countries should not be considered to suit only the aspirations of the powerful. So bitter were the exchanges between Stalin and Churchill, that by late April 1945 they wondered about each other's honesty, trustworthiness and willingness to compromise.

Despite the agreement to set up the United Nations – a noble act under the circumstances – trust between the three leaders had seriously faltered, if indeed it had been there in the first place. Having learned from the mistakes of the League of Nations, the formation of the United Nations was the first significant post-war achievement of the 'major' allies;[7] however the price paid for its inauguration was that Stalin's plans for Europe were allowed to prevail, with Poland being placed firmly behind the Iron Curtain.[8] The resulting agreement also saw Hungary, Romania, Czechoslovakia, Bulgaria, Latvia, Estonia, Lithuania, Ukraine and Eastern Germany become integral components of the Soviet 'sphere of interest' (empire), whilst Greece, Italy, Austria and West Germany remained in the 'western family of nations'. Churchill, forgoing idealism, claimed that this arrangement was the best deal that could have been expected under the prevailing circumstances in 1945. This was a pragmatic argument, and one that was never considered to be completely just in the West. The discontent regarding the post-war conferences eventually precipitated the Cold War, which at the time was just as dangerous as a 'hot war'. The *Daily Telegraph* boomed, 'Eight day talks in Crimea: Poland Agreement.'[9]

> Agreement was reached on the conditions in which a new Polish Provisional Government of National Unity may be formed. The Provisional Government should be reorganised on a broad democratic basis with the inclusion of democratic leaders from Poland itself and from Poles abroad. Mr Churchill, President Roosevelt and Marshal

---

6   The development and dropping of the Nuclear Bomb.
7   Britain, America and the Soviet Union.
8   Metaphor for the division of Europe into two political camps.
9   *The Daily Telegraph*, 13 February 1945.

Stalin consider that the eastern frontiers of Poland should follow the Curzon Line.[10]

Churchill bristled when he returned to London from the Crimea, for he knew that he would have to face the members of the Allied Polish Government (exiled in London), who were bound to protest about what had been agreed, or indeed not agreed. How could Churchill have betrayed the Poles after their valiant contribution to the war and what was he thinking when it had been agreed to cede approximately half of Poland's pre-war territory to Moscow? The pragmatic view, that this was 'the best that could be expected under the circumstances', did not wash with the Allied Poles, who continued arguing from idealistic and ethical principles. For them it was a moral (idealistic) duty that one does not betray an ally just because loyalty becomes difficult. Churchill also knew that he would have to face criticism from the House of Commons and explain why the Anglo-Polish Agreement (signed in 1939) had failed to save the Second Republic of Poland. The British Prime Minister was also well aware of the fact that the Yalta agreements threatened to portray Britain as a country which does not honour her international obligations. In order to sidestep such sentiment, the Cabinet embarked on a propaganda campaign designed to snatch the narrative from the Poles in the hope of shifting some of the blame for the problems onto 'unrealistic' Polish foreign policy. For example, London called the allied Poles 'intransigent', 'unrealistic' and 'naïve' for drawing unnecessary public attention to the prevailing difficulties. Churchill even went so far as to unofficially 'rewrite' the 1939 Anglo-Polish agreement by arguing that Britain had never guaranteed Poland's territorial and political integrity in 1939, only the country's continued existence.

When the exiled Polish Government in London received details from the Yalta conference, the British Prime Minister could not have been surprised by its response. Predictably, and probably expectedly, on 13 February the Poles rejected all the decisions that had put Poland behind the Iron Curtain. The reason for the rejection was that they had not been party to any discussions on the matter (nothing about us without us), and the issue concerning the political nature of their country after the war was an 'internal matter'. These were powerful arguments for Churchill to face, but as the British and Poles continued to argue, the impasse between them grew increasingly bitter and eventually turned into a stand-off. The British press set aside any pleasantries that may have existed, calling the Polish Forces in the West a 'bunch of hooligans'.[11] To dispel any further embarrassment, the British Government decided to remove its recognition of the Polish Allied Government in July 1945, eradicating at a stroke its authority to speak on behalf of the Poles,[12] whilst at the same time closing down the Polish Radio station in London. This action removed the possibility of further damaging discourse; however, in order to solve the 'Polish problem' completely, the British government also had to dispose of the Polish Forces in the West who had refused to stand down in protest. The Polish High Command pointed to the 1939 Anglo-Polish Agreement, where it was stated that 'neither of the contracting parties would lay down their arms until both parties had achieved independence'. Technically, this required both the Poles and the British to continue fighting until the Red Army had been removed from Polish territory. This reasoning was most troublesome, for not only was it based on international

---

10   *Telegraph*, 13 February 1945.
11   Mieczysław Młotek (ed.), *Trzecia Dywizja Strzelców Karpackich, 1942–1947, Tom I*, (London: Zarząd Główny Związku Karpatczyków, 1978) p.764.
12   Completed on 5 July 1945 by the British Interim Government.

Cartoon 2: The Polish Army is transferred to Britain for resettlement.

agreements, but it also implied the unenviable necessity of starting a war with the mighty Red Army. Despite not being fully convinced by these Polish arguments, Churchill's strong anti-communist views made him explore the possibility of such a confrontation, even if it also meant using 'de-nazified' German forces in the operation. He secretly instructed British General Headquarters (GHQ) to evaluate the feasibility of an attack on the Russian army in Europe.[13] Churchill understood that if such an action was successful, it would not only solve the Polish problem, but free Central and Eastern Europe from Russian domination, removing the curse of communism from spreading beyond Soviet borders. The Poles energetically signalled that they were ready to take part in such action. Whilst GHQ went to work, the British Prime Minister secretly presented the idea to the Americans who rejected it out of hand. The Americans replied that they would not take part in any military action against the Russians, as their focus was now on finishing the war with Japan – where Soviet help could still be needed. By 1945 it was clear that the American administration was not prepared to go to war with Russia, especially over Poland. A few days before his death, Roosevelt is reported to have castigated Arthur Bliss Lane, the post-war American ambassador to Poland, by shouting, 'What do you want? Do you want a war with Russia over Poland?'[14] Acheson, who was well known for his astute and clinical mind added that, 'Geography betrayed the Poles: not the Allies.'[15]

When news from GHQ landed on Churchill's desk he read it very carefully. Written on 22 May 1945, the document concluded that,

> If we are to embark on war with Russia, we must be prepared to be committed to a total war, which will be both long and costly ... Our numerical inferiority on land renders it extremely doubtful whether we could achieve a limited and quick success. Signed G. Grantham, G.S. Thomson and W.L. Dawson

The implication was that a confrontation with the Red Army would almost certainly

---

13 Operation Unthinkable.
14 Sebestyen, *1946: The Making of the Modern World*, p.180.
15 Dean Acheson, Advisor to the President.

result in a long and protracted war of attrition, without any certainty of success, especially if the Americans refused to take part. Quietly, the plans were dropped, with Churchill returning to inform the Polish High Command, that there would be no war with the Red Army and that the Poles would have to lay down their arms and return home. The Poles continued to resist and, since London did not want to repeat the debacle concerning Cossack refugees, who were forcibly marched under British bayonet into Soviet hands never to be seen again, it decided not to use coercion or force the Poles to comply. However, the question still remained; what to do next?

4

Trouble in the House (the Crimea Conference Debate)

It was perhaps inevitable that difficult questions would be asked of the British Government regarding Poland when the Yalta Agreement was discussed in the Houses of Parliament.[1] Britain had always insisted that one reason for going to war was to protect the freedom and integrity of Poland and to prevent the domination by a strong nation of its weaker neighbour. When the details of the Yalta agreement[2] were released to the House on 11 February 1945, many MPs saw that the document contained some fundamental contradictions, which could be construed as being unfair to the Poles, something which could easily jeopardise Britain's reputation as an honourable ally. It was clear from the text, for example, that far from protecting Polish freedom and integrity it seemed that Polish rights had been violated and, in some cases, completely ignored. It was the view in the House that this was certainly not the kind of conclusion to the War that the British people had envisaged. Time and time again Members of the House lamented that, despite the defence of Poland being the immediate cause of Britain's entry into the war, the country was destined to lose almost half her pre-war territory to Russia with a communist government being imposed on Warsaw which, incidentally, contravened Article Eight of the Atlantic Charter. This, to some, constituted a betrayal of a loyal ally.[3] As a result 33 percent of Poland's pre-war population was relocated to within the borders of the new communist Polish state. 85 percent of her oil and natural gas, 48 percent of her timber and peat, 50 percent of her chemical industry and nearly half her chemical production capacity was now part of the Soviet economy. She also lost half her grain and flax, together with 40 percent of her water power and potassium and phosphate mines. During subsequent debates the House was reminded that, when a country has been defeated it must bear the consequences, but this was not the case with Poland, for it had not lost the war. Poland had fought as an ally throughout and was on the winning side. There were other concerns regarding the Yalta Agreement that troubled the House. The document appeared to cast doubt on Britain's willingness to honour her international obligations. What would the world think if it was allowed to appear that Britain had let her loyal ally down so publically and decisively; an action which appeared to endorse the old Arabian proverb; 'If you are Britain's enemy, she will buy you, if you are her friend, she will sell you'.[4]

There was also concern from Members of Parliament about whether the Yalta Agreement stood any chance of bringing lasting peace to Europe. The view was that there could be no lasting peace, unless the sanctity of treaties confirming boundaries entered into freely were recognised and honoured. However, Doctor Guest (MP for Islington North) believed

---

1 Discussed from February to June 1945.
2 The Conference was held at Yalta on the Crimean Peninsula, February 1945.
3 Sebestyen, *1946: The Making of the Modern World*, p.177.
4 Nanke, *Cena Bycia Innym*, p.206.

that there was no reason for the Government to fret unduly over Russian plans to 'adjust' Poland's borders, because the territory passing to the Russians was originally taken from the Soviet Union when Poland attacked her in 1921.[5] This territory, he argued, was established through military conquest and subsequently, owing to the weakness of Russia, embodied in treaty. He could not see why this conquest was thought to be sacrosanct and that nothing afterwards could be regarded as having any justification. In his opinion, the protests being voiced against the Yalta Agreement by the Poles were nothing more than an expression of 'anti-Soviet prejudice of the worst possible kind'. Major Guy Lloyd (Member of Parliament for Renfrew East) wondered why the question of Poland's eastern border could not have been left until the end of the conflict; but Stalin was working for a *fait accompli* on the matter and even pursued it with vigour before the capitulation of the Germans had occurred. Lloyd then read out a statement to the House which was issued by the Ministry of Information on 17 September 1939, the day the Russian armies entered Poland,

> This attack made upon Great Britain's ally at a moment when she is prostrate in the face of overwhelming forces brought against her by Germany cannot in the view of His Majesty's Government be justified ... But His Majesty's Government take the opportunity of stating that nothing that has occurred can make any difference to the determination of His Majesty's Government, with the full support of the country, to fulfil her obligations to Poland.

He considered the statement was as a solemn pledge to Poland which was now being deliberately ignored and broken. He argued that it was 'adding insult to injury, not only to break Britain's pledge to Poland but to compel her people to accept a prefabricated government, something Britain should be ashamed of'. William Brown (Independent MP for Rugby 1945–1950) reminded the House that, at the Potsdam Conference, it was agreed to run elections in the country and that this should solve many of the outstanding issues regarding the Polish ally. He reasoned that for Poland to be 'truly free, truly democratic and truly independent', the matter of free elections was vital.

He enquired whether the post-war elections in Poland would be held with the Red Army in occupation and in towns and villages 'under the control and iron grip of the Soviet secret police?' Brown doubted whether the artificially approved and cynically named 'Government of National Unity' would override the intense desire of the *NKVD*[6] to communise Poland. He had looked upon Britain as the trustee of Poland and, with the Yalta Agreement, it appeared to him that London was 'ready to let her down', something he would look upon with great shame. However, he acknowledged that, the effect of no agreement will be infinitely worse than the worst that would happen under this document'. Major Lord Willoughby de Eresby (MP for Rutland and Stamford) reminded the House that Britain did not go to war to protect a Poland as decreed by the Soviet Union, but a Poland with similar frontiers to those that Britain had guaranteed. Willoughby called on the government to make a gesture as part of its duty to the Poles who did not want to return to a 'Sovietised' Poland, and to offer them safe haven either within 'our shores or within the Empire'.

Mr Price (Morgan Philips Price, Labour MP for the Forest of Dean) asked the Foreign Secretary whether he would reconsider the whole status of the Polish Government in London,

---

5 See the Polish-Soviet War, 1921.
6 The People's Commissariat for Internal Affairs, Soviet Secret Police.

if the Yalta Agreement was accepted. The reply quashed the chance of this happening, for it was explained that when the Provisional Government of National Unity had been formed, the British and the American Government, together with the Union of Soviet Socialist Republics would establish diplomatic relations with it. Mr Petherick (Maurice Petherick, Conservative MP for Penryn and Falmouth) noted that the Provisional Government was to be chosen by 'three eminent men and a brace of Ambassadors, together with a Foreign Secretary'. He wondered if Britain would 'like that very much' and if the British people would 'show much confidence in a government so chosen?' He went further by asking whether any country in the whole wide world would accept such a government. He then referred to the Atlantic Charter, which stated that people should be free to choose the type of government they wish to live under, and went on to say that the government the Soviets were establishing was 'chosen for the Poles', which was wrong and showed a 'poor treatment of Poland'. Nevertheless, speaker after speaker rose to their feet, shrugged their shoulders and, using pragmatic rather than idealistic argument, indicated that there was nothing that could have been done better under the prevailing circumstances. Petherick warned, however, that Britain's treatment of the Poles 'will be the touchstone by which Britain's post-war relationships will be measured'. Major Lloyd then rose to his feet and protested that the intention of the Yalta Agreement was to 'downright annex large portions of Poland's territory without the consent of her government and, what's more, without the consent of her people'. In his view this was a very definite moral breach of the Anglo-Polish Charter, which had now been whittled down to a mere 'meaningless symbol'. Reginald Manningham-Buller (Conservative MP for Daventry) then rose to his feet and said that, as a lawyer, he did not like anything that was 'unconstitutional' and reminded the House that the Polish Allied Government in London was not party to the Yalta Agreement. This he found 'very difficult to accept'. Victor Raikes (Conservative MP for Liverpool, Wavertree) returned to the question of British honour and lamented that the Atlantic Charter was finally repudiated at Yalta. He appeared to castigate Clement Attlee[7] for saying that; 'in any case, Poland would have been utterly destroyed if it had not been for the Russians' and continued that the Prime Minister reminded him of 'a man that regarded Poland as a defeated country, which has to get the best it can after defeat'. Petherick questioned whether the Prime Minister, together with the Foreign Secretary, turned to Poland after the Polish guarantee had been given to say, 'We are sorry, but in view of the fact that Germany and Russia have come together, total destruction is all that you can hope for if you stand up to Germany, whatever the democracies may do.' He was also astounded that the legitimate Polish Government in London, recognised as legitimate throughout the War, should not have had one word of consultation. Brown argued that he could not see any escape whatsoever from what the Prime Minister had agreed at Yalta. He explained that the accusation that the 'London Government was not consulted' was not the real difficulty for, although the London Poles 'regard themselves as representatives of the Polish people', a very large section of the Polish community do not. Likewise, if the Lublin Committee[8] regards itself as the true representative of the Polish people, there are many Poles who do not agree. What better line of approach could have been advanced, Brown argued, than to form some sort of Government of National Unity? He wondered whether it was the Lublin Committee or the Allied Government in London

---

7   Prime Minister from 26 October 1945 to 26 October 1951.
8   Also known as the Polish Committee of National Liberation, considered by many as the puppet Provisional Government of Poland.

that was the true government or both. If it is either, he said, one could not get a settlement, if it is both one would get chaos. He ended by informing the House that the PM's purpose at Yalta had to be to keep the Allies together, and that there were other pressing issues besides Poland and even more important ones.

Clearly, MPs were falling into two camps, those who believed that it was a shame that the Poles had been betrayed and those who ascertained that the deal at Yalta was the best that could be hoped for. This group of MPs believed that the Poles were suffering with inflated aspirations and that they should, 'get real, get over it and go back'. The view was that if the Yalta Agreement was acceptable to Churchill at the time of signing, then it should be good enough for the Poles now. Perhaps it was Douglas Savory[9] who asked the Foreign Secretary the telling question whether the President of Poland,[10] also exiled in London, had been consulted on the matter as being the only person entitled to appoint or dismiss a Polish Government. The answer was that he was not.

By May 1945, the Polish military under British command believed that the rug had been pulled from under their feet. They were unable to accept that the government they had sworn allegiance to had been so effortlessly disenfranchised by the British *de facto* accepting Russia's occupation of Poland. Nor could they accept that they were being asked by an ally (Britain) to return home and live under Soviet domination. The Allied Poles were convinced that justice delayed is nothing more than justice denied and therefore continued to protest.

It could be said that these Polish Forces were the second generation of modern Poland[11] which was called upon to defend their country and, despite fighting hard and loyally on the winning side, they felt they would have failed in this endeavour if they laid down their arms in 1945 as Britain was recommending. Accepting Yalta for them would have meant that they had failed in doing their duty in protecting their country. As the Polish leader, Józef Piłsudski,[12] had said 10 years earlier, 'To be vanquished and yet not surrender, that is victory.'

Following the 1945 British elections, it fell on Clement Attlee and his administration to resolve the situation and, to his credit, he accepted Churchill's pledge to treat the Poles as a 'special case'.

---

9   South Antrim.
10 President Raczkiewicz.
11 The Second Republic.
12 Józef Piłsudski, 1867 to 1935, one time leader of the Polish Second Republic.

5

On the Question of Repatriation

For the Polish Forces fighting alongside the British 8th Army in Italy, the end of conflict came at 2pm on 2 May 1945. For those fighting in north west Europe (the First Armoured Division) it came on 4 May, in Germany. The official act of German surrender was signed at 2:41am on 7 May with Victory in Europe Day coming on 8 May. For the second time in history, Europe had passed through some of the most horrendous episodes ever instigated by mankind. The continent was tired and spent. For the first time in six long and arduous years people were able to lift their eyes from the toils of war and gaze on a peaceful and tranquil though devastated landscape. And once again, just as it had been in the aftermath of the First World War, wartime leaders vowed that such horrors must never be repeated; but, as with most wars, the end of conflict in 1945 was a fractious time, particularly when, on 5 July, the communist Committee of National Union was 'ordained' as the legal Polish Government in waiting. However, the immediate issue was the repatriation of soldiers and millions of civilians displaced by the fighting. Consequently, between 1945 and 1948, Europe witnessed some of the largest mass movement of people ever seen in history and, although the process was commendable and welcome for those being moved on humanitarian grounds, this was hardly the case with those who were being relocated for political expediency as the map of Europe was redrawn once again. This is what had occurred with German and eastern European populations in Ukraine, Poland and Belarus, as Russia went about rearranging nation states in order to build her new empire. However, despite Soviet foreign policy being in line with the Yalta accord, by July 1945 and the Potsdam Conference the trust between Churchill, Truman[1] and Stalin had evaporated to such an extent that it unavoidably spawned suspicion and mistrust. The European continent cleaved into two huge, opposing, political power blocks, usually described as The East and The West. Excluding the special arrangements made for Austria, Greece, Turkey and Italy, it was conceded by western governments that the countries liberated from German occupation by the Red Army would remain under Soviet domination.[2] As disconcerting as this was, it forced Washington to embark on a huge initiative which was designed to dissuade other countries from being forced (or tempted) to join the 'Soviet family' of nations. One response in Washington and London was to approve the indefinite stationing of American and British troops in West Germany as a military counterbalance to the Red Army in the east of the country. The British Army on the Rhine,[3] as the British contingent of these forces was named, was formed on the 25 August 1945 from 21st Army Group and was entrusted to resist the threat from the Red Army across the north German plain. This policy precipitated a military standoff which became one of the major components that underpinned post-war peace. The second response to Moscow's foreign policy was the provision of 13 billion American dollars for reconstruction and the rebuilding of liberal

---

1 Harry Truman replaced Roosevelt as the American President, April 1945.
2 Later known as the Warsaw Pact countries after military agreement.
3 BAOR.

democracy in the countries outside the Soviet sphere.[4] The initiative became known as the Marshall Plan, after the newly appointed American Secretary of State, George Marshall. However, even here, problems remained when Berlin became trapped deep inside the Russian zone of occupation in Germany when the Russian front line swept beyond the agreed demarcation line.[5]

Despite British authorities being preoccupied with developments on continental Europe and the standoff which had developed between the Soviet Union and the 'Western Allies', they were at the same time grappling with the continuing 'Polish problem'. By February 1945, Churchill could not have doubted Polish attitudes to the Yalta agreement for General Anders[6] had bluntly informed the British Prime Minister during a series of fractious meetings held in London that, in his view, Britain had betrayed her Polish ally and had openly broken the 1939 Agreement of Mutual Assistance. These were 'high voltage' criticisms which openly displayed Anders' feelings regarding the events unfolding regarding Poland, and explained why relations between the British and the Allied Poles in the West deteriorated to such an extent that Churchill was minded to say to Anders, 'Go, we don't need your forces anymore'. Consequently, General Anders, who believed that peace without justice amounted to nothing more than tyranny, was never sympathetic to the suggestion that the Poles should repatriate to communist Poland. More than once had tempers flared in London over Anders' outspoken views and his veiled suggestion that the British Prime Minister was unable to stand up for the higher ideals of loyalty, honesty and decency. Suddenly, in an attempt to deflect the criticism and diffuse Polish intransigence, Churchill made an unexpected and extraordinary statement in the House on 27 February,

> In the event, His Majesty's Government will never forget the debt they owe to the Polish troops who have served them so valiantly and, for all those who have fought under our command, I earnestly hope that it may be possible to offer the citizenship and freedom of the British Empire, if they so desire.[7]

This statement, sometimes called 'Churchill's Pledge', had turned the Polish issue into a British problem and resulted in extraordinary plans being made in London to dispose of the Polish forces in the West.

In June, Clement Attlee unexpectedly won a landslide victory in the first post-war election on a ticket of 'Let Us Face the Future'. Although the British people respected and were grateful to Churchill for the way he had led them during the hard years of conflict, they were at the same time looking for change and expected 'good old Clem' (Clement Attlee) to modernise the country and take it out of wartime austerity. Despite social reform and moral renewal being the nation's primary objectives, it also fell on the new Prime Minister and his Foreign Secretary, Ernest Bevin, to put together the governmental machinery which would be used to resolve the 'Polish problem'. Perhaps it was fortuitous that Attlee won the election, for he was noted to be a principled man who had a strong sense of justice – arguably the two most important qualities required for working with the disgruntled Poles.

---

4   The Marshall Plan.
5   See the Berlin Airlift.
6   Acting Inspector General of Polish Forces from October 1944 to May 1945.
7   Hansard volume 408 1284, 12 February 1945.

```
                                                    Form B. zał.nr.3.
          APPLICATION
          --------------------

     FOR TERMINATION OF SERVICE /OFFICERS/ OR DISCHARGE /ORs/ FROM
     THE POLISH RESETTLEMENT CORPS ON REPATRIATION OR EMIGRATION.

     and Christian Names
     sko i imiona/
```

Throughout the Resettlement Programme, Polish personnel were given the option to repatriate. For members of the Polish Resettlement Corps this required an application to be made to terminate service. This form was used for the purpose.

Attlee's first action was to endorse the caretaker Government's[8] decision to remove Britain's recognition of the allied exiled Polish Government and transfer allegiance to the communist Polish Government of National Unity in Warsaw. His second move was to have another attempt at persuading the Poles to repatriate. The interim Treasury Committee for Polish Affairs, which took over the responsibilities of the defunct Polish Government's functions in Britain, was to take the leading role in the matter. On 24 August, Attlee informed the Polish Ambassador[9] that Britain would take full charge of demobilising all Polish forces that had fought under British command and were outside Poland. This decision was a game changer, for it meant that London had finally decided to take sole responsibility for the 'Polish problem'. Another reason for the decision was Attlee's belief that the 'ordinary' Polish soldier was being unfairly pressured by a politicised Polish High Command not to repatriate, as such an action, according to the Command, would constitute nothing more than a betrayal of the Colours and 'selling out' to Stalin. Attlee's view, on the other hand, was that most Polish soldiers would return if this pressure was removed and he could reassure them that they would get a hearty welcome, despite the presence of communist rule in Warsaw. Attlee approached the new administration in the Polish capital in order to obtain such an assurance and he received a positive response. The new Polish administration issued the following statement to all the Polish soldiers under British command;

> Poles! The time to return to Poland has arrived. It is time to unite all our forces in the name of the Government of National Unity, which the whole nation supports. All obstacles that existed previously have been removed by the democratic authorities of the People's Republic of Poland and now you can return to your homeland. All Polish nationals, wherever they find themselves, should now accept the authority of the new Government of National Unity. Poland needs you to rebuild a ruined country and to secure the frontiers of the nation. Your heroic efforts, far from our homeland, executed in the name of the fatherland against Nazi Germany, cannot bar you from returning. Heroes of Narvik, Tobruk and Monte Cassino, it is time to return home and unite with your brothers in arms who fought at Leningrad, Warsaw, Gdańsk and Kaliningrad;

---

8 Caretaker Government in office between Churchill's resignation and the Elections, July 1945.
9 Edward Raczyński.

who spilt blood on the banks of the Odra and Nysa rivers and who unfurled the Polish flag in defeated Berlin. The Polish Government of National Unity is providing you with the means by which you can return. There will not be, and must not be, any Polish Army that does not recognise the Government of National Unity.[10]

Having approved the statement, Attlee agreed that it should be included in a pamphlet to be distributed to every Polish serviceman and woman. However, before releasing the pamphlet, he asked Bevin to include a British declaration with a message from His Majesty's Government. The section read,

> Announcement: 1) The British Government is at this time making arrangements for those Polish soldiers who want to return to Poland. 2) If you want to take advantage of these arrangements pass your name to your Commanding Officer. 3) After informing your commander you will be transferred to a transit camp, where the details of your transfer will be given to you. 4) These special arrangements are for those who want to be repatriated immediately or for those who feel they may want to return in the near future.[11]

In September the Polish and British statements were combined into a single pamphlet and made ready for distribution.[12] The War Office reiterated that the distribution was to take place under strict British supervision with no interference from the Polish High Command. To ensure this, the War Office in London sent a top secret cipher telegram to British officers attached to the Polish forces. The one sent to Italy, where the Polish 2nd Corps was stationed, read:

> Report on Polish Press in Italy. In view of forthcoming announcement giving His Majesty's Government policy on return of Poles it is essential you ensure that no articles advising refusal to return to Poland or questioning *bona fide* terms of Warsaw Government should appear in papers run by Polish forces. Short of refusing publication all together, a step we do not desire, repeat NOT desire, the only solution appears to be to refuse publication of all questions of controversial political matters. Such steps have already been taken for Polish papers in UK with satisfactory results.[13]

British officers involved in the distribution of the pamphlets were also instructed to make it known that it was an inescapable fact that Britain could not continue maintaining and paying for any Polish forces under British Command, estimated to be £2,500,000 per month, and therefore they must disband and return home. The War Office also warned British officers in Italy that General Anders might attempt to put pressure on his men not to return to Poland and that this should be 'avoided at all costs', although the War Office was certain that 'the General was aware that His Majesty's Government had exercised great

---

10 *Polska Emigracja Polityczna*, ADIUTOR and the *Institut Pamieci Narodowej, Warszawa* 2004, pp.VII–VIII.
11 Keith Sword with Norman Davies and Jan Ciechanowski, *The Formation of the Polish Community in Great Britain 1939–1950* (London: School of Slavonic and East European Studies, University of London, 1989), p.258.
12 Operation Keynote.
13 The National Archives of the UK (TNA), WO AP/46, Operation Keynote.

patience in dealing with this matter'. London stressed that everyone receiving the publication should be encouraged to read it carefully and take time in making their decision about the future. Finally, it was emphasised that on no account should the Polish soldier come away with the belief that he could settle on British territory, as Churchill's pledge suggested.[14]

The distribution of the pamphlets went ahead as planned on 18–20 March 1946 with the publication being given to all Polish Forces in the Middle East, Italy, north west Germany and Britain. The only Polish personnel who did not receive a pamphlet were cadets in training schools and what the War Office called 'mental cases' in Polish military hospitals. It was of the upmost importance to the British Government that as many Poles as possible chose to repatriate and so it was decided to maintain high morale during the distribution, by exalting the fighting spirit and loyalty of the Polish Forces.

Bevin waited with trepidation in London for reports to arrive on how the distribution had gone. He knew that, if things had gone well, many of the Poles would feel confident to return to a communist Poland, and in so doing, begin to unravel the 'Polish problem'. He did not have to wait long for reports to land on his desk. One of the first came from Italy where the Polish 2nd Corps was stationed. It did not make good reading,

> Distribution of pamphlets completed without incident. Evident that General Anders caused no problems. Men perplexed that their officers had not issued any clarification. Men confused because no date included for decision. Personal suspicion because Warsaw's terms not signed. Mr Bevin's statement not dated and the pamphlet is in poor Polish.

There was also little joy in the report received from the Middle East. Apart from containing the usual evaluation on how things had gone, the report also included some statistical data which provides us with some insight as to the scale of the operation. The report informed the War Office that in Egypt, 4,000 pamphlets were distributed and included Polish schools in Qassasin Camp. 1,500 were distributed in Kontara Camp, 500 in Alexandria Camp and 400 to bases in Cairo. In Palestine, 500 were distributed to Kafr Bilu Camp, 700 to camps in Tel Aviv and 300 to bases in Jerusalem. The report also indicated that Polish schools run by the Polish forces had received pamphlets with 500 going to Barbara, Italy, 500 going to Nazareth, 100 going to Ki Ryit Motzkin, 50 to Beit Mabala and 20 to Tiberias. In total some 116,000 pamphlets were distributed in these regions. The report from Egypt and Palestine had concluded that the distribution was carried out, completed impartially and undertaken with the maximum of good will. However, the report did state that some Polish personnel refused to accept the pamphlet or only agreed to read the British section. It appeared that some personnel had decided beforehand that they would have nothing to do with publications emanating from the communist regime. There was no evidence of Polish officer influence and no propaganda against repatriation had appeared. It was also reported that some men wanted to know whether General Anders knew about the contents of the pamphlets and what his views were on the matter. They also enquired about what would happen to men who did not repatriate. The report concluded that there would be 'no general flow of men' for repatriation and that the Poles believed that His Majesty's Government was being pressed to end the problem of the Polish Army outside Poland, but

---

14   TNA, WO AP/46, Operation Keynote.

they still had faith that the British Government would not fail them.

The government agonised about what to do next, and carried out an analysis of those who had decided to repatriate in order to find out what factors had persuaded them to return in the hope that they could be used to encourage others to follow suit. It found that the overriding reason for returning to Poland was the desire to 'reunite with families'.

For example one soldier reported,

> I cannot see any future for me here and in any case I have family responsibilities at home ... My wife and children were moved from Novogrod and now live near Warsaw. They are living in destitution and I must return to help them, after all I gave my word in front of God to my wife that I shall not leave her until death.[15]

Another soldier wrote,

> I am returning home. I am growing old now, 56, and wish to spend the rest of my life with my family. I am extremely tired and cannot see myself living in England, even on a temporary basis.[16]

Such information convinced the War Office that family ties were an overriding reason for returning, particularly for older members of the Polish forces. However, the analysis also uncovered a worrying trend which showed that many men were receiving letters from parents and siblings still living in Poland, urging them not to return to the country which was in total 'disarray'. This development alarmed the Attlee government for such sentiment put a huge brake on the process of repatriation.

Likewise, the report from Scotland, where Polish troops were also stationed, contained little comfort for the British Government,

> Issued pamphlets 20 March, received calmly. Main criticism, Warsaw Government proclamation is anonymous, Bevin not titled under signature. The men thought that Churchill promised citizenship, but now presented as his opinion – is it not the case that the statement by made Bevin is also an opinion and not government policy? General Maczek is silent on the matter of repatriation. Majority will not return – though a sizeable group will, even up to 30 percent. Conclusion – distribution has not raised anti-British feelings and some believe that hard core refusers will be organised into a Polish Legion.[17]

These reports were indeed gloomy reading for Attlee and his Cabinet for not only did they indicate that the majority of the Polish Forces under British command could not be persuaded to return to Poland, but that a misconception was emerging that Britain would be establishing a British Foreign Legion, made up of Poles, for their zone of occupation in West Germany. The emergence of such inaccurate and troublesome rumours was a worry, for despite the government's attempt to quash such hearsay they continued to persist. In September the final tally of those choosing to return to Poland was published; 33 percent

---

15   Paraphrased from Polish. See *Dziennik Polski i Dziennik Żołnierza, Numer* 286, 4 December.
16   Paraphrased from Polish. *Dziennik Polski Numer* 286, 4 December.
17   TNA, WO AP46, Operation Keynote.

from the UK, one percent from Germany, 14 percent from Italy and four and a half percent from the Middle East. This gave a grand total of 52.5 percent of Polish forces under British command who would repatriate which meant that out of 207,000 men 107,000 would return.[18] However, the whole pamphleting exercise was suddenly and unexpectedly stopped in its tracks, when the Polish Government of National Unity in Warsaw turned on its heels and announced that it would no longer recognise Polish forces under British command as units of the Polish Sovereign Army, and would not take any further responsibility for them. If any man wanted to repatriate, he would have to apply as an individual. Warsaw's about-face broke like a tidal wave across Attlee's desk, for the reason for this decision was far from clear. Speculation today suggests that what Warsaw was trying to prevent was a huge influx of anti-communist forces into Poland, where they could become a beacon of resistance to communist rule. Meanwhile, Warsaw secretly re-wrote its policy towards the Polish forces in the West and distributed it to Polish diplomatic missions. The objective now was to 'destroy the Polish Exiled Government's Polish Armed Forces and to extinguish traitors, bandits and murderers of reborn Poland'.[19] This development was obviously a serious blow to Attlee's repatriation policy, but the British Prime Minister also recognised that Warsaw's about-face had provided him with a free hand to deal with the Polish question which could be exploited without hindrance from outside interference. As far as the Poles under British command were concerned, the Warsaw announcement had only confirmed what they had always believed; that there was no point in returning to a communist homeland where lies and deceit was the norm. In the light of these developments Attlee had to rethink his approach to the Polish problem. As of 30 September 1949, 8,984 PRC personnel (excluding PRC Naval Wing) were repatriated.

---

18 *Dziennik Polski I Dziennik Żołnierza*, Rok 3, Numer 64, 15 March 1946.
19 'Poland under Soviet Occupation' in *Goniec Karpacki*, Issued in London 1984, p.458.

6

On the Question of Emigration

During April 1946, the British government agonised about the pamphleting of the Polish Allied Forces under British command. The operation had failed to reassure the Poles that repatriation was the best future for them, although it would be wrong to believe that it had no effect, for the number of returners increased to 9,000 after the operation which approximated to one percent of all the men in the West. In order to find what else the Government could do to encourage repatriation, Attlee embarked on finding out what factors were influential when the decision not to return home was made. He found that those least likely to repatriate were individuals who had originally lived in eastern Poland; territory where Soviet terror was rampant during the war. He concluded that the presence of the Russians in Poland in 1946 was the overriding factor which prevented many of the men under British command from returning. As soon as Attlee realised this, he reasoned that if the men were given an opportunity to settle in countries absent of communism, in particular Soviet communism, the likelihood that they would do so would improve substantially. This reasoning seemed sound and so he embarked on an 'assisted emigration programme' to non-communist countries, although the offer to repatriate remained.

The word 'emigration', as used by the British in this context, meant resettlement in a country other than Poland or Britain.[1] The resulting Assisted Emigration Programme was the second attempt at solving the Polish problem after the disappointing 'repatriation initiative'. The Foreign Office began by promising to take care of all the formalities required by receiving countries, including the paying of travel expenses for the men and their dependants. The aspects of emigration the British had control over were dealt with relatively quickly but those it had little control over, such as the issue of travel documents and visas by foreign embassies, had to be painstakingly negotiated. The task for Bevin[2] now, was how to persuade countries to accept Polish personnel as migrants. Although he was helped by the fact that there were extensive labour shortages at various levels in many of the countries which had made a contribution during the war, they were nevertheless preoccupied with repatriating and employing their own nationals before considering others. It fell on the Foreign Office to work alongside the Inter-Governmental Committee for Refugees and send out feelers to countries which appeared willing to receive demobilised Polish servicemen. But it was not just a question of the numbers of men that had to be considered but their age, skill set and qualifications. Strategies were designed and employed to match the skills of the Poles to the labour requirements in receiving countries.[3]

Numerous countries were approached about the possibility of absorbing the Poles, starting with those in Western Europe. Europe was considered to be the most obvious starting point, but it soon became clear that progress here was dependant on the attitude of the French, who in turn were being influenced by a flourishing communist movement in

---

1   TNA, WO 315/4, Cipher telegrams October–November 1945, Repatriation to Poland.
2   British Foreign Secretary.
3   TNA, WO 315/4, Cipher telegrams 1945, Repatriation to Poland.

```
                    FORM OF APPLICATION
                    FOR EMIGRATION TO: . . . . . . . . .

1. Name in full . . . . . . . . . . . . . . . . . . . . . . . .
   /Surname first in block capitals/

   Nationality . . . . . . . . Religion . . . . . Date of birth . . .

   Country, province & place of birth . . . . . . . . . . . . . . .

   Military number . . . . . . . Rank . . . . . . Unit . . . . . . .

   Present Address . . . . . . . . . . . . . . . . . . . . . . . .

2. Father's name . . . . . . . . . . . . Nationality . . . . . . .

   Mother's maiden name . . . . . . . . . Nationality . . . . . .

3. Passport or other travel document No: . . . . . . . . . . . .
```

If a member of the Resettlement Corps decided to emigrate to a country other than Britain, an Application Form for Emigration had to be filled in.

the country. Nevertheless, given that France was an important ally during the war, London expected that the country would play a significant part in absorbing substantial numbers. However, when the French Interior Minister informed Bevin that, owing to the uncertainty of Mr Blum's[4] position in the forthcoming elections, the moment would be inappropriate to press Paris to take any Poles, even though there was a labour shortage in the country. The Minister added that France would be prepared to accept Poles 'on loan'.

Apart from Holland, other European countries also made little or no contribution to taking in Polish soldiers. Belgium was minded only to accept those individuals who had been resident in the country before the war, whilst a reply from Scandinavian authorities was so long in coming, that the prospect of absorbing any significant number by them was thought to be 'highly unlikely'. Holland was perhaps the only shining light in Europe, agreeing to take 5,000 men, but even here there was anxiety at the Foreign Office for London had just ignored Holland's request for 3,000 miners.

Hopes of resettling the Poles outside Britain were temporarily lifted when the British Ambassador in Washington informed London that the United States had decided to extend its Displaced Persons Bill[5] which suggested that the country could accept some 18,000 men. But caution was advised when America took a second look at its 'quota system' and wondered whether it could offer much assistance within the existing framework as priority was being given to displaced orphaned children. However, trying to be accommodating to London, the State Department indicated that it would seriously consider a proposal it had received from Lieutenant General John C. H. Lee[6] to provide a safe haven in the United States for a large proportion of the 107,000 Polish soldiers of General Anders.

Meanwhile, the Inter-Governmental Committee for Refugees had noted that some

---

4   President of the Provisional Government of the French Republic.
5   Displaced Persons Act 1947.
6   Commander of American Forces in the Mediterranean.

members of the Polish Armed Forces had made their own arrangements and had already emigrated to South America. It wondered whether the fact that countries in this part of the world were Roman Catholic had anything to do with attracting Polish men to settle. Having decided that the existence of Catholicism was an important factor, the committee approached the Vatican to see whether the Pope could use his influence with the governments of South America in order to encourage them to accelerate the absorption of Polish settlers. However, following a lack of response from Rome, the Foreign Office instructed committee members working in the Italian capital to seek assistance from individual Vatican staff, especially in the case of the 1,750 Polish soldiers who had married Italian women. Some Latin American countries, in particular Chile, Brazil, the Dominican Republic, Bolivia and Guatemala, responded favourably to Vatican staff and it was calculated that they might ultimately absorb approximately 20 to 30,000 men. The only disappointing news came from the Argentine mission in Rome which indicated that, 'at present it was only considering Italian and Spanish speakers'. The Inter-Governmental Committee for Refugees believed that the best country for the Poles to settle in was Canada. It justified its opinion by pointing out that Canada had huge expanses of wilderness which required clearing and that its summer climate was very like Poland's. When the Canadian Government was approached to take some Polish men, it reported that many of the men who had already arrived in the country were suffering from tuberculosis and, as a result, it had to be highly selective. It was agreed that the Canadians could send medical staff to Polish bases in Europe in order to sift through the applications for healthy individuals. Officials were instructed to concentrate on recruiting young, single, fit men.[7] The *Polish Soldiers Daily Newspaper*, published in Britain, carried a long article with advice for those contemplating emigrating to Canada.[8] The article made clear that the Canadian government's priority was the repatriation of its own citizens and that it had not even started to consider foreign nationals: also, that men who could work in agriculture would be given priority to enter the country. The article continued that travel to Canada was in the sole control of the country's government and therefore those who wanted jobs other than agriculture would find it difficult to obtain travel documents. Polish soldiers were also warned that, if they decided to settle in Canada, they would initially receive a five year work permit and would only be able to apply for Canadian nationality after this time. It was also pointed out that a clean bill of health was necessary as well a good character reference. On a more positive note, articles informed the paper's readership that there was the possibility of applying for loans of up to 2,000 Canadian dollars to purchase farms costing between 3,500 and 10,000 Canadian dollars on the open market.[9] Finally, it was made clear that those who had lived in Canada before the war, or had served in the Canadian Forces, or had spent time in military training in Canada during the war, or had married a Canadian national whilst in service, would be given preferential consideration. Canada's intention was to find workers for agriculture and gold mining and took a further 4,000 men who were added to the 2,900 already accepted. The Inter-Governmental Committee for Refugees also reported that approximately 8,000 men had applied to the Canadian government but that only 4,500 names were ever submitted to the Canadians by Polish authorities. The Committee, therefore, put pressure on the Poles to process applications at a more reasonable pace.

---

7   TNA, WO 315/52, Repatriation, Emigration, Enlistments.
8   *Dziennik Polski i Diennik Żołnierza Rok 3 Numer 121*, 25 March 1946.
9   *Dziennik Polski Numer 121*, 25 March 1946.

South Africa also had an immigration mission working in Rome. Its task was to recruit individuals with a variety of representative skills and professional qualifications without discriminating on nationality. It advertised for individuals who did not necessarily have connections with South Africa and even considered those who had limited English language skills. Meanwhile, the Foreign Office in London had noticed that no arrangements had been made for transporting migrants to Africa and offered the South African government ships on the condition that favourable treatment was offered the Poles. Australia and New Zealand were also actively recruiting in Italy but Australia, just as Canada, was seeking young, single men, whilst New Zealand was concentrating on resettling Polish orphans.

On 1 May 1946 the Foreign Office produced a report on the state of affairs regarding Polish Forces' emigration.[10] The report informed Attlee that even by putting the most 'favourable construction on the situation', it was clear that Britain could not rely on a significant contribution being made by other countries in solving the 'Polish question'. The British Prime Minister was disconcerted to read that finding a home for some in the colonies was proving so difficult that early indicators were that the number they would absorb would not be large. The report concluded that when all of these possibilities had been exhausted, the problem of disposing of a very considerable number of Poles would still remain.[11]

Approximately 10 percent of the Polish forces in the West decided to take up the offer of emigrating. This is how Marian Januszewski describes his departure to Australia:

> Chippenham Camp[12] accommodated those who had decided to emigrate to Australia. Following a medical examination, various interviews and a fond farewell from our beloved commander, General Kopański, who wished us 'God speed', we left the camp by rail for Southampton Docks with our Chaplain's words ringing in our ears: 'Do not forget your homeland and be faithful to God'. On arriving at Southampton we embarked on the SS *Asturias*[13] and on 1 September 1947 we departed from England. As we slipped towards the open sea, our thoughts turned to our homeland and our nearest and dearest from whom, rather than getting closer, we were sailing even further away.
>
> After a short stay in Port Said and Aden, we finally reached the west coast of Australia on 21 September. At Freemantle Port we disembarked and were temporarily housed in downtown Perth at an army camp near Karrakatta. Following more form filling, we were transferred by rail to Melbourne with a stopover at Adelaide. At Melbourne, where we were welcomed by some local dignitaries and members of the Rats of Tobruk Association, we were taken by bus to a camp at Butler's Gorge. The conditions in the camp did not fill us with any optimism. I was billeted in a two persons' room with beds covered by straw filled bedding. The walls were so thin that one could hear everything that was going on in the neighbouring room. Unfortunately, we had left our blankets, coats and winter undergarments in England because we were told we would not need them as we were going to a warm climate … Dressed in light weight battledress we stood on the porch watching the falling snow.

The total number of Polish personnel, including dependants, emigrating as of 1955

---

10   TNA, WO 315/4, Cipher telegrams 1945, Repatriation to Poland.
11   The report was signed by H. McNeal, May 1946.
12   See chapter on the 'Camp System'.
13   See <http://www.ssasturias.net> (accessed 12 March 2019).

was calculated to be 29,000 of which 14,000 travelled to the United States of America, Argentina and Brazil. 7,000 remained in France and 8,000 in Italy.[14] As of 30 September 1949, 12,275 PRC personnel emigrated to countries other than Britain. 1,414 of these were from the PRC (RAF).

---

14 Witold Leitgeber, *Rok Decyzji w Sprawie Rozwiązania Polskich Sił Zbrojnych na Zachodzie, Zeszyty Historyczne nr 42*, Paris 1977, pp.54–95.

7

Nascence of the Polish Resettlement Corps

The Foreign Office's report on the success or otherwise of the Assisted Emigration Programme only served to endorse what the British Government had already realised; that a new initiative was required, if the complete disposal of Polish Forces under British command was to be achieved. It accepted that the new approach would have to be radical, creative and probably unique as the Polish problem 'must not be allowed to fester any longer'. After short deliberations the Government decided that there was nothing for it but to demobilise and resettle the Polish forces in Britain. This lateral jump in logic was a brave decision as such a thing had never been tried before with a foreign army, and it was far from clear how the British population would view such an initiative. Bevin,[1] acknowledging that many details still needed attention, announced the proposal to the Cabinet on 21 February saying that the Poles would be demobilised and settled in 'this country' and that shortly he would be meeting the Polish High Command where he would present the plans.

On 15 March 1946 at 10 o'clock in the morning, Bevin met with General Anders,[2] General Kopański,[3] General Maczek,[4] General Rudnicki,[5] General Wiatr,[6] Vice-Admiral Świrski,[7] and Air Vice Marshal Iżycki.[8] Bevin began by saying that a 'critical stage had been reached in Polish affairs'. He informed the Polish generals that the British Government and people 'feel a deep sense of gratitude' to all Polish forces, land, sea and air, for the magnificent contribution they had made to the common victory but that the time had come for demobilisation to begin. He continued, saying that retaining the Polish Forces would 'cause serious difficulties for Britain at the Security Council of the United Nations', if it was thought that the forces were being maintained for 'anything other than military purposes'. The Foreign Secretary explained that the demobilisation of the Polish forces was by no means a simple task and requested that all officers present cooperate with British authorities in persuading their men to go back to Poland. However, regarding those who did not want to return, he wanted it known that His Majesty's Government would not renege on its assurances that Polish forces 'would not be abandoned'. Bevin requested that the High Command work closely with the British government on the matter so that a suitable scheme for demobilisation could be created, and servicemen and women could settle into civilian life successfully. Bevin promised that the British 'will proceed steadily in order to ensure that the best possible arrangements can be made' and stressed that it would require the transfer to Britain of all Polish forces in the West, including the Polish 2nd Corps, which was currently stationed in Italy. The officers were reassured that no undue pressure would

---

1   Foreign Secretary.
2   Commander of the Polish 2nd Corps.
3   Polish General Headquarters, London.
4   Commander of the Polish 1st Corps.
5   Commander of Polish Forces stationed in Germany.
6   Commander Middle East.
7   Polish Naval Forces.
8   Polish Air Force.

be put on the men to accept the British offer, and that Attlee would be making a statement in the House that there would be no British Foreign Legion made up of Polish soldiers. Bevin, turning specifically to General Anders, asked for full cooperation. Although General Anders was disappointed that Poland had finally been lost to Russia, he understood that the announcement represented a convergence of interest for both sides in solving the Polish problem. He was, nevertheless, minded to ask why the British were being so coy about their plan and why was he being given only a few days to discuss the proposal with his officers? He also reiterated that encouraging his men to repatriate constituted an error of judgement, as Warsaw's assurances that a friendly welcome awaited every man on his return was not true. General Anders also lamented that the decision indicated that Britain had lost interest in the Polish soldiers' attempts to resist 'sovietisation'. Bevin retorted that he could not allow others to think that the Polish corps was being used as a diplomatic tool against the Soviet Union and repeated his request for cooperation. Anders, who believed that it was his duty to continue the fight for a free Poland, was not ready to back down and protested that the announcement was nothing more than a *fait accompli*. Bevin reassured the Polish general that the policy was a logical outcome of the Potsdam Conference, and reminded Anders that the British Prime Minister had often made it clear in the House that the attainment of Polish freedom would best be served by the return of these 'good, sensible and experienced men' to Poland. Tensions eased when Anders stopped arguing from first principles, which were difficult to counter, and started to discuss the practicalities of demobilisation, which suggested that he was coming around to accepting Britain's point of view. Anders asked Bevin when the transfer of Polish forces to Britain would commence. Bevin informed the General that such details could be fixed until the extent of the task was known. The meeting concluded with the Foreign Secretary saying that he understood Anders' concerns, but it was the future of the men and Poland that were uppermost in his mind.

On 21 March a second meeting was arranged at the War Office to announce further details. Anders began by expressing his concern regarding the timing of demobilisation, informing the meeting that he had only learnt of the details from 'yesterday's morning newspapers', which had put him into a very difficult position. He protested that if he was asked by any of his men for an opinion on the plan, he would not be able to answer them with any convincing authority. Major General Lyne[9] in the Chair informed Anders, in a rather patronising manner, that he was very sorry about the general's difficulties, but that 'it often happens' and 'is one of the penalties' of a free press. Anders was not pacified and informed Lyne that it was only 'this morning' that he had received a written draft of the proposal, followed by an amendment which he could not understand. As a result he had some immediate questions to address the meeting:

1. How would the demobilisation affect the two and a half Polish divisions on special guard duty in Italy?
2. How would the British deal with any political unpleasantness which might arise towards the Polish Forces in Italy as the size of the Corps diminished?
3. How would London reassure the Italian population who feared an exodus of allied forces from the country in the face of communist agitation?

---

9   War Office.

General Anders was also afraid that the people of Britain would not be particularly welcoming to such a large body of foreigners arriving in the present stringent conditions and, despite wishing to keep up the high reputation of the Polish 2nd Corps, he foresaw difficulties in keeping up morale and discipline when gradual demobilisation commenced.[10] Lyne, alluding to the incremental character of the resettlement programme, answered by saying reassuringly that these issues would be dealt with as they arose, and continued to present fresh details on the process of demobilisation. He announced that the War Office had decided the easiest and smoothest way to achieve demobilisation of Polish forces in the West would be to bring them to Britain, where they could enlist into a resettlement corps. According to his information, said Lyne, the corps would be a British military formation administered by Polish officers under British supervision. This, of course, meant that the troops would have to be transferred to Britain – a process which was envisaged to take approximately eight months. On arrival they would be distributed, as equally as possible, between the various Home Commands – although the exact procedure for enlistment into the corps had not yet been finalised. However, he reassured those present that this would become clear just as soon as the Conditions of Service were finalised and British advisers were appointed. Anders returned to the question of whether the Polish 2nd Corps would remain under his command until all units had arrived in Britain? Lyne informed the general that every Polish unit would be enlisted in the resettlement corps on its arrival in the country, and reminded Anders that the PRC would be a British military unit, not a civilian one. He continued to say that, upon enlistment, the men would be answerable to Britain's military law and subject to War Office disciplinary procedures. Lyne added that the British envisaged one central Polish headquarters being established in London, with group headquarters in each Home Command. The distribution of Polish units was expected to be as follows;

Eastern Command	3rd Carpathian Division, 14th Armoured Brigade
Northern Command	2nd Armoured Division
Southern Command	5th Kresowa Divisions
Western Command	7th Division Corps Troops and most Base troops
Scottish Command	training units and remaining Base troops[11]

General Anders again returned to the question of command and asked whether the Polish 2nd Corps would remain under his command when it arrived in Britain? Lyne replied, rather sharply, 'No!' and added that Polish troops (1st Armoured Division) would be arriving from Germany later, and envisaged that a new single overarching British command structure for the whole of the Resettlement Corps would be required. Anders responded with alarm and explained, rather melodramatically, that 'his' corps was a special case as it was more than a fighting formation. He went on to describe the Polish Second Corps as 'one large organism' and a 'family' where divisional commanders had jurisdiction over divisional matters, coordinated and supervised by Corps Headquarters. Furthermore, the corps had its own press corps, welfare funds, theatre groups and military courts and so on, and that is why he was recommending that the Polish 2nd Corps was not disbanded piece meal as it arrived in Britain. Lyne, not wanting to enter into a lengthy and complicated verbal

---

10 TNA, WO 315/50, Policy statements, messages, telegrams, minutes of meetings.
11 TNA, WO 315/50, Policy statements, messages, telegrams, minutes of meetings.

combat, replied that he felt quite sure General Anders wished the absorption of the men into civilian life to take place as smoothly and as soon as possible and, for this reason, it was not practical to wait until the whole Second Corps had arrived in Britain before enlistment commenced. Anders moved on, but only after he had informed the meeting that, in his view, it would be far more advantageous if the Polish Corps was transferred *en masse* and kept as a whole until plans for it could be prepared 'properly'. He warned that it was only under these conditions that he could be held responsible for the discipline of his men. This veiled threat did not concern the British unduly as they had already decided to establish a new British command structure for the Poles, once they were in Britain. General Morgan, also present at the meeting, tried to reassure Anders by saying that the difficulties outlined by the General were not as great as he was suggesting, and that the rolling programme of transferring the troops to Britain would take place at a rate determined by the availability of transport. The Poles were competing with hundreds of thousands of American troops being sent home and the demand for shipping was very great. As a result, he said, the process would inevitably be gradual but, more importantly manageable. General Anders then asked for reassurance that para-military groups attached to the Polish Second Corps, such as the YMCA and the Polish Red Cross, would also be transferred alongside the troops. The answer was that they would, together with dependants who were under British protection so that they could be reunited with their menfolk. Brigadier Davy continued by saying that the men would be issued with identity documents which would be valid all over Britain as well as other countries in which the men might want to settle. Anders pointed out that some countries did not recognise the communist regime in Warsaw, but still recognised the disenfranchised Polish government, and wondered whether this would cause any difficulties for his men down the line. Lyne replied that this was still being studied at the War Office. He also could not give any assurances regarding extraordinary categories of personnel, such as those suffering with tuberculosis, 200 men undergoing long-term sentences for disciplinary reasons and 1,000 'bad characters and lunatics'; matters which were currently being considered. Despite not being able to give any further information, Lyne asked that the Poles appoint an officer who could attend Brigadier Davy's future committee meetings in order to advise on such matters that were important to them. The session was brought to a close with General Anders being asked to bring along any other outstanding issues to Davy's next meeting. These were: the future of Polish high schools being run by Polish forces in the Middle East, 1,200 Polish soldiers who were studying at Italian universities, Category E personnel, soldiers' savings accounts, Polish welfare funds, army archives and philanthropic institutions.

Despite the exchanges between the Poles and British degenerating into near 'psychodramas'. it is possible to begin outlining what the British policy towards the Polish forces under British command was going to be. It was clear, for example, that Britain would be responsible for arranging transport for all Polish forces and that the Americans would help in the transfer by providing ships. It was also clear that the transfer of Polish forces to Britain would be a rolling programme, and therefore enlistment into the resettlement corps would be a gradual process and not held back until the last Polish serviceman had landed. It was also the case that Polish personnel would be issued with British identity documents and serve in the Resettlement Corps under British military codes. This was required because Polish codes were not legal in British courts. It was also evident that Polish officers would not stay in command of their units and that a fresh command structure under British control would be established.

8

Further Consultation and Clarification

On 23 May, a further meeting was convened at the War Office in order to continue the discussion on the disposal of Polish Allied Forces who had refused the offer of repatriation or emigration. Bevin, who chaired the meeting, began by saying that much thought on the Polish issue had taken place since the last conference.[1] He explained that the British government was very anxious to ensure that the settlement of the men into civilian life was smooth, orderly and satisfactory to all: consequently, the immediate task after their arrival would be to find the men suitable employment which would then trigger full demobilisation. Bevin warned the Polish officers at the meeting that a delay in doing this would be undesirable, both politically and psychologically. He also added that time was of the essence because the government had just secured the co-operation of trade unions and professional federations on the matter of employing the Poles, and did not want to frustrate them by allowing the resettlement programme to drag on. The British government's expectation was, he continued, that the employment of Poles would be managed by the service ministries which had experience in dealing with the labour market. Bevin was also pleased to announce that families and dependants of the troops would be brought to Britain from British 'safe havens' just as soon as those individuals could be located and verified so that they could reunite with their menfolk but, he warned, no guarantee could be given that they would travel on the same ships as the troops. However, he reassured the Polish generals that 'care will be taken not to keep families apart for longer than absolutely necessary'. The Foreign Secretary continued, saying that further discussions would continue on the matters of rates of pay, conditions of service and the payment of gratuities for those who enlisted in the resettlement corps, and as soon as these points were settled he would quickly publish the information. He advised the Polish officers present not to worry unduly about the details of the programme for the British Government had vowed to deal with the Poles fairly, and that the Treasury had been instructed to treat the troops 'on the same basis as British soldiers'. Bevin also made it known that His Majesty's Government was anxious that employment made available for Polish soldiers should be honourable civilian work which would go some way towards reassuring public opinion on the contribution the Poles were making to the rebuilding of the nation. He also emphasised that the work the Poles would undertake would bear no resemblance to that carried out by prisoners of war in Britain during the war, which would do justice by the gallant Polish soldier. The meeting concluded that the resettlement programme would be organised in such a way as to allow His Majesty's Government to fulfil its pledge to Poland in an orderly and honourable fashion.

The Polish view, on the other hand, was that this was all well and good, but how would the ordinary soldier be persuaded to join a resettlement corps, especially if this was not what he had been fighting for or necessarily desired? After all, one thing was clear, if the peace that the Allies had subscribed to in 1945 was real, then why were the Poles being asked to join a

---

1 TNA, WO 315/50, Policy statements, messages, telegrams, minutes of meetings.

foreign army and live in exile? To Polish men, their country was being ruled by people not of Polish nationality and, according to their understanding, the majority of Polish people back home were looking to Polish forces in the West as the only remaining symbol of national freedom and independence. Furthermore, to demobilise now would be nothing more than a sign that the Allies had sacrificed Poland's war aims on the altar of expediency. General Anders suggested that demobilisation be postponed until the planned 1947 elections in Poland had taken place because, if the communists lost, he and his men would gladly return home. The British, however, believed that this suggestion was nothing more than a stalling tactic designed to delay the disbanding of the Polish forces and so rejected the idea. General Anders then returned to the point he had made earlier about enlisting the men in the resettlement corps *en masse*, arguing that this would maintain morale. The reply he received had not changed from the one before which was that the management of a large group of foreign troops awaiting enlistment was prohibitive. In any case, continued Bevin, urgency was now required because the Americans had just made available three transport ships which would be ready in Naples on 26 May with a fourth expected to be available on 4 June following repairs. General Anders was asked to limit as much as possible the time these ships lay idle and to approve the start of the transfer immediately. It was recommended that the first personnel to be brought over should be advance parties with practical skills in order to prepare accommodation in the service camps for the main body of men. Anders, by now not strong enough to obstruct British planning and, in any case, sensing that the British proposals gave Polish forces a way out from the dilemma they had found themselves in, agreed and approved a list of troops which could sail immediately. Following a request from the general, however, a direct communication link was established between Polish headquarters in London and the Polish 2nd Corps command in Italy. In concluding the meeting, Bevin reassured General Anders that the procedures to be used in the transfer of personnel would be transparent, with no distinction being made between officers and men. He took his leave by saying that his staff would be at the general's disposal if help was required. Anders ended the discussions by enquiring how the British would ensure that the 'wrong men' did not arrive first, while the 'better men' remained abroad. Bevin explained that individuals with skills required in Britain would be given priority to travel. But in any case, he continued, chances were that most of the men would probably require some kind of retraining, and he did not want to wait for months while long winded selection procedures took place on the continent. He recommended that the general need not worry unduly about such details, as the British had extensive experience in resettling Poles from the transfer of Polish forces from the continent when France fell in 1940. He described how General Sikorski had cooperated fully with the resettlement scheme devised then, and how labour exchange offices were open for Polish servicemen in Cavendish Street, London. He was proud to remind the Polish officers that approximately 20,000 men had been dealt with successfully and the experience gained there would now be put to good use. The point was also made that, in 1940, the Ministry of Labour only learned of the skill level of the men once they had landed in the country, and he envisaged that the same would probably happen with these new arrivals. Bevin also slipped into the conversation the fact that Polish troops would be disarmed before travelling to Britain.

For the Polish High Command in the West, discipline and order in the ranks was a priority (as it was for the British) and it expressed satisfaction that the arrival of dependants and wives in Britain would go some way towards pacifying the men. General Anders expressed concern about the resettlement of paramilitary units such as military hospitals, schools for orphans, the Polish military press corps and entertainment groups (Polish equivalent to ENSA)[2] attached to the Polish 2nd Corps. And then there was the issue of approximately 7,000 women in the Polish Women's Auxiliary Service,[3] which had also served in the 2nd Corps. Bevin reassured him that all such units would be offered the chance to settle in Britain, including female service personnel, if this is what the Polish High Command wanted. He explained that all His Majesty's Government was trying to do was to carry out Britain's pledge to the Poles as smoothly and fairly as possible, whilst putting pressure on the Provisional Government in Poland to do likewise. Bevin argued that the British Government's objective in the whole affair was to place the Poles on as good a footing as British personnel and this was why the British government was prepared to provide every facility necessary for their successful resettlement.

Bevin understood that to achieve the cooperation of the Polish High Command, in particular General Anders who was the most vocal of all the Polish generals in expressing Polish opinions on the resettlement programme, was vital if the initiative was going to be a success. However, the British Government was not only responding to her treaty obligations with Poland, but to growing Italian pressure for a quick and final removal of Polish troops from Italian soil. Belgrade was also expressing anxiety about Polish troops stationed so near Yugoslavia's northern border in case they crossed in unauthorised operations to confront communist partisans. Unsurprisingly, Stalin also joined the protests saying that Polish forces in the West had to be demobilised as they posed a serious threat to peace in Europe.

Manpower shortages in Britain existed in trade, agriculture and industry and the plan was to match the skills and abilities of Polish soldiers to these requirements. The Poles were informed that the Minister of Labour[4] was already compiling a list of potential employers who had indicated that they would be prepared to employ Poles, and that extensive discussions were underway with trade unions and professional bodies in order to secure their support. However, what Bevin did not want to see happening was too rapid an entry of men onto the labour market which could create a backlog of personnel waiting to find suitable work. Admiral Świrski asked whether a man could bypass enrolling in the resettlement corps if his skills were urgently required by British industry. Pointing to the agreements that government had negotiated with the trade unions, Bevin indicated that he did not see any situation where a man would enter the job market directly from the Polish forces, but explained that if a man could be placed in work quickly, he would pass through the Corps rapidly in order to realise the employment. This condition was necessary because the men had to be placed under British law first, and only then could they enter employment. He also explained that British people would probably not accept the placement of men in employment straight from foreign forces, and that the resettlement plan must be made to fit the 'psychology of the people' if it was to work. General Anders expressed concern about getting all this information across to his men, to which Bevin replied that he was sure that if they were told that the British Government wished very sincerely to help them in every possible way, and if the plans were properly explained, then they would understand and be receptive to the procedures being planned for them. He reassured the Polish officers that, if the men were met with friendship and full cooperation from all sides, then nobody would

---

2   Entertainment National Service Association.
3   *Pomocnicza Służba Kobiet*.
4   George Isaacs.

be able to say that duty had not been done. Air Vice Marshal Iżycki wondered whether a small Polish Air Force could be maintained as part of the RAF otherwise, he argued, 'there would be no Polish Air Force to speak of'. His second point was on the question of British citizenship for his men. He was of the opinion that on the strength of Polish pilots being so closely associated with the RAF during the war, almost becoming part of it, they were surely entitled to special treatment regarding British nationality. Bevin promised to look into the matter: however, he did not want to provoke the Polish Government of National Unity in Warsaw, so would not make any quick statements on his deliberations in order not to hurt the men's interests.

The meeting then moved on to the enlistment of other categories of combatants. The question was whether soldiers from the Polish 1939 Campaign and members of the underground Home Army were eligible to join the resettlement corps, despite not serving under British command.[5] Bevin explained that the resettlement corps was only for those who had fought under British command during the war, but promised to look into this wider matter. On 18 July 1946, the War Office issued further details by reiterating that entry into Britain was for those who had fought under the British command, although further discussions were taking place about those members of the Home Army who had been released from German captivity. However, the most significant announcement was the official declaration made by the Army Council, in accordance with Cabinet decisions, that formal authorisation had been given for the formation of a new corps of the British Army called the Polish Resettlement Corps (PRC) and would be comprised of Polish personnel who had fought under British command and who had to date elected not to return to Poland. The formation of a resettlement section, designated ATS (Polish Resettlement Section), was also announced and was designed for Polish female personnel. On returning to Italy, General Anders addressed the men of the Second Corps:

> Ancona, Italy,
> Soldiers! Polish Colours are swathed in honour, victories and names of many battles, fought for the independence of Poland. After seven years of confronting our enemies we now face a fight with international political forces who want to divert us from our road to freedom ... Today we must endure and conquer so that we do not lose our national honour for the convenience of others ... As you know Minister Bevin announced that we are to be demobilised ... Our work, therefore, is to prepare soldiers, sailors and airmen to fight on under new circumstances whilst we are working in British factories ... We will not depart from our path to freedom and will continue the struggle for the kind of Poland we have been fighting for – free and independent.[6]

---

5   The Polish Home Army was the only underground formation given official recognition as being part of Poland's Sovereign Army and therefore bestowed rights under the Geneva Convention.

6   Paraphrased from the Polish Language Quoted in *Dziennik Polski i Dziennik Żołnierza, Rok 3 Numer* 130, 23 May 1946.

9

The Polish Resettlement Bill

On 20 March 1946, the British Foreign Minister, Ernest Bevin, addressed the House regarding the Polish Resettlement Bill. He said,

> I have explained the principle underlying the policy of His Majesty's Government on this matter. While we will not use force to compel these men to return to Poland, I have never disguised our conviction that in our view they ought to go back in order to play their part in the reconstruction of their stricken country. As the House knows we long ago made it known to the men that transport facilities would be available for those wishing to return. But from the start I felt that one of the principal causes that prevents a large number from returning was the lack of certainty in their minds about the conditions upon which they would be received. For this reason His Majesty's Government have, for many months, been urging the Polish Provisional Government to clarify the conditions which would apply. Agreement has now been reached with the Polish Provisional Government and we have arranged to issue a document in Polish to every individual member of the Polish Armed Forces. To my great surprise and regret, agreement had hardly been reached upon the text of this document, when the Polish Provisional Government addressed to His Majesty's Government and published a note in which they declared that they could no longer consider the Polish Armed Forces under British command as a formal part of the Polish Forces of Poland. They asked that these units should be disbanded forthwith and stated that the men who wished to return should make individual applications to Polish consulates abroad.[1]

On 22 May, Bevin returned to the House in order to announce the latest planning concerning the resettlement of Polish Forces,

> In this House on 20th March I expressed the hope of His Majesty's Government that as many members of the Polish Armed Forces under British command as felt able to do so, would recognise it is their duty to return to Poland in order to take part in the reconstruction of their country. As to those who do not wish to return to Poland, it is our aim to demobilise them as quickly as possible and to arrange for their settlement in civilian life, either in Great Britain or overseas. Those serving abroad will be brought back to this country starting with those in Italy. Since it would be impracticable and unfair to these gallant men, many of whom do not know our language, to launch them wholesale upon the labour market here and leave them to their own resources, His Majesty's Government are going to enrol them into a specially created resettlement corps, which will be a British organisation, and for convenience be administered by service ministers. Enrolment in this corps will give them an assured status to

---

1 Hansard Volume 420, Number 106.

its members.

The resettlement corps will be essentially a transitional arrangement designed to facilitate the transition from military to civilian life. They will, therefore, be discharged from the Polish Armed Forces and enrolled into the resettlement corps with a view to transfer to civilian life as soon as possible.[2]

Bevin continued to inform the House that the personnel of the Resettlement Corps, for whom approved jobs could be found, would go to them immediately, whilst the others would be fully employed by the government in productive national projects, such as coastal mine clearing. He also said that, in appropriate cases, training would be provided to prepare personnel for civilian employment. Although the conditions of service and rates of pay had not yet been finalised, the government had decided to take the first step in demobilising the Poles starting with the forces stationed in Italy. The minister confirmed that, on arrival, the Poles would be distributed amongst the Home Commands; a policy designed to facilitate assimilation into civilian life. Bevin reassured the House that the Poles would be under military control and responsible to the laws of Britain. He continued that the Poles would be obliged to sign a two year contract with the PRC, during which time jobs would be found for them. During question time, Churchill asked the Foreign Secretary whether he had closed his mind entirely to the idea of using these 'fine, well-disciplined troops' as part of a garrison holding Germany, in positions far removed from the Russian line. Bevin answered that it would be a very bad thing for British policy if a foreign legion was used to undertake 'our responsibilities' and in any case, he continued, the resettlement corps would not be an armed force. Mr Piratin enquired of the Secretary of State for Foreign Affairs whether the resettlement corps would be 'officered or administered by personnel at present officering'. Bevin answered yes, but that they would be under British supervision and would adhere to British Service Law. He explained that assistance would be provided for the settlement of the men, and so British officers would be appointed as interpreters to assist in administrating the service code and provide guidance on British standards.

On 8 July the debate continued. Mr Hynd enquired whether the Secretary of State for War[3] had fixed a date beyond which General Anders' army would not be entitled to wear military uniform? Jack Lawson replied that the personnel of General Anders' army would, in due course, be enlisting into the Polish Resettlement Corps which required the wearing of uniforms. However, when civilian employment was found the men/women would be demobilised and the wearing of military uniform would cease. He continued by saying that no date could be fixed beyond which Polish personnel would not be entitled to wear military uniform.[4] Mr Piratin asked why Polish soldiers were expected to sign a two year contract with the Resettlement Corps? Lawson replied that the purpose of the two year contract was to cover the maximum period which was thought likely to be required, before all the Poles were settled into civilian life.[5] The Secretary of State for War explained that men would, within this period, obtain civil employment and be relegated to the Reserve. At this point they would be treated as civilians. Mr Hynd was concerned about the command structure of the Resettlement Corps and asked whether it would be ensured, that units of

---

2   Hansard Volume 420, Number 106.
3   Jack Lawson.
4   HC Debate, 9 July 1946 Volume 425 cc 48–9.
5   HC Debate, Volume 425 cc 48–9.

the Corps did not remain under the control of Polish Officers. Mr Lawson answered that Polish Officers would necessarily be employed in the PRC, but as many British officers as possible would be made available. Mr Piratin asked which districts in England and Wales were being considered to provide facilities for the housing and training of members of the Polish armed forces brought to this country, and what type of accommodation would be made available? The reply he received was that the Poles would be housed in existing military accommodation wherever it was available. As a result the Poles would be widely dispersed throughout disused bases in England and Wales, as well as Scotland. When asked about the estimated cost of this endeavour, the Secretary of State for War estimated that £250,000 would probably be needed for transport and £200,000 for the provision of accommodation.

During July 1946, the House was informed that the preparation for the transfer of Polish forces to Britain and enlistment into the Polish Resettlement Corps was almost complete. The government predicted that enrolment would begin at the end of August at the rate of 6,000 men in the first week, followed by 12,000 per week thereafter. In fact, the transfer of men had already begun in July with 30,000 men of the Polish 2nd Corps arriving from Italy.

There were, however, some issues the government had yet to resolve. For example, it had not decided what to do with those men who wished neither to return to Poland nor join the Polish Resettlement Corps, although it had decided that these individuals should not expect any assistance from British authorities regarding their resettlement. The issue of the men's nationality also became a vexed question, since the Polish Provisional Government in Warsaw had made it known that, as a result of entering into service for a foreign power, men who joined the Resettlement Corps would lose their Polish nationality. This threat was founded on a Polish military law dating back to the 1920s. Mr Bevin informed the House that some of the Polish officers, such as General Anders, had already lost their nationality under this ruling which was supposed to serve as a warning to other ranks if they decided to join the Corps. The Warsaw announcement alarmed London, only to the extent that it could dissuade men from enlisting, hence perpetuating the Polish problem. Bevin reminded the House that it was hoped Warsaw understood that the Corps came under British military law and its purpose was to disperse the men into civilian life. Professor Savery wondered whether special representations could be made to the Polish Provisional Government on behalf of General Anders in view of his distinguished service to Britain and the allied cause? Bevin answered in the negative, for he believed that the idea was 'not to the moment' and, in any case, it was clear that the British government could not distinguish between General Anders and other ranks also affected. He went on to reassure the House that he would not 'single out a General over a Private'.

The British Foreign Secretary went on to say that all help would be given to the men to resettle successfully, and that general education and pre-vocational training would be made available on similar lines to that provided for British troops under the Army Education Scheme. Course material, with an emphasis on English subjects, British institutions and way of life, based on the book *The British Way and Purpose*, was already being prepared. According to Bevin, the soldiers with a good command of English would be encouraged to enrol in 'formation colleges' and would be eligible for War Office correspondence courses. Vocational training would be under the control of the Ministry of Labour and National Service. Further education for the Poles would be supervised by the Interim Treasury Committee on Polish Affairs in consultation with the Board of Education. It was also planned that the Committee would be responsible for the education of dependants and Polish children until they could be absorbed into the British school system.

The debate in the House finished with Bevin saying that Britain had incurred a debt to the Poles in the war. That debt was acknowledged by the coalition government and was being confirmed by the new Attlee government. The Polish Resettlement Bill was an effort by Britain to discharge that debt honourably. The Bill passed its reading in the House and was written into law as the Polish Resettlement Act 1947 in March, and formed the legislative framework for the resettlement programme.

10

The Polish Resettlement Act 1947

Once His Majesty's Government had decided to dispose of the Polish Allied Forces in Britain it faced two unique problems. The first concerned the fact that the Poles were a foreign sovereign army over which British authorities had no legal jurisdiction and, secondly, Polish individuals had no legal status in the country. The first problem was solved by encouraging Polish service personnel to join the British Army (the Polish Resettlement Corps) which placed them under British military law.

This gave His Majesty's Government jurisdiction over their future prospects. The second problem was solved by providing Poles with legal status (but not citizenship) in Britain through the provisions of the 1947 Polish Resettlement Act. Although these policies were designed to smooth the way for the disposal of Polish forces in Britain, certain issues remained unresolved. For example, in Polish military law, men who enlisted in the forces of another power opened themselves to court martial for desertion. This is why obtaining reassurance from the Polish High Command that no man would be prosecuted for enlisting in the Resettlement Corps was so important. General Kopański, Commander of the Resettlement Corps, published the following reassuring statement;

> Polish authorities in exile do not consider enlistment into the Resettlement Corps as service in a foreign army as the aim of the Corps is to prepare you for civilian life and not for any future military action.[1]

Another issue facing the government was how to persuade the House that granting legal status to such a large number of foreigners was a reasonable thing to do, especially under the prevailing conditions.

The Act was the legislative framework used to resettle the Polish Allied Forces in Britain and to provide them with social welfare rights in the country. The Act did not only apply to those in uniform, namely Polish Naval units, the Polish Airforce, Polish staff attached to the RAF, Polish Land Forces, the 'Unseen and Unheard'[2] of the SOE,[3] the Cadet School in the Middle East and Polish auxiliary staff in Britain and France, but also to their dependants as defined by the War Office. The government defined what it meant by 'dependant' very precisely in order to prevent the exploitation of the resettlement programme by individuals who wanted to get to Britain under false pretences. Five categories of people were identified as dependants:

1. Wives and children of serving members of the Polish Resettlement Corps
2. Wives and children of ex-serving members of the Polish Resettlement Corps

---

1 *Dziennik Polski i Dziennik Żołnierza*, Numer 209, 5 September 1946.
2 *Cicho Ciemni* (Polish Special Forces).
3 Special Operations Executive.

Cover of the Polish Resettlement Act, 1947. The Polish Resettlement Act provided the legislative framework for the Resettlement Programme. The Act provided social welfare rights in Britain for all Poles who had arrived as part of the Resettlement Programme. (Crown copyright)

3. More distant relatives than wives and children of serving members of the Polish Resettlement Corps
4. More distant relatives than wives and children of ex-members of the Polish Resettlement Crops
5. Persons not related to any individual member or ex-member of the Polish Resettlement Corps but under the care of the Polish High Command.[4]

Later the War Office clarified categories three and four:

1. Father of soldiers or father-in-law
2. Mother of soldier or mother-in-law
3. Brother younger than 21 years, who is single, widowed or divorced
4. Grandparents or grandparents of a wife of a soldier
5. Sister younger than 21 years, who is single, widow or divorced
6. Widows
7. Orphans
8. Single daughter older than 21 years
9. Single sister older than 21years
10. Sister-in-law
11. Brother in law younger than 21years
12. Aunt younger than 21years
13. Cousins younger than 21years
14. Sister younger than 21 years and married
15. Niece under 21years
16. Nephew under 21 years
17. Grandson under 21years

The Polish Resettlement Act gave powers to ministries to provide for the needs of the various categories of Poles to facilitate settlement in the country. For example, the Minister of Pensions was empowered to apply Royal Warrants to pensions and periodical payments in respect of the disabled.[5] The Assistance Allowance Board was empowered to provide payments to Poles who had no work, or only such part time or intermittent work which

4   HMSO Polish Resettlement Act, 1947–27 March 1947.
5   HMSO Polish Resettlement Act 1947, 27 March 1947.

enabled an individual to earn insufficiently for his needs. The Board was also permitted to provide accommodation in service camps, hostels or other establishments and to make provision to meet welfare needs.[6] Such assistance could be made in a manner convenient to the Board and could include goods and services or by payment to other agencies to provide what was required.

The Minister of Health had the authority to provide such help to meet medical needs as defined in the Unemployed Assistance Act 1934.[7] This provision provided support for mental as well as physical illness. The Health Ministry was also authorised to make arrangements with any other government department for the provision of services to meet medical needs. The Board of Education was empowered to meet the educational needs of the Poles, including children who had arrived in Britain or been born to ex-members of the Corps and to do any such thing as required under the Educations Acts 1944 and 1946.[8] The Ministry of Labour and National Service had the responsibility of finding suitable employment, whilst overseeing arrangements for the repatriation of those who had decided in the course of resettlement to return home.[9] In 1947 the British authorities had decided not to recognise any Polish pre-war academic or vocational qualifications other than medical and dental degrees. Doctors and dentists were in short supply and it was therefore necessary to reduce any shortfall by employing qualified Polish medical staff. Such personnel were contracted to the Ministry of Health in the service of the Polish Resettlement Corps. A similar arrangement operated for pharmacists. The Polish Resettlement Act allowed the British Medical Council to register medical staff on a fast track system, permitting them to practise in the United Kingdom. Personnel were rushed through training courses designed to align their skills with British law regarding the dispensing of drugs, medicines and poisons so that they could begin their work as soon as possible. Finally, the Act made it clear that all personnel employed in Britain on politically sensitive assignments had to be supervised by British persons, especially if they were appointed to work for the Secretary of State for War.

By late 1946, Britain was ready to receive Polish Allied forces, the first and last foreign formation to be demobilised on British soil. All that remained was to disseminate information to the Poles on the options open to them and to ensure that the resettlement programme ran as smoothly and fairly as possible.

---

6   HMSO Polish Resettlement Act 1947, 27 March 1947.
7   HMSO Polish Resettlement Act 1947, 27 March 1947.
8   HMSO Polish Resettlement Act.
9   HMSO Polish Resettlement Act.

11

Conditions of Service – Polish Land Forces

In August 1946, the War Office published the Conditions of Service for the Polish Resettlement Corps. They were distributed to every serving soldier and written in the Polish language. The document reads:

> The Polish Resettlement Corps is a unit of the British Army. The objective of the Corps is to prepare men and officers of the Polish Land Forces for civilian life. The British Army is committed to do everything in its power to help its brothers in arms who fought with the British throughout the war.
>
> Those of you who refuse to enlist in the Polish Resettlement Corps cannot expect any help or support from the British Army. If you want to avail yourself of this help you should enlist into the Polish Resettlement Corps. If you enlist the British Army will welcome you into the army and will support you in your settlement into a new life in the United Kingdom or abroad if you so wish. If at any time during your service in the Corps you decide to return to Poland your travel will be paid for by the British authorities. If you decide to join the Corps you will have to sign an attestation that you agree to enlist for two years. The form you will have to sign will be written in the Polish language and the form will explain in detail the things you need to know. During enlistment you will have to answer a series of questions on a questionnaire. When you have completed the questionnaire and signed it you will automatically become a member of the Polish Resettlement Corps. After you have signed you will have to be ready to serve for two years. However, this does not necessarily mean that you will have to spend the full two years in an army base for if you accept employment you will pass to the reserve. The decision to enlist you for two years was taken to allow work to be found for you.
>
> Once you pass into the Polish Resettlement Corps you will be answerable to British law and discipline. Whilst in the Crops you will follow orders just like any soldier in the army. If you break a serious law you will be tried in a British military court which will follow British protocol.
>
> You will be enlisted as a Private as British law does not allow for the enlistment into the army individuals above this rank although you will receive payment according to your rank you held in the Polish Army. If you are employed full-time in the service of the Corps you could receive a slightly improved rate of pay. Polish Officers of high rank will be enlisted as lieutenants. The rates of pay will be as follows:

Table 1: Daily Rate of Pay Resettlement Corps (Polish Land Forces) shillings/pence			
Rank	Enrolment	After three years	After four years
Warrant Officer 1st Class	14/6	15/6	16/0
Warrant Officer 2nd Class	11/6	12/6	13/0
Staff Sergeant	9/6	10/6	11/0
Sergeant	6/8	7/9	8/0
Corporal	5/0	5/10	6/1
Lance Corporal	4/3	5/1	5/4
Private	3/3	4/0	4/6

Note: Pay referred to in the columns 'after three years' and 'after four years' only applied to those who had completed three or four years' service in the Polish Army, under British Command, during the period ending 1st July 1946. Other rates of pay applied to service before 1 July 1940 and after 1 July 1946.

You will be paid by the British Government and you will be liable to pay British taxes as all British soldiers are. Families and wives of officers and other ranks that are in the United Kingdom will be entitled to accommodation and certain allowances paid in cash.

As members of the Polish Resettlement Corps you will be billeted in army barracks or military dormitories just like any other British soldier. You will be entitled to time off and 'leave' as British soldiers and will be approximately equal to 10 days every 4 months. Your Commanding Officer will have the discretion to give you one off passes of up to 48 hours. You will also be entitled to time off for illness. Just as any British soldier you will be entitled 3 journeys per year by rail within the United Kingdom free of charge.

Whilst in the Polish Resettlement Corps the British Army is committed to providing you with welfare help on a par of other British soldiers. No doubt you will want to learn the English language whilst serving in the Corps. The British Army guarantees lessons for this and will also provide sessions to introduce you to the British way of life.

One of the aims of forming the Resettlement Corps is to find you civilian employment but until this can be done you will be employed as a soldier in variety of meaningful and useful roles. This work will be military in nature and will be done within groups of other Polish men or alongside British soldiers. This work may include agricultural or industrial work. There is a large need for manpower in Great Britain particularly in the building trades. You will be paid by the War Office during this work or if in civilian employment the employer will pay your wages.[1]

At any time in the service of the Polish Resettlement Corps you will be entitled to return to Poland if you so wish. Your transport will be paid for by the War Office and you will be discharged from the Corps. If you decide to do this you will be entitled to

---

1 TNA, WO 315/56, War Gratuities, Release Benefits, Compensation.

56 days of pay plus a war gratuity for the years of service and rank in the Polish Army under British Command. You will also be able to apply to join the professional forces of Britain if you are younger than 30 years, fit and healthy. If you apply you will have to pass a medical whereupon you will serve as any other British soldier in the service of the Crown. If you enrol in the professional army you will not be entitled to any discharge benefits from the Polish Resettlement Corps.

You can also apply to emigrate. Once you get permission to travel from the receiving country the passage for your journey will be paid for by the British Government. You will be discharged from the Resettlement Corps and be entitled 56 days' pay together with the war gratuity you are entitled to.

When you are employed in civilian work that you have found yourself you will be entitled to 21 days' pay and you will be relegated to the Reserve. If for any reason you resign from that employment you will be recalled to the Polish Resettlement Corps. You will not be entitled to any benefits of demobilisation until this happens. You will not receive any army pay whilst you are receiving pay from a private employer.

Every effort will be made to find you work that you like and will be happy with. To help the British Army in this task you will be asked to fill in a questionnaire about your education and employment history.

The British Army is committed to giving help in any way it can to your family and dependants once they arrive in Britain. Your family will, in the first instance, be housed in reception camps. Due to the shortages of housing in Great Britain it is not possible to move them out of the camps quickly although every effort will be made to do so. In the event of a return to Poland or other country outside Britain family expenses will be paid for. Transport, hopefully on the same ship, will be arranged as quickly as possible. Those of you who choose employment in this country will have families moved close to where you are working if accommodation can be found. Once you start earning a wage the responsibility of looking after you family will fall on you.

Remember, the Polish Resettlement Corps has been organised primarily to help you – if you do not enrol in the PRC, the British Army will not be in the position to help you, but if you do enrol the British Army will do everything in its power to find you suitable work.[2]

One significant footnote to this information was a warning that no Polish troops or individual in the service of the Corps was permitted to involve himself in political activity. Special conditions of service were written for Polish individuals who had been forced to serve in the German Army during the war, but later transferred to Polish units when Germany capitulated. On 1 May the British Advisory Staff to the Polish Resettlement Corps clarified the situation, explaining that men who were transferred into the Polish Armed Forces under British Command on or before 12 October 1945 were eligible to join the Corps. Later this policy was tightened when it was decided that only those who had enrolled between 1 June 1945 and 12 October were eligible to join the Corps. No individual, however, was eligible if he had a criminal or unsatisfactory war record.[3]

---

2   The War Office August 1946, translation from Polish.
3   TNA, T 236/1369, Polish resettlement employment policy, 1946–1948, translation from Polish.

Table 2: Approximate number of men in Polish units eligible to join the PRC	
Unit	Number of Men
Polish 2nd Corps	62,000
1st Armoured Division + Parachute Brigade	16,000
Polish Staff in Great Britain	35,000
Auxiliary Staff in France and Middle East	85,000
Total	**198,000**

12

Conditions of Service – Polish Air Force

The Polish Resettlement Corps (Royal Air Force) was under the control of the Air Ministry. Every Polish pilot received the following communique from the Ministry on 14 October 1946:

At this moment, when the Polish Air Force is about to be disbanded, I wish to express on behalf of the officers, airmen and airwomen of the RAF our deep gratitude for the most valuable services rendered by the officers and airmen of the Polish Air Forces to the allied air effort during the war. The RAF will always remember the magnificent qualities of your fighter pilots, the fearless and determined bravery of your bomber and coastal crews and the expert skills zeal and energy of your staffs. The whole of the Polish Air Force is a splendid team. You are now invited to join the Polish Resettlement Corps the RAF has formed, solely the help you settle down in suitable employment in the United Kingdom or elsewhere.[1]

And then:

To join the PRC (RAF) you will be required to complete and sign an appropriate form. You are asked to sign a two year contract to give plenty of opportunity to find suitable employment for you. On employment you will be temporarily released from the Corps. When you take civil occupation you will be released and receive a grant in lieu of leave. Should you cease to be in civil employment you will be recalled to the active list for duty with the Polish Resettlement Corps (RAF). While in civil occupation you will not receive any Air Force pay or allowances and you will responsible in supporting your family. The Polish Resettlement Corps (RAF) will advise you when opportunities for emigration occur in case you want to emigrate and help you fill in the appropriate documentation. It will also tell you what training you should undertake. You will be eligible for discharge from the Polish Resettlement Corps (RAF) to civilian life in the United Kingdom when British authorities are satisfied that you can look after yourself and your dependants or at the end of your two year service unless engagement is extended. On discharge you will be given civilian clothing.

Personnel of the Polish Resettlement Section of the WAAF[2] will be allowed to obtain release or discharge from the Corps to join their husbands in approved cases. When you join the Polish Resettlement Corps you will belong to the RAF and will wear an RAF uniform and badges except that the shoulder flashes will read 'Poland'. British medals ribbons will take precedence over Polish ones and Polish insignia, badges of rank and squadron badges will not be worn. RAF flying badges and corps badges together with RAF buttons will also be worn.

---

1   TNA, WO 32/17573, Polish Land Forces Polish Air Force and Polish Resettlement Corps.
2   Women's Auxiliary Air Force.

The emoluments you will receive in the Polish Resettlement Corps (RAF) will be subject to British income tax under normal rules and the tax free rates of pay which you receive as a member of the Polish Air Force, will cease to be payable, instead you will paid as from the date of appointment to the Resettlement Corps. The rate payable to you whilst a member of the Resettlement Corps will be that appropriate to the rank, branch of service or group in which you will serve in the Corps.

Marriage Allowances in respect of civilian wives and/or children resident in the United Kingdom will be payable at the normal British rates applicable to new recruits in the RAF on or after 1 July 1946. If food and accommodation are provided your family/marriage allowances will not be payable in addition. Marriage allowances will not be payable in respect of wives who are also members of the Resettlement Corps. Ration Allowances will be payable at normal British rates where applicable. If public accommodation is provided on Resettlement Corps stations, lodging allowances will not be paid.

If you are released to take up civil employment you will receive a grant in lieu of leave equivalent to 21 days' pay and marriage allowances where issuable together with ration allowances. In the event of your recall to the Corps a similar ration grant will be made on subsequent release to civil employment but all such grants except the first will be deducted on final discharge. If you are discharged from the Corps to proceed overseas you will receive a grant in lieu of leave equivalent to 56 days' pay and allowances in addition to pay and war gratuity.[3]

Female personnel of the air wing were not enlisted in the Resettlement Corps, instead being enrolled in the Auxiliary Territorial Service (Polish Resettlement Section).

Table 3: Approximate number of men in Polish Air Force Squadrons	
Number of Personnel (excluding those who returned to Poland after the war)	10,500

---

3 Air Ministry 14/10/1946.

13

Conditions of Service – Polish Naval Wing

Naval operations of the Polish Navy based in Davenport, Oakhampton and Woodford Green during the war comprised 787 convoys, 1,162 combat patrols, the sinking of two U-Boats and 39 German transports and the shooting down of 20 enemy aircraft. The total number of nautical miles covered by the Polish Navy during the War amounted to 1,213,000.[1] The Admiralty wrote to every rating of the Polish Navy units in January 1947. It advised the men that, if they did not want to return to Poland, they should enlist in the Polish Resettlement Corps (Naval Wing) or, for female personnel, in the Polish Resettlement Section of the ATS (ATS/PRS).[2] Members of the Polish Navy were informed that enlistment would commence on 3 February 1947 and cease on 17 February 1947. As with the other Services, personnel were notified that the Polish Resettlement Corps and the Auxiliary Territorial Service (Polish Resettlement Section) were British military units organised to help prepare Polish personnel for civilian life in the United Kingdom; alternatively, they could be helped to emigrate at Admiralty expense if they so wished. Ratings (non-commissioned sailors in the navy) had to apply through their detachments or sections. The enlistment would last for two years, during which time suitable employment would be found for them in Britain. Emphasis was placed on the fact that enrolment in the Polish Resettlement Corps or the ATS/PRS would mean that they would become members of the British Army and would be subject to British military law. The War Office added that, despite being in the navy, personnel would come under the responsibility of the military and would be treated as ordinary members of the Resettlement Corps. They would still be allowed to wear their naval uniforms. Also, although they would be given military ranks whilst in the Resettlement Corps, they would continue to be addressed by their naval rank, which would be a courtesy title.

Members of the Naval wing could be employed on military as well as civilian tasks in exactly the same way as other members of the Resettlement Corps except that, in some cases, they could be employed on naval tasks organised by the Admiralty. Orders would be issued by Military Advisory Staff and passed to the units of the Naval wing of their Command.[3] Female personnel of the navy were not enlisted in the Resettlement Corps, instead being enrolled in the Auxiliary Territorial Service (Polish Resettlement Section).

---

1 <http://www.ostrycharz.free-online.co.uk/polish_navy.html> (accessed 19 March 2019).
2 Auxiliary Territorial Service (Polish Resettlement Section).
3 TNA, WO 315/19, Polish Navy and PRC (Polish Resettlement Corps) Naval Wing: reorganisation, pay and personnel, also history of Polish warships attached to Royal Navy.

Table 4: The Admiralty published the daily rates of pay as follows		
Officers (Daily Rate)		
Rank in PRC	Equivalent in Polish Navy	Officers employed by the PRC
Lieutenant General	*Wiceadmirał*	90s 0d
Major General	*Kontradmirał*	75s 0d
Brigadier Colonel	–	60s 0d
Colonel	*Komandor*	55s 0d
Lieutenant Colonel	*Porucznik*	40s 0d
Major	*Kapitan*	31s 0d
Captain	*Porucznik*	20s 0d
Lieutenant	*Podporucznik*	14s 6d
2nd Lieutenant	*Podchorąży*	7s 6d

Other Ranks (Daily Rate)		
Rank in PRC	Equivalent in Polish Navy	ORs employed by the PRC
Warrant Officer	*Chorąży*	**16s 6d**
Staff Sergeant	*Starszy Bosman*	**13s 6d**
Sergeant	*Bosman zawodowy*	**12s 0d**
Corporal	*Starszy marynarz*	**8s 8d**
Private (Able seaman)	*Marynarz zawodowy*	**8s 0d**
Private	*Marynarz*	**3s 3d**
PRC – Polish Resettlement Corps, ORs – Other Ranks		

Table 5: Approximate number of men in Naval units	
Unit	Number of Personnel
Polish Naval Units	3,000

14

Conditions of Service – Female Personnel and Members of the Home Army (AK)

The Polish Women's Auxiliary Service,[1] Polish 2nd Corps, was established when the Polish Army in Russia was formed after the Soviet Union changed sides in the war in 1941. As with most of the men in the Corps, these women had been released from Soviet captivity after approximately two years' enslavement in Russia. 75 percent of the women in the Corps (about 1,400 in number) originated from pre-war eastern Poland (occupied by the Red Army in 1939) and had been deported to the Soviet Union. The Auxiliary Service, which was under the command of Władysława Piechowska (later replaced by Bronisława Wysłouchowa)[2] played a crucial role in the Polish forces between 1941 and 1945, performing a variety of supportive tasks. Uniquely, their work was shared between the needs of the Polish forces and the welfare of civilians (including orphans and the aged) who had also been released from Soviet captivity and placed under the care of the Polish High Command. Those with nursing experience cared for wounded and distressed soldiers in field hospitals or worked in pathology laboratories, where they were responsible for infection control, the dispensing of medicine and diagnostic support. Other members of the Auxiliary Service trained in military communications where they were responsible for building field transmitter stations, sending ciphers and deciphering incoming messages. Others trained as drivers and mechanics and were members of transport divisions responsible for moving ammunition, fresh food and water to the base units behind the front line. Finally, a large cadre of female personnel served as administrators involved in the writing of Corps diaries, translating orders between British Command and Polish General Headquarters, archiving the Corps' records and taking care of the day to day running of army bases.[3]

No female personnel, whether having served in the Polish 2nd Corps, the 1st Armoured Division, the naval wing or the air wing, were permitted to join the Polish Resettlement Corps. Instead they were enlisted in the Auxiliary Territorial Service (Polish Resettlement Section). The conditions of service were very similar to those of British personnel in the ATS, apart from being given a two year contract which included an early release clause if they wanted to leave to marry, to reunite with their husbands or if they fell pregnant. Expectant mothers were entitled to clothing coupons for maternity wear as soon as pregnancy was confirmed, as well as to supplementary rations supplied by local food offices. However, not all female personnel were required to enlist. The following did not have to sign up: pregnant women (whether married or unmarried); married women whose husbands had been relegated to the unattached list, or in the reserve of the PRC, and had obtained civilian accommodation; aliens who were not members of the Polish Armed Forces, but had been

---

1 *Pomocnicza Służba Kobiet* – 2,000 in number.
2 Anna Bobińska, *Pomocnicza Wojskowa Służba Kobiet 2 Korpusu 1941–1945* (Warszawa: Krupski i S-ka, 1999), p.270.
3 TNA, WO 315/20, Polish Auxiliary Territorial Service, Polish Nursing Service.

accepted as civilian residents in the UK; women whose husbands were awaiting relegation to the reserve of the PRC and had found civilian accommodation. Women whose husbands had opted for repatriation also did not have to enlist, provided they accepted repatriation with them. Those who did not wish to be repatriated with their husbands were eligible to enrol in the PRS.[4]

Training offered to female personnel in the PRS included sewing, tailoring and cooking. Other classes provided were similar to those offered to the men, including lessons in the English language, and Spanish for those who had shown an interest in emigrating to Argentina (a popular destination for some displaced Poles). If they decided to leave Britain, they were entitled to war gratuity payments relating to the duration of their service under British command, and were eligible to repatriate or emigrate at War Office expense.

During the war the Poles had organised one of the largest, clandestine, underground armies in occupied Europe. It was called the Home Army[5] and was recognised by the Allies as a regular unit of the Polish Sovereign Forces and therefore had rights under the Geneva Convention. On the strength of this fact, it was argued that Home Army personnel who had been incarcerated in Germany should be eligible to enrol in the Polish Resettlement Corps if they so wished. The problem for the War Office was that these underground formations, which had been under the control of the Polish Government in London during the war, had not fought under British command (a condition for enrolling in the Resettlement Corps). A compromise was struck when it was decided that members who had been freed from German captivity and were still in the West could enrol. Members of the 'Silent Unseen'[6] who had been parachuted by the RAF on SOE missions into occupied Poland to fight alongside the Home Army, and were in the United Kingdom on 1 July 1946, would also be eligible for enrolment. However, the War Office reserved the right to make the final decision on a case by case basis, therefore any individual who wished to enrol would have to be available for interview at the headquarters of the Resettlement Corps in London at an agreed date. The conditions of service for these individuals would be similar to the regular Polish Land Army who had served under British command, once permission to enlist was granted.[7]

Table 6: Approximate number of personnel in these units	
Unit	Number of Personnel
ATS/PRS	2,000
Members of the Home Army in German captivity	10,000 estimate

---

4   Polish Resettlement Corps (Polish Resettlement Section).
5   *Armia Krajowa* (Polish).
6   The 'Silent Unseen' [*Cichociemni*] were a special operations unit of the Polish Army in exile, created in Great Britain to operate in occupied Poland.
7   TNA, WO 315/40, Home Army, ex POWs.

Table 7: Pay for members of the ATS/PRS

Officers	£.s.d/Week	ORs	£.s.d/Week
Controller	32s 6d	Warrant Officer Class I	9s 5d
Chief Commander	28s 6d	Warrant Officer Class II	7s 6d
Senior Commander	18s 6d	Staff Sergeant	6s 4d
Junior Commander	11s 6d	Sergeant	5s 0d
Subaltern	9s 0d	Lance Sergeant	4s 3d
Second Subaltern	3s 0d	Corporal	3s 9d
		Lance Corporal	2s 9d
		Private	2s 4d

15

Accommodation – The Camp System

The War Office decided to use the many disused military bases, mainly occupied by Canadian and American forces during the war, to temporarily accommodate Polish Allied forces once they had been transferred to the United Kingdom.[1] Many of these bases were built in the early 1940s and stood idle after Germany's capitulation. They were situated on a number of different sites, either on Ministry of Defence land, Royal Air Force airfields, Royal Navy docks or land requisitioned from wealthy landowners. Although the bases were originally built to last for approximately 10 years, they were pressed into further service to accommodate the Polish arrivals after a short renovation programme. These camps were constructed using prefabricated methods, as cost and speed were of the essence during wartime. This method of building, where components are manufactured off-site to be assembled into ready-made structures, also did away with the need for skilled labour, such as carpenters and tilers, which was in short supply during the war years. Approximately 400 camps were built during the period 1940 to 1942 and were also used as repatriation depots for American and Canadian troops at the end of the war. However, their demolition was postponed indefinitely as the Polish problem loomed.

The most common buildings used in the construction of these bases were wooden barracks (sometimes called Yukon huts if the timber had come from the Yukon forest) and Nissen huts, which had been designed by Major Peter Nissen during the First World War. The barracks were of wooden construction standing on concrete platforms or foundations. The outer walls were made of feather edge, overlapping timber planks (weather boards) held in position on a wooden frame to give a weatherproof barrier. The planks were treated with a preservative such as creosote, or other tar-based paint, to prevent water penetration and pest infestation. The barracks were lined with 12mm fibre board which doubled as a heat and sound insulating layer. The roofs were covered with thick, black, interlocking felt tiles. These structures were also supplied with tall, iron-framed windows built by the Crittall Window Company of Essex and were glazed with shatterproof glass. Each window was also supplied with a blackout blind. The barracks were heated using freestanding, cast iron wood and coal burning stoves and were provided with running water from regional supplies. Some of the water supply was heated in boiler houses to provide hot running water for kitchens, laundries and showers. The heated water was distributed throughout the bases via asbestos-clad overground pipes. Low voltage electric power was provided using cables slung over wooden pylons. Remote camps were provided with their own water treatment facilities which included filter beds, sedimentation tanks and pumping stations. The camps, where the predominant buildings were wooden barracks, were sometimes called 'Hutted Camps' in official documentation.

Crittall products were also used in dormer windows in the second type of building, the Nissen hut. These structures were of a completely different construction and were formed

---

1   TNA, AST 7/1553, Polish resettlement: Poles in War Department camps.

Model of a barracks block: Polish Resettlement Camps, where barracks were the predominant building, were sometimes called 'Hutted Camps'.

from galvanised sheet steel which was corrugated and shaped in such a way that they could easily be bolted together to form the 'skin' of the structure. They had a tunnel-shaped profile (cross section) and were robust enough to be used as medical stores, infirmaries, ammunition dumps and air field hangars as well as dwellings. But such military considerations were irrelevant by the time the Polish forces had arrived. The concern now was whether the condition of these aging camps was suitable for the Resettlement Programme. The view of the War Department was that it would be prudent, for political reasons, to ensure that the standard of accommodation offered to the Poles was higher than that provided for POWs[2] during the war, and so it was decided to refurbish the camps before releasing them to the Resettlement Programme. In 1946, the War Office adapted the camps to the demands of the Programme. It informed general headquarters that the resettlement of Polish troops would begin in 'reception camps'. It estimated that approximately 230 of these would be required to process the number of personnel expected to be landed in Britain. Whilst in these camps, the Poles would remain as members of the Polish Armed Forces under the command of Polish officers who would be operating under strict British supervision. Once the personnel had enlisted in the Polish Resettlement Corps (PRC), they would become members of the British forces and be transferred to so-called 'PRC service camps' (resettlement stations as regards Polish Air Force units). If for any reason an individual changed his mind about staying in Britain, and decided to repatriate during this procedure, he would leave the service camp and be transferred to a 'repatriation camp'. Three repatriation camps were established; Camp

---

2   Prisoners of War, usually German and Italian.

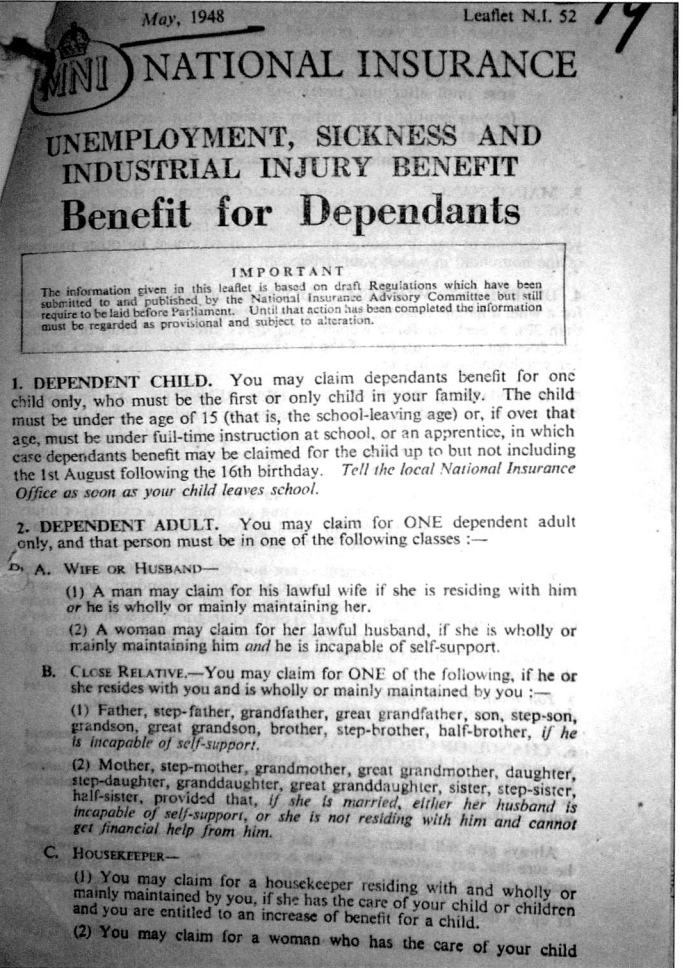

Information leaflet issued by the Ministry of National Insurance describing benefit rights for dependants of the Polish Resettlement Corps.

number 94 – *Polkemmet* – with a capacity for 2,000 men, Camp number 95 – Stewarton – with a capacity for 2,000 and Camp number 99 – Fairfield – capacity 500. The repatriation camps ensured that those wishing to return to Poland did not come into contact with those who had refused to return, thereby reducing the chance of unsightly incidents occurring between the two groups. A similar arrangement was made for men who wanted to emigrate, but in this case they would be moved to 'emigration holding camps' before leaving the country. Emigration camps were usually located near departure points such as Chandlers Ford near the Port of Southampton, where the men would await transport and be assisted in applying for travel documents and visas required by the receiving country of their choice. The camp system also included medical facilities, such as hospitals and infirmaries, which were previously used during the war such as Diddington Camp in Cambridgeshire. The British authorities decided to recognise three types of pre-war Polish qualifications which

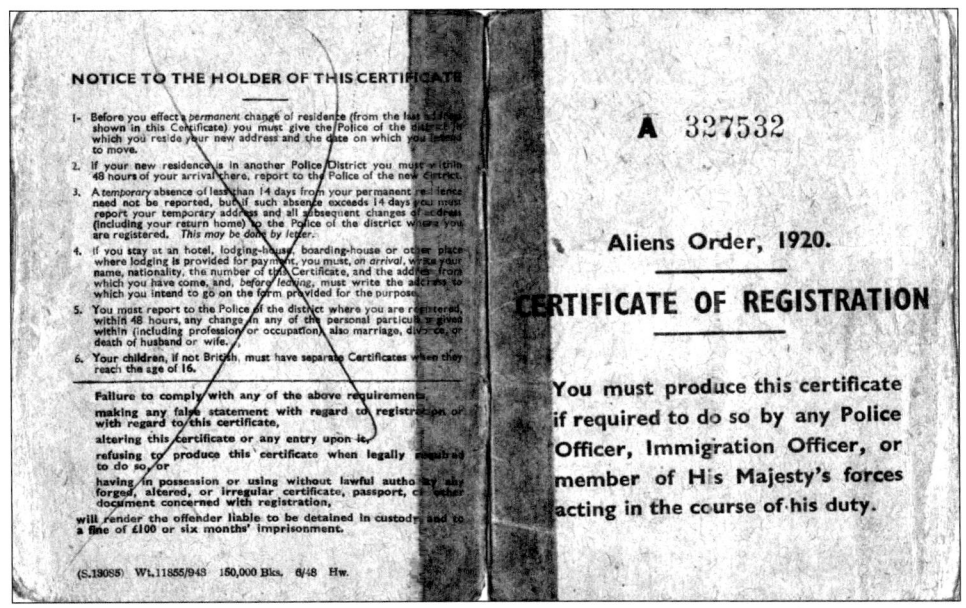

Certificate of Registration: Polish dependants in Britain were issued with this document under the Aliens Order 1920. Demobilised personnel were also issued with this document on becoming civilians.

were in short supply in Britain; medical, pharmaceutical and dental. Personnel with these qualifications would be employed in the treatment of Polish individuals, thus preventing undue pressure being put on national medical resources. An integral component of the 'camp system' included 'workers' camps'. These camps were operated by the National Services Hostels Cooperation for individuals who were billeted in PRC service camps which stood in isolated areas where employment was not available.

His Majesty's Government had also agreed to resettle the dependants of Polish soldiers who had decided to remain in Britain. Most of these people had spent the war in British 'safe havens'[3] and were expecting to return to Poland; however, since their menfolk were being resettled in Britain, they too were given permission to transfer to this country. The expectation was that they would reunite with their menfolk on arrival. They were brought to Britain from the safe havens on British ships. For example, RMS *Arundel* sailed from Cape Town with 600 women, children and the elderly from northern and southern Rhodesia, arriving in Southampton on 30 May 1948. Travelling from Bombay, the SS *Empire Brent* (Ministry of Transport) sailed into Southampton on 26 September 1947 with 968 Polish displaced persons from camps in India c/o Headquarters Polish Resettlement Corps London. HMS *Scythia* sailed from Mombasa to Liverpool arriving 15 August 1948 with 490 Polish displaced dependants from camps in Uganda and Tanganyika c/o Polish Resettlement Corps Cirencester.

Being civilians, they were not received in military reception camps but were welcomed in civilian 'holding camps' (sometimes called 'transit camps'). For example, Daglingworth

---

3   TNA, AST 18/115, Admission of refugee Poles from East Africa.

Camp served as a transit camp for displaced persons arriving from Africa and Europe, including Germany. Dependants were issued with Certificates of Registration under the authority of the 1920 Aliens Act.

Employment for civilian adults was not available, and so work permits were not issued to these individuals until the early 1950s when employment policy changed. The primary task for these individuals was to reunite with husbands and, in the case of children, with fathers. Once wives were reunited with their husbands, they were transferred to 'families' camps' which were initially run by the War Office but later the Assistance Board after the man's demobilisation. Families established in Britain, that is men and women who had met and married in this country, were also accommodated in these camps, although many new wives were required to remain in transit camps until suitable housing was available.[4] Some camps were used solely for the accommodation of Polish orphans and were classified as Polish orphanages. These were staffed by British personnel. Whilst in the orphanages, the children were provided with special care which included rations of milk and food. Psychological support was also provided for children who required it. Reports coming from such camps concluded that the children in these camps were very happy and contented.[5] A special category of camp was reserved for those who refused to sign up to the PRC having stated in the attestation that they would do so. These were called 'recalcitrant camps' and were used to separate them from those who agreed to enlist as it was feared that the friction which had been noticed between the two groups would spill out into physical confrontation.

As demobilisation from the Polish Resettlement Corps continued, the character of the displaced diaspora changed into a civilianised population. This necessitated the responsibility for the Poles to pass from the War Office to civil departments. For example, workers' camps became the responsibility of the National Services Hostels Corporation[6] which had originally been established by the War Department in 1945 to provide accommodation for single workers (usually men) who were far from home whilst in employment. All it would take, the War Office argued, for the corporation to be able to take over these camps would be to add to its charter the phrase, 'to provide accommodation for persons who, by reason of circumstance connected with war and enemy action, are in need of accommodation'. The corporation agreed to this amendment but was not particularly pleased when it later discovered that a number of families were living in some of the workers' camps. Their expertise was limited to running hostels for unmarried men who were employed nearby and not families, some with children. The War Office suggested that the family quarters could be removed, or at least kept to a minimum and located in remote parts of the camps.

The National Services Hostels Corporation established a special department to run its Polish sites; however, before accepting responsibility for a camp, it carried out a structural survey, in order to ascertain the viability of buildings and infrastructure. If its surveyors highlighted serious problems, the corporation insisted that the War Office make the necessary improvements before relinquishing responsibility, thus ensuring it carried the financial burden for any renovation work. If a camp was rejected, the corporation had to produce a formal report explaining the reasons for the decision. Minor improvements, however, were carried out by the corporation's own mobile labour force and, when it had completed the work, a warden was appointed and an official transfer date was arranged. The

---

4   *The Polish Daily* and the *Soldiers Daily* Number 199, 24 August 1946.
5   *The Polish Daily* Number 199, 24 August 1946.
6   TNA, AST 18, ref: PRO 57/703 National Service Hostels Corporation: files and papers.

warden was answerable to a regional board made up of representatives from the Ministry of Labour and the War Office as well as the corporation's management team. Monthly reports were written and circulated to all members of the managing committee for discussion. By 1 April 1948 the corporation had successfully taken over 23 camps, but this rose rapidly as demobilisation from the Resettlement Corps continued.

Responsibility for the families' camps and service camps where civilianised individuals were accommodated passed to the Assistance Board and were invariably renamed 'hostels'. The Board had extensive experience in providing accommodation and welfare services for needy individuals and families, and had accepted the responsibility for the 'greater good of keeping families united' and 'relieving the War Office of its responsibility for civilians'. However, it pressed the government to make other arrangements for the Poles so that it could relinquish its responsibility as quickly as possible. In hostels where the individuals were self-sufficient, the Board employed a 'light touch' management regime by merely appointing a warden to oversee the day to day running of the hostel. Vulnerable individuals or families, who for one reason or another could not reunite with their men folk or were widows, were housed in hostels where more resources and specialist support was provided. Apart from lodging, these hostels also offered full board with regular meals based on healthy menus as well as medical services, which included maternity help and 24 hour care for the old and infirm.[7] The staffing and equipment in these hostels was comprehensive and included kitchen facilities, canteens and medical rooms all staffed by qualified personnel. The Assistance Board's policy was to make monthly inspections of its establishments with reports being published on what was found. It would examine such things as the qualifications of staff, the suitability and serviceability of medical and kitchen equipment and operational procedures being employed in order to ensure safe and economic practices. Families in Assistance Board hostels were required to contribute to the cost of their upkeep, so frequent audits of the accounting records were undertaken. These would cover the conditions of rent books and the cost of supplies being bought to run the hostels. The bywords here were 'good value for money'. It was also the policy of the Board to encourage the Poles to set up resident committees as self-help groups.[8] Although the Assistance Board envisaged that the Polish inhabitants would integrate into British society quickly, they still found themselves running some 19 Polish hostels with a total population of 8,860 until the mid-1950s. Seventeen of these were eventually reclassified as housing estates and taken over by district and municipal councils.

In order to encourage the Poles to leave the temporary hutted estates and transfer to more permanent homes, local councils gradually reduced the provision in the hostels and offered suitable dwellings from their own housing stock. As the hutted estates were emptied, they were quickly demolished to discourage squatters moving in. Many of the housing estates became enclaves of isolated Polish communities, a situation which ironically put a brake on integration and assimilation. Invariably, contact with the British community only occurred when the men entered the job market, or when illness occurred and, following the establishment of the National Health Service in 1948, doctors or district nurses were

---

7 TNA, AST 18/43, Women and children resident in maternity units in Polish Hostels: claims against Ministry of Health for maintenance.
8 TNA, AST 18/101, Assistance Board and successors: files dealing with problems arising out of the administration of the Polish Resettlement Act 1947 by the Assistance Board, the National Assistance Board and the Supplementary Benefits Commission.

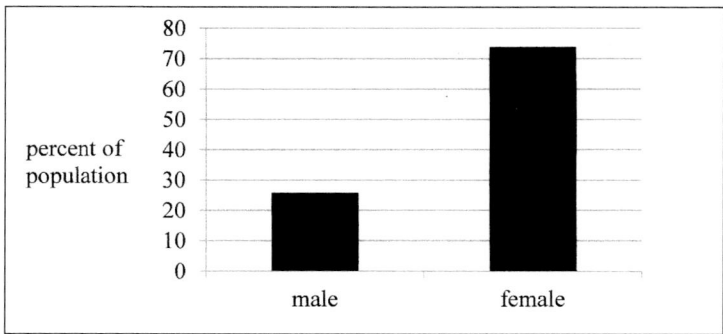

Figure 2: Gender breakdown of dependants brought to Britain.

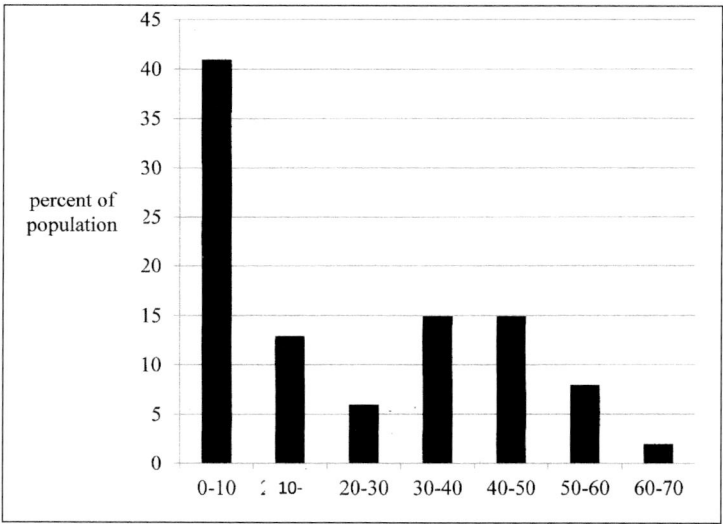

Figure 3: Age profile (in years) of dependants brought to Britain.

allocated to the estates. Children born on the estates only came into meaningful contact with the British population when they entered local primary schools and made friends with children in the playground. The policy of education authorities was to distribute Polish children amongst a number of different schools in their areas to ensure that no one school became overburdened with a sudden influx of foreign children with language difficulties. Otherwise, playmates of the children born in Polish hostels were usually other children on the estate which meant that many of them entered primary school with a very limited knowledge of the English language. (Ironically even Polish language skills of many of the children were restricted as the availability of Polish children's books in Britain was extremely limited.) This meant that making friends with English children was slow and difficult which left many of the Polish children feeling isolated and vulnerable. In order to avoid becoming ostracised by their classmates, many children used the normal psychological strategies of making oneself popular, siding with the majority and using humour as a psychological shield. Some education authorities managed to provide special language classes for the children, but learning to read and write tended to be a struggle, especially when parents could not offer appropriate support at home. As many of these housing estates stood in remote locations the local education authority provided free transport to and from school.

The camp system was a temporary expedient in the Polish Resettlement Programme. It was never the intention to keep these camps open for long, just until the Poles had left to live in the wider British community. Government departments, whilst accepting their fair share of responsibility for the Poles, insisted that they would prefer to rid themselves of this duty as soon as it was possible. Two things needed to occur before this could happen: one, a job had to be found for the men, which was responsibility of the Ministry of Labour; and two, permanent accommodation had to be made available so that individuals could leave their camp/hostel. This was the responsibility of civil authorities such as municipal or rural district councils and, although their priority was the rehousing of British families who were also in need of homes, a proportion of newly built dwellings were reserved for Polish families which allowed for the eventual dismantling of the camp system. Camps that stood on Ministry of Defence land were demolished by War Office staff or their subcontractors. The same service was available to land owners who had a camp on their land, although they could choose to receive money from the War Department and hire their own workforce.

The data above suggests that the greatest number of dependants brought to Britain were female (mothers) and children. The next largest group were dependants between 30 and 50 years of age probably because they were too old to enrol in the Polish forces during the war. Individuals between 50 and 70 years of age also formed a significant group which indicates how heterogeneous this diaspora became.

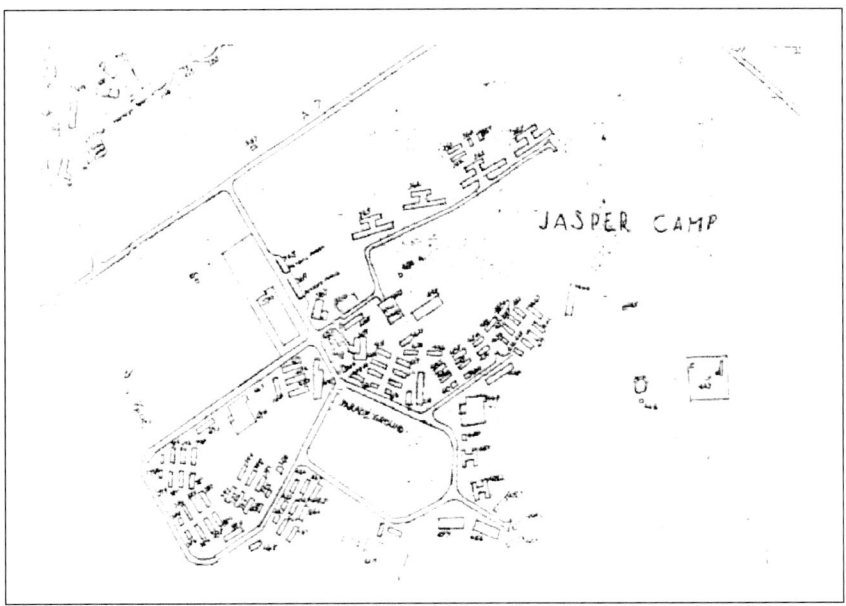

Figure 4: Jasper Camp, Surrey - later used in the Polish Resettlement Programme.

88 THE POLISH RESETTLEMENT CORPS 1946–1949

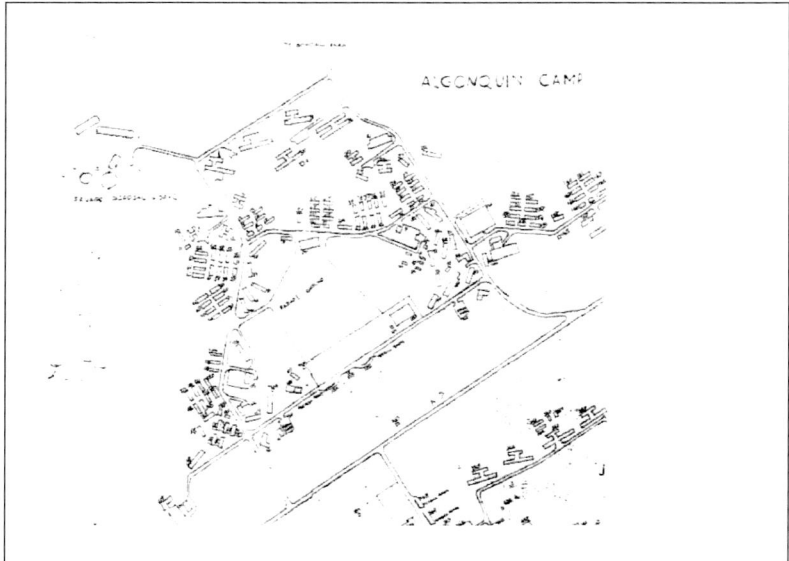

Figure 5: Algonquin Camp (Canadian base in Surrey) – used in the Polish Resettlement Programme. Note the water treatment works top left.

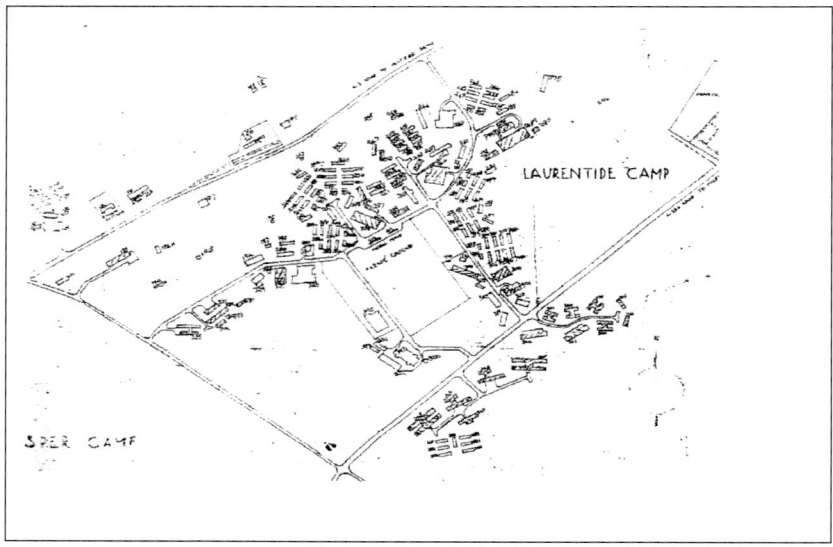

Figure 6: Laurentide Camp (Canadian base in Surrey) – used in the Resettlement Programme. Note the parade ground.

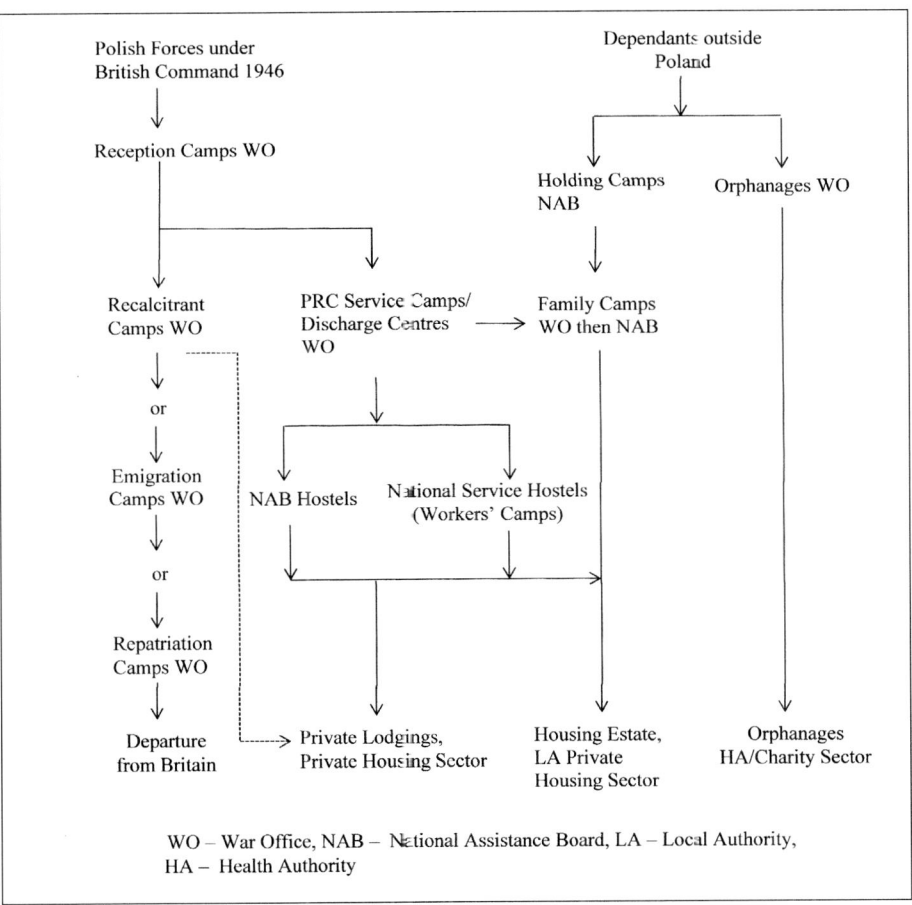

Figure 7: The camp system as used in the Resettlement Programme.

Part II

The Resettlement Programme

Man is a political creature and one whose nature is to live with others.
(Aristotle, Ethics, 1169b 18)

16

The Transfer of Polish Land Forces to Britain

The transfer of Polish forces to Britain began in July 1946 and proved to be a demanding task. It was not only the sheer number of personnel that made the process difficult but the nature and variety of units, such as medical companies, signal companies, theatre groups and cadet schools, which added to the complexity. The number of men in the Polish 2nd Corps in Italy was approximately 62,000 to which approximately 3,000 female personnel of the Women's Support Unit had to be added. Those in the 1st Armoured Division amounted to approximately 16,000 men, and they too had to be transferred back to Britain, having taken part in the liberation of the Low Countries and Northern Germany during the second phase of the D-Day landings. Those in the Middle East numbered approximately 21,000, and to this it was necessary to add 11,000 personnel who were in France. Once cadets and special groups such as theatre groups were added, the total rose to approximately 116,000. The transfers followed a precise procedure which ended with personnel being billeted in reception camps in various Home Commands. The usual mode of transport was shipping to ports such as Liverpool, Glasgow and Southampton, although rail transport was also used with a ferry crossing from Calais to Dover. Clearly, Polish squadrons in the RAF based in the Middle East would fly directly to British airfields. The transfer process began with what the War Office called 'extraction' which involved locating and concentrating personnel at departure points which could either be railway stations or ports. International railway stock was employed for overland transfers whilst British and American shipping was used for sea routes. For example, three British and two American ships were made available for those being transferred from Italy; the RMS *Mauretania*, with a capacity for 4,500 men; the SS *Queen of Bermuda* with a capacity for 2,600 men and the HMS *Cilicia* with a capacity for 2,500 men were provided by the British. The Americans provided the SS *Medina Victory* with a capacity for 1,089 men and the SS *Colorado Springs Victory* with a capacity for 1,123 men. From these figures it is possible to estimate that a total number of sailings required to complete the transfer from Italy alone was 10 round trips.

Extraction was followed by the second stage which the War Office called 'embarkation' but, before this was allowed to happen, the men were disarmed and required to sign an attestation which stated that they would join the Polish Resettlement Corps on arrival in Britain. The transfer process would end with the men being accommodated in reception camps where the process of enrolment into the Polish Resettlement Corps commenced. Polish officers, who were positively predisposed to the resettlement programme, were entrusted to manage this sensitive stage although British officers administered enrolment. Following enlistment, personnel ceased to be members of the Polish Sovereign Forces becoming members of British forces subject to British command and military law. Once the men had signed to join the Polish Resettlement Corps, they were moved from the reception camps to Polish Resettlement Corps service camps or 'PRC camps'.

The first units to be transported to Britain were advance parties which were expected to refurbish the disused service camps earmarked for use in the resettlement programme. An administrative department under British supervision had also to be established, ready to compile statistics on PRC enrolment. The extraction of the Polish 2nd Corps from Italy began in September 1946 with the following units: Rear HQ 2nd Polish Corps from Ancona, HQ Polish Enclave, from Forti, Rear Party Base Two Polish Corps, Bari Casamassima, HQ 10 Polish Company, together with 101,102,130 Polish Field Companies, Bologna. The Signals Unit was also transferred from Ancona, alongside the Polish Mobile Petrol Filling Station from Falconara. Also brought to Britain during the early stage was the 16 Polish Field Ambulance Company from Naples, 62 Polish Mobile Field Dental Unit, 344 Polish Advanced Depot for Medical Stores, both from Loreto, and the Polish Bacterial Laboratory from Ancona. All units of the 3rd Carpathian Infantry Division (approximately 14,000 men) travelled during June and October 1946. Their route took them overland by rail through Austria, Germany and France via the cities of Verona, Bremen, Stuttgart, Strasburg, Nancy and Calais and took three days to complete. Following the short crossing of the English Channel, they landed in Dover. The units transported by sea left Italy via Naples and sailed to Liverpool or Glasgow. The sailing time took seven days. The Division's Headquarters was brought to Britain on 14 July and 29 October and quartered in Camp Hedgemoor in Buckinghamshire and Penn Wood Camp near Amersham. The 1st Brigade travelled by sea on 7 and 10 September, whilst the 2nd Brigade was transferred on 24, 25 and 29 September and quartered in Camp Gosfield near Halstead. The 3rd and 4th Brigades also travelled overland by rail between 25 August and 17 September, but excluded the 8th Battalion which was transferred by sea. The brigades were based in Buckinghamshire, with the Officer Corps of the 8th Battalion being quartered at Piper Wood Camp near Amersham. The Officer Corps of the 7th Battalion was based at Waddeston near Beaconsfield, whilst the officers of the 9th Battalion were stationed at Wotton Wood near Aylesbury. This is how the diary of the 1st Transport Company of the 3rd Carpathian Infantry Division describes the units departure,

> We prepared to relinquish all the vehicles by cleaning them and conserving all spare parts in the stores. All Company records were brought up to date. Items which we were to be disposed of were thrown into a huge pile of junk. Everything had to be left behind, even the Lorries we had planned to use for our return journey to Poland. The staff receiving the equipment was made up of German POWs, who made no effort in compiling itineraries of the items we passed to them.[1]

Soldiers travelling from Italy were allowed to bring 9,000 Lira (£10) with them which was changed into pounds sterling in Naples or Calais. Undeclared money was later changed in Britain. Men who had decided to emigrate directly from Italy, or wanted to remain in Italy with their new wives, were allowed to demobilise immediately.

The transfer from the Middle East started in February 1947 as soon as transport was available. The principal units transferred from this region included the 12th Polish Defence Security Squadron from Jerusalem, the 9th, 10th and 17th Polish Defence Squadrons from Qassasin, the 4th Polish Guard Company from Kantara and the 6th Polish Guard

---

1   M. Młotek, (ed.) *Trzecia Dywizja Strzelców Karpackich 1942–1947, Vol. 1* (*Związek Karpatczyków*, 1978), p.800. Paraphrased from Polish.

Cartoon 3: Making the decision to join the Polish Resettlement Corps.

Company from Barbara. The 546th Polish Base Signal Company, the Polish Cipher Section, the Training Signals Section, the HQ Polish Provost Company, the medical units (which included the 8th Polish General Hospital), the Polish Convalescence Depot and the Polish Tuberculosis Section based in Kantara were also transferred from this theatre. Welfare units, including the Polish Soldiers Families Office in Qassasin and the Polish Soldiers Families Number One Palestine Section in Jerusalem were included in these transports. The British were responsible for the transfer of 1,736 cadets from the Polish 2nd Corps Cadets School. Polish 2nd Corps medical facilities were moved in three echelons and included the 8th General Military Hospital and staff from two hospitals for tuberculosis and mental departments; however, 800 patients, who were too weak to be moved, remained in Palestine until they became strong enough to travel.

Polish orphans, whom the Polish Army had undertaken to care for during the war, were moved into British orphanages run by the War Office or by private charities. Children who were over 17 years of age were allowed to enlist into the Polish Resettlement Corps, whilst the younger ones continued with their studies in technical schools run by the Ministry of Labour.

The transfer of the Women's Auxiliary Service, 2nd Polish Corps[2] took place during October and November 1946. Before leaving Italy, the unit left a plaque in Holy Ghost Church in Bologna which read, 'In this church between 1945 and 1946 members of the Polish Women's Auxiliary Service of the Polish 2nd Corps which had liberated Monte Cassino, Ancona and Bologna, prayed to God to bless their military service and to help them to return to a free and independent homeland'.[3]

Polish personnel in France were given the option of remaining in France if they could

---

2 *Pomocnicza Wojskowa Służba Kobiet, 2 Korpus.*
3 Bobińska, *Pomocnicza Wojskowa Służba Kobiet 2 Korpusu 1941–1945*, p.305.

find employment, otherwise they were given the option to transfer to Britain and join the Polish Resettlement Corps. The Liquidation Mission in France divided the Polish personnel into four categories:

Table 8: Aims of the Liquidation Mission in France	
Cat. A (Polish Army under British Command)	Transfer to UK
Cat. B (Lived in France prior to 1939)	Dispose of in France
Cat. C (Member of the Polish Forces in France 1940/ Ex-POWs/DPs)	Dispose of in France
Cat. F (Ex-Wehrmacht of Polish extraction who joined the French Resistance)	Dispose of in France

The War Department produced a table of the principal units and the number of personnel involved in the transfer from France.[4]

Table 9: Unit Name	Officers	ORs	ATS
Polish Liquidation Mission	44	63	
Polish Court Marshal, La Courtive	5	14	
Military Camp, La Courtive	187	352	3
Polish OR Record, La Courtive	2	9	
Polish Military Camp No 3, Lille	159	964	22
Poles in French Zone of German occupation	5		
Polish Graves Registration Section	1	2	
Polish Graves Registration Section, Belgium	1		
Polish Demobilisation Centre	18	242	
Polish Military Hospital, Calais	6	48	
Polish Senior Officer's Club, Nice	38	16	
Polish Guard Platoon, Istres	2	61	
HQ Polish Units in the South of France	2	6	
Total	470	1,777	25

The instruction to the Liquidation Mission in France was to find employment for those who wanted to stay in France, and then discharge them from the Polish forces. This had to be achieved before 15 March as no transport to Britain after this date would be available. As with all Polish personnel brought to Britain, the men in France were required to sign an attestation stating that they would join the Polish Resettlement Corps on arrival. If, for whatever reason, they did not sign the document they risked a dishonourable discharge. All the men who required transport to London had to be available at Calais no later than 15

---

4 TNA, WO 315/18/11, Polish Military Mission in France.

March, otherwise they would be subject to immediate dismissal from the forces.

The Polish Camp in Lille was closed on 15 March, with personnel being transferred to Britain *en masse*. As far as the Polish Officers' Club in Nice was concerned, officers could travel to Britain during the last days of February.[5] Medical units were transferred on 20 March whilst staff at the Polish Demobilisation Office at Istres wound up operations on 25 March and were transported to the United Kingdom on 30 March.

The grand total of displaced Polish personnel in Britain was, therefore, approximately 250,000. This is how Stanisław Cieślewicz described his journey from Italy to Britain,

> On 18 September we left Resin and travelled to a transit camp called Lamie where we waited for transport to Great Britain. Whilst we waited we had to fill in travel documents. Five days later we were taken to the port where the *Colorado Victory* was waiting. We were scheduled to sail on 21 September but no sooner had we boarded than we had to disembark as there was a technical fault with the ship. No one complained about having to unload their baggage. Whilst we waited, Captain Westalewicz from the Liquidation Company, arrived to wish us *bon voyage*. He had also brought the good news that I had been given a promotion.
>
> On a sunny 23rd September at 13.20 hours we finally set sail for Britain. The ship was pushed from its moorings by two tugs. Everyone stood on the open decks to take a last look at the coastline of Italy where every road and square held a memory for us. As the ship moved slowly into open water, a lone girl was standing on the quayside waving a handkerchief in tears. She slowly disappeared from view. *Addio Bella Italia!* We made our way through the Straits of Gibraltar and then into the Atlantic. During the journey we had to hand in our side-arms which we did with great sadness for we knew that we would not see them again. I handed in my Colt pistol.
>
> During the night of 28 to 29 the ship approached Liverpool Docks. My first night in Britain was spent on board and on 30 September at 11.00 hours we began disembarking. Double decker buses stood by to take us on our onward journey to Liverpool Railway Station. After an eight hour rail journey we arrived at Halstead in Essex, about ninety kilometres north of London. We then marched in formation to our reception camp, which was called Grosfield Camp and stood near an airfield used by the American Air Force during the war. On arrival we were given leaflets which read, 'Your arrival in Great Britain gives the many friends of Poland in this country a chance again to congratulate the achievements of the Polish Armed Forces on land, sea and in the air'. We were then required to enrol in the Polish Resettlement Corps.[6]

Tomasz Arciszewski, Polish Prime Minster of the disenfranchised Polish Allied Government in London, welcomed the first Polish troops to arrive in Britain with the following statement;

> I welcome you to Britain where fate has brought you though you must know that we are still on the road to a free and independent homeland … Whilst in Britain you will need to continue to be true to your traditions and unbending in the belief of a future

---

5   TNA, WO 315/18/11, Polish Military Mission in France.
6   Stanisław Cieślewicz, translation from *Diary of a Carpathian Soldier 1939–1947 Dziennik Karpatczyka 1939–1947* (Self-Published by Lulu, 2009), pp.506–511.

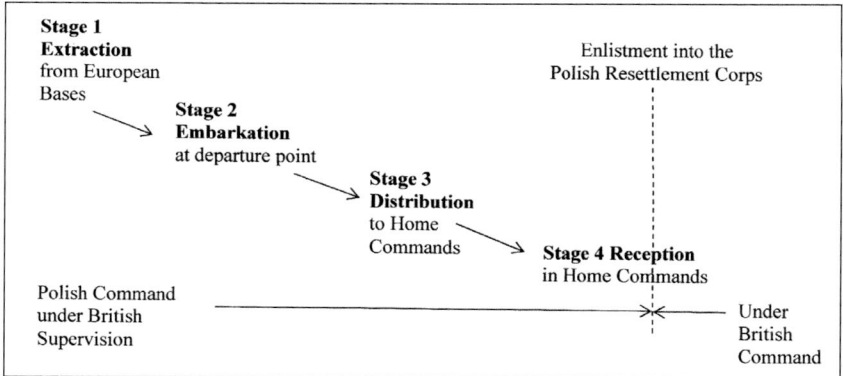

Figure 8: Transfer of Polish Allied forces to Britain (1946–1949).

Poland ... For six years the British have hosted the Polish President, our government and Polish Forces who after the fall of France took part in the defence of the British Isles ... Try to take advantage of what Britain has to offer for this will help you to reach your ultimate goal of returning to our homeland ... The British are a friendly people who respect those who fight for their rights ... I know that you have been through horrendous battles and that now you are in personal turmoil, but I believe even now that you will continue to work for the objectives our nation has set us, the realisation of a free and independent nation.[7]

The transfer of Polish Forces to Britain also included paramilitary units, such as entertainment groups. Ten groups were brought over and distributed throughout the Home Commands where Polish troops were stationed (these are listed in Table 10). The War Office considered these to be military companies, because they were destined to perform mainly to audiences made up of soldiers. They were organised on the same lines as the British Central Pool of Artists which meant that they would not receive any assistance from public funds apart from the normal pay and allowances of other personnel; but, they could retain admission fees which would be at the same rate as those performing for British Forces; namely 3/-, 2/- and 1/- depending on the seat number. Polish troops brought with them various foreign banknotes which were changed into British currency when declared.

---

7   *Polish Daily and Soldiers Daily* Number 199, 24 August 1946, translated and paraphrased from Polish.

THE TRANSFER OF POLISH LAND FORCES TO BRITAIN

Table 10: Forces Entertainment Groups

Name	Parent Unit	Camp Accommodation	Manager	No of Artists	No of Admin	Total
Revue Theatre	2 Corps	81 Transit, Kirby	Second Lieutenant Krakowski	40	19	59
Dramatic Theatre	2 Corps	Milfield	Mr Domański	42	19	61
Revue Ref Ren	2 Corps		Mr Konarski	48	15	63
Cyrulik Warszawski	2 Corps	78 Camp, Maghull	Mr Jarossy	11	2	13
Representative Orchestra	2 Corps	78 Camp, Maghull	Lieutenant Dembogórski	62	6	68
Theatre Silesian	2 Corps	Hereford	Lieutenant Sikorski	49	24	73
Lwowska Fala	1 Corps	Edinburgh Welfare Section	Mr Rapacki	11	4	15
Theatre Team	1 Corps	Crieff Welfare Section	2 Lieutenant Starzyński	14	2	16
Artistic Musicians	1 Corps	Crieff Welfare Section	2 Lieutenant Pankiewicz	10	4	16
Revue Plankowa	London		Mr Karpiński	11	4	15

Polish 100 Złoty banknote, reverse.

Polish 100 Złoty banknote.

Egyptian five Piastres banknote.

Egyptian five Piastres banknote, reverse.

Italian 10 Lire banknote.

Italian 10 Lire banknote, reverse.

German 50 Pfennig banknote issued by Nazi Germany.

A British Military Authority two Lire currency note.

Currency of the British Military Authority 10 Shillings.

Currency of the British Military Authority 10 Shillings, reverse.

17

Procedure for Enlistment into the Polish Resettlement Corps

To the great credit of the British Government, enlistment into the Polish Resettlement Corps was never made compulsory, although it was expected that all those eligible would enrol. To encourage this, soldiers were promised work, accommodation, and healthcare as well as food coupons, pay, war gratuity and education. This support and help was designed to assist successful resettlement in Britain. The threat for those who refused to sign up was to be cast into an isolated 'wilderness'. However, the Government repeatedly made it clear that, if any individual decided they wanted to repatriate or emigrate during any time in the resettlement process, he could do so at the British Government's expense.

Enlistment into the Polish Resettlement Corps commenced as soon as personnel arrived in the reception camps. This meant that recruitment was a rolling programme which took up to three years to complete. Officers in the Polish Army, who were positively predisposed to the resettlement programme, oversaw the men's reception and were entrusted to promote the merits of enlisting.

The newly appointed Inspector General of the Polish Resettlement Corps, General Stanislaw Kopański, wrote an open letter to Polish officers in reception camps,

> As we may no longer exist in our present form, it is the duty of leaders to inform their subordinates what they should do. I consider it my duty to declare that everyone who does not wish to return to Poland should join the Polish Resettlement Corps. To do this is not contrary to a soldier's oath or to our principles, and it is absolutely necessary on account of the personal interest of the soldier. Besides, those of us who remain abroad have a duty to educate ourselves. and give to the nation what our fellow countrymen in Poland under occupation cannot give. Service in the Resettlement Corps leaves open the road to Poland and, if at any time the situation in Poland should change, we will be able to return. The staff of the Corps should do all in their power to prepare the soldier for civil life.[1]

The procedure for registering and enlisting into the Polish Resettlement Corps was designed not only to verify personal information such as name, place and date of birth, but to glean as much personal information on life aspiration, military service, education and preferred employment as possible. This information was deemed necessary if suitable work was to be found for the men, and ensured that appropriate data for the statistical department at the Ministry of Labour and the War Office was obtained. Personnel were expected to sign a two year contract with the PRC, although officers over the age of 50 could enrol for one. Information obtained from the troops was summarised and encoded on punch cards called

---

1   TNA, WO 315/9, Polish Resettlement Section, Polish Resettlement Corps.

3. NOMINAL ROLLS.

(a) The documents, after endorsement as above, will then be placed in sequence of British Army Numbers and separate nominal rolls in QUADRUPLICATE for each unit in groups as enumerated in para 2 above, will be prepared in accordance with the following proforma :-

UNIT.................................(in English and Polish)

P.R.C. Army No.	Rank (in English)	Name.	Initials.	Date of Enlistment.	Polish Army No.	Documents sent.

Station...................... (Signature)...........................O.C.

Date.......................... (Unit)..............................

(b) Three copies of the nominal roll must be attached to the Former Service Documents, one of which will be returned to the unit as acknowledgement.

It was important for the War Office to keep records of enlistments into Polish Resettlement Corps for statistical purposes. This form was used to record the nominal roll of men who had agreed to enrol.

'paracards' and filed at the Polish Records Office.

These cards would accompany the individuals throughout their service in the Corps. The protocol for enlistment, which was administered by a British officer, comprised four stages: 1) filling in a questionnaire 2) attending a one-to-one interview 3) encoding and summarising the information, and finally 4) copying the encoded data onto the personalised paracard. The interviewing officer was responsible for the accuracy of the information entered on these cards, and was not allowed to provide advice on what individuals should do about their future.

The questionnaire comprised eight sections with a clear margin on each page which was used for verifying remarks and summarising information furnished by the candidate. They were to be completed in a calm atmosphere so that the men remained relaxed and were not put under pressure when filling his form. The men were first organised into groups of no more than 30 individuals, so they could work in an intimate atmosphere, and allocated a space at a table before being provided with a sharpened pencil. Once all the soldiers were settled, general remarks were read out,

> As you have been told, it is the intention of the British Government to arrange for gradual demobilisation and to find you a job either in the United Kingdom or in other countries. In order that the British authorities may have as much information

as possible about your past experience, qualifications and wishes, they have arranged for you to complete a questionnaire. You will be given assistance to fill it in. The information you provide about your plans and wishes will be sent to London and given to the British authorities.[2]

This was followed by the distribution of questionnaires so that everyone was in possession of his own form. They were given five minutes to peruse the form and familiarise themselves with its layout. The group was then brought to attention and the interviewing officer went through the questionnaire using a conversational tone.

On the table in front of you is a questionnaire which you will have to fill in. Now look at section A, called 'Personal Information'. This section has been filled in for you. Read through it carefully and check that the information given is correct ... [3] You will then have to complete all Sections including Section 8 which deals with your education.[4]

Once the interviewing officer was satisfied that the men understood what was needed to be done, he brought them back to the beginning of the form so that completion could commence. (Assistance was given to anyone who was illiterate.) The final question was particularly important for the War Office as it was here that an individual described the aspirations they had for the future. An individual interview then followed where the written responses were verified, encoded and entered onto the individual's paracard. The questionnaire for Polish officers had a similar layout as for other ranks, except it contained an application for an officer's commission in the British Army.

The procedure for enlisting Polish Air Force personnel was identical to that of the Land Forces, except that their questionnaire contained an application section for enrolment into the Polish Resettlement Corps Air Wing. As with the Land Forces enlistment, it was for two years in order to give plenty of opportunity to find suitable employment for personnel. However, the procedure for air staff differed in that the interview was organised by the Air Ministry and included regional representatives of the Ministry of Labour and National Service. The questionnaires were initially distributed to air bases by British Advisory Staff in each Home Command. The enrolment of naval personnel was similar, except the enlistment process was carried out through Naval Detachments. The paracards of naval personnel were initially passed to British Advisory Staff in Detachments who would copy it to the Polish Records Office.

The completed questionnaires comprised the first stage in a paper trail designed by the War Department in May 1946. The trail, however, could not function successfully until a Polish Statistical Section at the War Office and a Polish Records Office were established.[5] Information from the questionnaire was transcribed onto a punch card called a 'paracard' which was lodged with the Officer-in-Charge (OiC) in the Home Command. He (she) would then send a copy to the Polish Records Office which passed a duplicate to the Polish Statistical Section at the War Department. Thus every man's details were kept in three places. The War Department compiled the information and used it in official statistics. Applications

---

2 TNA, WO 315/9, Polish Resettlement Section.
3 TNA, WO 315/9. Polish Resettlement Section.
4 TNA, WO 315/9. Polish Resettlement Section.
5 TNA, AST 18, Assistance Board and successors, Polish Resettlement, Registered Files (PR and PLH Series).

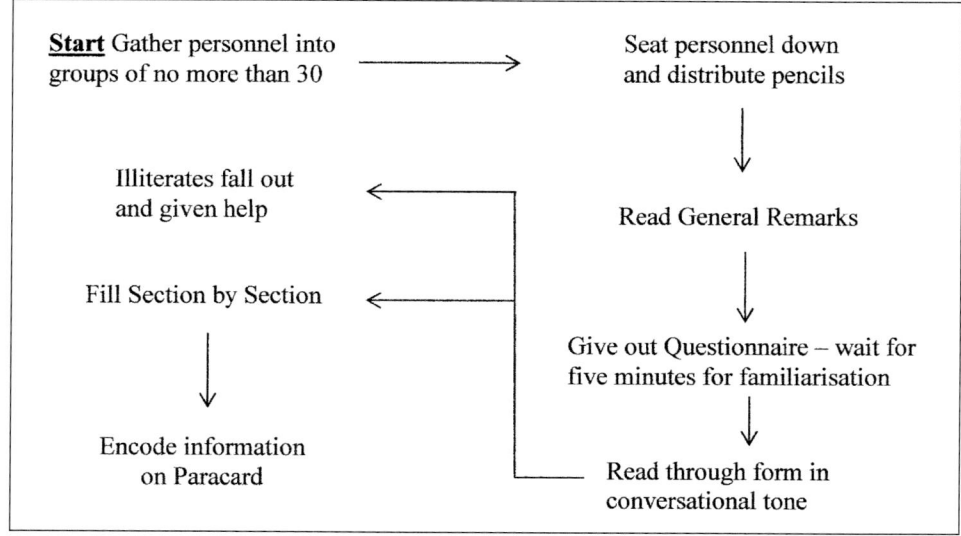

Figure 9: Protocol for filling in the War Office questionnaire.

for commissions, however, were first passed to British Advisory Staff before being sent to the War Department via the Polish Records Office (PRO). Any alterations to a man's particulars had first to be recorded by the Polish Records Office before a copy was sent to the Statistical Section for updating. The War Office also made it clear that it would be unable to deal with any queries regarding an individual soldier as 'even one enquiry would throw out the working of the machinery'. It ordered that any enquiries received on any individual should be passed directly to the Polish Records Office at Witley Camp to deal with.

One difficulty facing the War Office regarding enlistment into the Resettlement Corps was what to do with individuals who could not decide, or refused to sign up despite agreeing to do so in their attestation. The official term used by the War Office for these individuals was 'recalcitrant'.[6] There were numerous reasons why men refused to enlist; the first was the mistrust which had developed during the closing stages of the war between the men and their officers. By this time, many of them were fed up with hearing yet more promises from their officers who had banged on throughout the war about 'right being on our side', 'we are on the road to victory' and 'Britain will not let us down'; all so much poppycock. Soldiers with this view concluded that they would not be hoodwinked again. Many also feared that the communist regime in Warsaw would take reprisals on their families back in Poland if they enlisted. Others believed that enlisting in the Polish Resettlement Corps constituted nothing more than capitulation and represented a failure to deliver independence and freedom for Poland. In any case, they argued, enrolment would require the breaking of their solemn oath to the Second Republic which for them was a step too far.

Options that were considered for dealing with recalcitrant individuals included deportation and the reduction of pay levels. One suggestion, for example, was to deport waverers to Germany or Austria where they would be registered as Displaced Persons (DPs) and placed under the care of UNRAA.[7] On 2 February 1947 the War Office gave

---

6   TNA, HO 213/1235, Recalcitrant Poles: use of deportation orders, 1947–1948.
7   United Nations Relief and Rehabilitation Administration.

an ultimatum to those still vacillating, warning them that they had only one week to make up their minds or they would be transported to Hull and then shipped to Cuxhaven near Osnabruck in Germany where they would be demobilised.[8] There they would be paid 400 Marks as a settlement for their war service and provided with a demob suit. They were also informed that, once deported, they could no longer rely on British help regarding their future. However, this rather harsh policy was quickly reversed when members of Parliament protested that the War Office had no right to deport Poles forcibly without going back on the government's undertaking to treat the Polish Forces fairly. There was also the concern that it was highly unlikely that the Central Control Office in Germany would accept Poles under such circumstances.

Further thought on the matter resulted in two classes of recalcitrant being identified; those who were willing to work, but for one reason or another were unwilling to join the Corps, and the hardcore who were considered to be agitators and habitual criminals, who refused both to work and enlist. The War Office introduced interim pay scales amounting to 90 percent of Corps pay for those who volunteered to work but not enlist, and pocket money for those who refused both, but this was only done once the hard core were separated from the rest. However, an announcement concerning these pay scales was not made until 1 September 1947. Recalcitrant individuals went through the same aliens' registration procedure as members of the PRC who were subject to military discipline. This meant that if they left their registered employment without permission, or came to the notice of the police in connection with some dubious activity, they would be recalled to their unit and dealt with as a serviceman.[9] However, the War Office decided not to take a firm line on this provision, for there was no compulsion to join the Corps and it would have been disingenuous to be firm with someone who was merely exercising his rights. As a result, the War Office resigned itself to demobilising recalcitrants and absorbing them into Britain as individuals, irrespective of whether they had obtained employment or had their own means of support. However, it would have been preferred if recalcitrant individuals had decided to emigrate rather than remain in Britain. In order to encourage this, the War Office made it known that, if the decision to emigrate was made before 31 August 1947, their passage would be paid. These individuals would also be entitled to retain the following kit: one battledress, one coat, one pair of shoes, one pair of socks, one pair of underpants, one vest, one shirt, one tie, one pair of braces, one shaving brush, one toothbrush, one shaver, one sewing kit and one towel on departure. However, after this date, the individual would have to make his own arrangement and pay for his own passage if he changed his mind about staying in Britain. Nevertheless, personnel were reminded that repatriation or joining the PRC was still available to them. Anglo-Polish commissions were set up for those who required further information on the options available to them. After this, if an individual continued to resist signing up or emigrating, he was reminded that, for him, remaining in the UK was not an option and the chance of employment would be removed. To isolate them from PRC personnel, recalcitrant individuals were accommodated in eight special recalcitrant camps as people who had enrolled were considered by some to have sold out to the British. In fact, the War Office was already aware of unpleasant episodes occurring in some recalcitrant camps where PRC Officers had been threatened in a 'most provocative

---

8 *Dziennik Polski i Dziennik Żołnierza*, Numer 39, 14 February 1947.
9 TNA, KV 4/286, Polish Resettlement Corps, Policy for the absorption and control of Polish Forces in the UK.

Male Officers:

Name_____ Commissioned into the Polish Resettlement Corps on_____ and allotted personal number _____ .

Female Officers:

Name_____ Commissioned into the ATS (PRS) on _____ and allotted personal number_____ .

Other Ranks – Male:

Name_____ Enlisted into the PRC on _____ and allotted Army Number _____ .

Other Ranks – Female:

Name_____ Enrolled into the ATS (Polish Resettlement Section) on_____ and allotted Army Number_____ .

Figure 10: Polish Authorisation Passes.

manner' by disillusioned individuals. PRC officers had no executive power in these camps and were therefore disrespected. Even Military Police had been assaulted, both physically and psychologically, in some camps. Eight camps were designated as recalcitrant camps: Falton Park, Plasterdown, High Ash, Greystone, Rampside, Haverford, Skitton and Downreay. Meanwhile, 43 recalcitrants had emigrated to France, 15 to the British Zone in Germany, 26 to America, seven to Brazil, 26 to Argentina, two to Venezuela, one to New Zealand, five to Italy, six to Canada and one to Australia.

Officers over 65 years of age were not enlisted in the Resettlement Corps; instead they were demobilised and made the responsibility of the Assistance Board on arrival in Britain. Officers over 50 years of age were enrolled on one year contracts. There were also 12 officers who were prevented from enrolling for being what the War Office called 'politically active'. However, General Anders was not included on the list as it was thought that this would inflame relations with the Warsaw Government. Five other officers were turned down for commission on the advice of MI5 who warned that they were 'working politically'. The Services Department negotiated with the Foreign Office and the Treasury on the individual terms of their discharge, including whether they should be granted pensions. Personnel with criminal records in the Polish forces were also prevented from enlisting; however, the Services Department promised to supply the Home Office with full particulars of the offences committed, and the sentences imposed, before a decision on entitlement to enrol was made. Where the evidence against an individual was insufficiently strong to warrant deportation, the individual was accepted into the Resettlement Corps but only after they had served their sentence. Prisoners under the control of the Polish forces could enlist, but only if they were in the United Kingdom on 19 October 1945. Deserters who returned to their units on their own initiative were eligible to enlist after serving out their punishment. Deserters who did not return (AWOL) [10] were dismissed from the Polish Army and treated on a case by case basis. Category 'E' personnel[11] were not enlisted owing to the nature of disability: they were discharged and passed over to the care of the Assistance Board.[12] On completion of the procedure the Polish Records Office issued an Authorisation Pass to remain in Britain.

At the same time, the Corps' Record Book at the Records Office was updated with the following statement,

Name_____ date enlisted into PRC or PRS_____.

Paid Rank held on date of enlistment into PRC_____Rank

Data held centrally was collated and summarised on a spreadsheet and shared with HQ Polish Resettlement Corps and the War Office:

Unit	Strength				Date	Allotted			
	Officers		ORs			male		female	
	male	female	male	female		from	to	from	to

Table 11: Collated Data for Enlistment

The following personnel of the Polish Forces were not required to enrol in the Polish Resettlement Corps:
1. Female staff with young children,
2. Female staff whose husbands were on the unemployed list, but had found other work,
3. Female staff whose husbands were on the reserve list,
4. Female staff whose husbands had applied for repatriation,
5. Those in the Polish Armed Forces who were in Britain briefly before the war were demobilised immediately

---

10 Absent Without Leave.
11 Infirm or Non-Effectives.
12 TNA, WO 315/21, Invalids, disabled and category E other ranks: resettlement, pay and discharge 1943–1950.

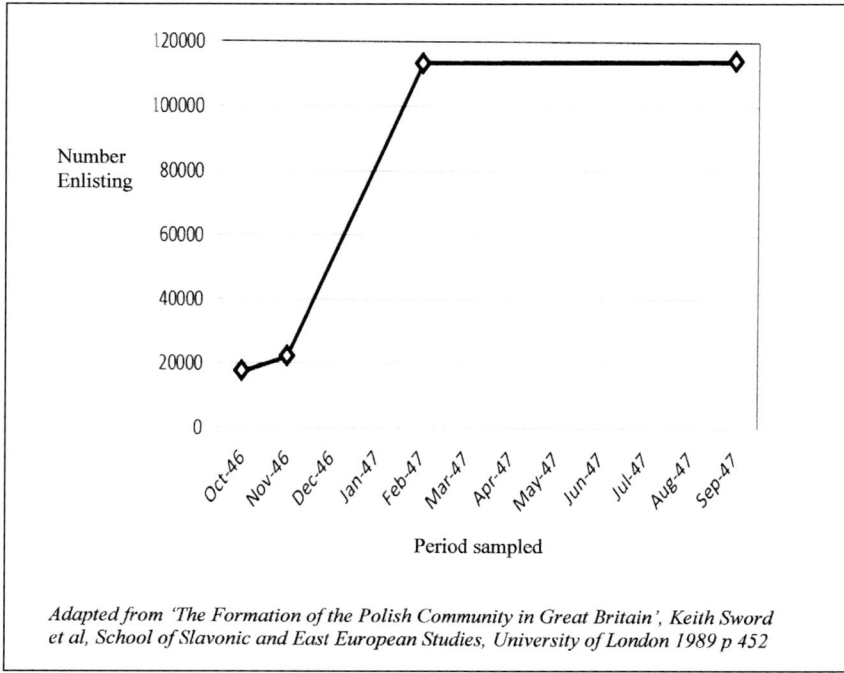

Figure 11: Total numbers enlisting, 1946–1947.

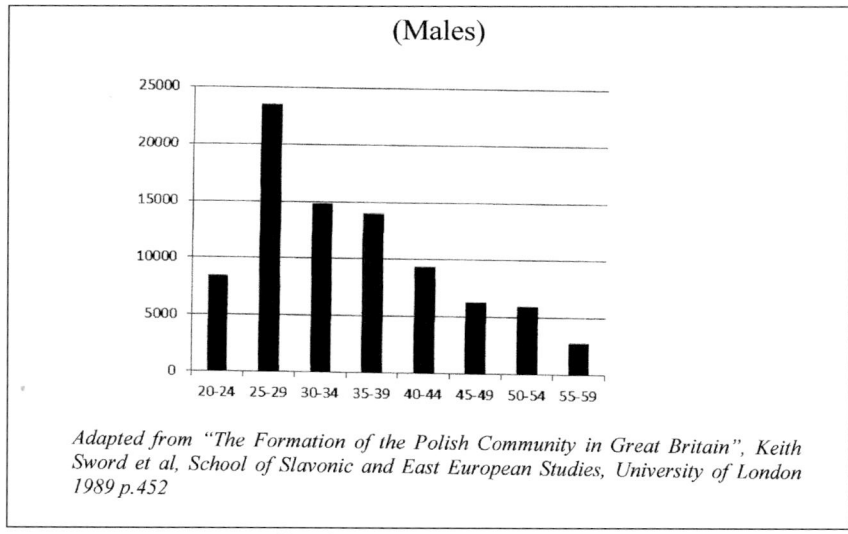

Figure 12: Age profile of Members of the Polish Resettlement Corps.

PROCEDURE FOR ENLISTMENT INTO THE PRC

Table 12: Recruitment into the Polish Resettlement Corps/Section by Home Command (February 1947)

	Eastern Command	Northern Command	Scottish Command	Southern Command	Western Command	London
Male Officers	1,491	1,059	3,477	1,420	2,865	968
Male ORs	16,660	12,441	25,836	16,840	25,393	874
Total	18,151	13,500	29,313	18,260	28,258	1,842
Female Officers ATS/PRS	59	186	103	105	275	34
Female ORs ATS/PRS	262	189	518	316	1,699	235
Total	323	275	621	424	1,974	269
Grand Total	**18,475**	**13,775**	**29,934**	**18,684**	**30,232**	**2,111**

ATS/PRS = Polish Resettlement Section for female staff
Source – The National Archives of the UK (TNA): WO 31

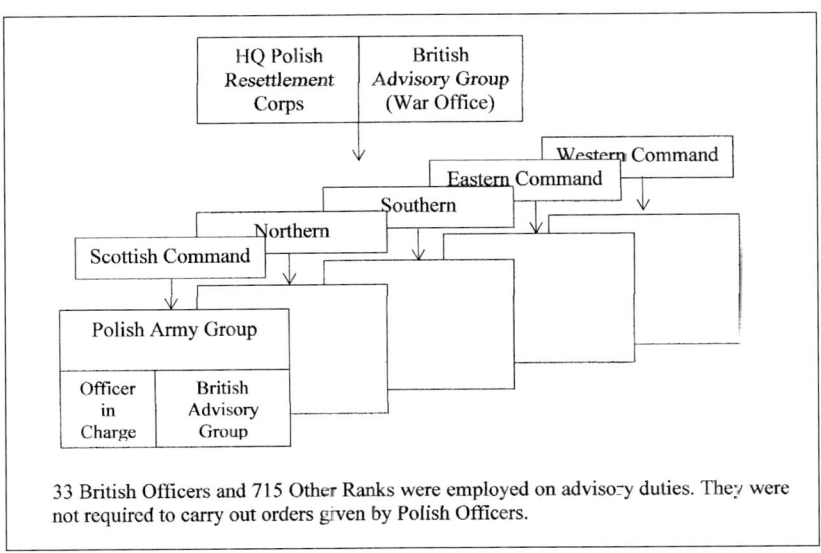

Figure 13: The distribution of Polish Resettlement Corps units into Home Commands.

RAF Squadron HQ	Naval Detachment HQ	Base Unit HQ
↓	↓	↓
Polish Records Office	Polish Records Office	Polish Records Office
↓	↓	↓
War Office (Statistical Office, Air Wing PRC)	War Office (Statistical Office, Naval Section PRC)	War Office (Statistical Office, Land Forces PRC)

Figure 14: Paper trail for PRC enlistment documents.

Form for enlisting into the Polish Resettlement Corps dated January 1947.

Before a Polish soldier could enlist in the PRC he would first need to leave the Polish Forces. This is a Polish Demobilisation Certificate which incidentally carries the same date as on the form used for enrolment into the PRC. This signifies that joining the PRC does not mean a break in service.

PROCEDURE FOR ENLISTMENT INTO THE PRC 111

Cartoon 4: Integration started with learning the English language.

In the meantime the Polish soldiers were introduced to their English allies through articles in army magazines. 'The English are a noble and principled people', they were informed, 'and are an island race that keeps itself to itself. Their outlook on Europe is not to meddle in any country, unless it challenges British interests'. This approach, the Poles believed, allowed the country to concentrate on running the British Empire. When Hitler challenged British interests in 1939, Britain was bound to respond. It was then that Chamberlain said that:

> Britain's border ends on the river Vistula. When Britain becomes involved in a country it anglicises it very quickly. In India, Afghanistan, on the banks of the Red Sea and central Africa, English order and attitudes are imposed and defended. The British love their royal family and follow precise etiquette as far as the King is concerned. For example, His dinner plate must be larger than his subjects' and his knife and fork have to be longer than anyone else's. British foreign policy is obsessed with three things: the road to India, Gibraltar and Flanders. In 1939 Britain confronted Hitler and by March 1941 it stood alone to defend freedom in Europe. It was then that Lords, Ladies, workers and servants had to meet in wartime shelters. To understand the British you have to appreciate what they appreciate in horses: blood and breeding. Victory belongs to us, they tell the world and the world believes them.[13]

---

13 Taken from a Polish article '47,000,000 Churchills' in Our Roads, The Magazine of the Carpathian Soldier, April 1941, pp.43–45.

18

The Rundown of the Polish Forces

All Polish servicemen and women who had chosen exile in Britain began their service during the War as soldiers of the Polish 2nd Republic; however, on arrival, they were placed under the authority of the 'Administrator of Polish Forces under British Command', a British officer simply known as 'the Administrator'.[1] He worked alongside Polish Officers according to Polish military law until the men had enlisted in the Resettlement Corps and began serving as British personnel. Unfortunately, enrolment in a foreign army was a court martial offence in Polish military law, so an assurance had to be made that no man would be disciplined by Polish authorities if he enrolled in the PRC. This assurance was given on 24 March 1946 by Władysław Raczkiewicz, the Polish President in exile, and was vital if enrolment into the PRC was to proceed as planned. With every signature entered on PRC documentation, the displaced Polish forces in Britain took a step closer to their tormented doom and historical oblivion. Finally, in January 1948, the War Office decided to close Polish Army Records which had been brought to Britain with the displaced units. The documents, which included medical records, disciplinary records, personal records and documentary evidence, were officially given the name, 'The Polish Forces Records' and subsumed into PRC records. They were lodged in the Polish Records Office at Witley Camp in Surrey and Hursley Park Camp in Winchester[2]. A list of all the documents which had been closed was sent to Polish Central Command in London.

As the Poles were now members of the British forces, the War Office decided that they were eligible to receive British campaign medals as long as they had not already accepted Polish equivalents. Two exceptions to this were the Polish Cross for Monte Cassino and the Italy Star. Furthermore, it was decided that those in receipt of campaign medals from other allied countries, such as France and Belgium, would not be eligible to receive the British War Medal. The War Office also declared that female personnel who had served in support units, such as the Women's Corps and the WAAF, would qualify for the British Defence Medal even if their service was undertaken abroad.[3]

The disposal of Polish Forces in Britain eventually meant that regimental colours and banners had to be placed in storage. They were eventually lodged in London at the Sikorski Institute, 20 Princess Gate, Kensington, following a solemn ceremony on 10 July 1947. At midday after a mass at Westminster Cathedral the Colour Parties, made up of one officer and a small number of NCOs in battle dress with side-arms, marched their banners to the Institute accompanied by the 3rd Carpathian Infantry Division Band.[4] The escort to the Colours wore service dress with berets and brown gloves. The officer in charge of the ceremony was Lieutenant General Szyszko-Bohusz who, in 1940, was the Commanding Officer of the Polish Independent Highland Brigade during the Battle of Narwik in the

---

1 *Dziennik Polski i Dziennik Żołnierza*, Numer 74, 27 March 1947.
2 *Oddzial Likwidacji*.
3 TNA, WO 315/49, Laying Up of Colours.
4 TNA, WO 315/49 Laying Up of Colours.

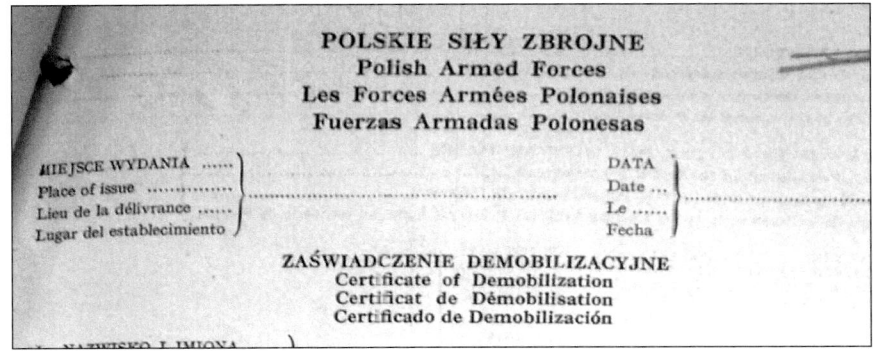

Discharge papers from the Polish Armed Forces in Britain – issued on enrolment into the Polish Resettlement Corps.

Norwegian Campaign. He had instructed all units to deposit their banners at the offices of the Inspector General, Polish Resettlement Corps Headquarters, London, in holdalls not later than the morning of 10 July where they would be received by Lieutenant General Fieldorf of the Liquidation Committee. Commanders of the colour parties were required to inform Fieldorf of the exact time and railway station at which they would arrive in London. This allowed for military transport to make a rendezvous. Before releasing their banners for the journey to London, units displayed their colours in their camps for a final farewell ceremony. On 8 July, for example, Colonel Łowczowski, the Commander of the 30 Battalion Group of the 3rd Carpathian Brigade, delivered a formal closing statement during its ceremony,

> Nations erect monuments and honourably preserve their military colours for they inform subsequent generations that they should be proud of their forbearers and be prepared to follow in their footsteps ... Our banners will remain in a foreign place in England until Poland is able to receive them with honour ... These banners say to those that follow, 'Polish soldiers marched under these banners and never lost faith during the most difficult stages in the War; under these banners they gave their all, their blood, their life, only to end up in exile.' They gave Poland everything they could.[5]

The guests of honour attending the event in London included the Head of Polish Civilian Authorities in London and the Inspector General of the Polish Resettlement Corps together with other representatives of the Corps, officers in charge of the Polish Navy and Polish Air Force and a delegation from the Sikorski Institute. Each Colour Party was led by its commanding officer during the solemn march through the streets from the cathedral to the Institute. The following formations laid up their Colours during this day; the Polish Navy, the Polish Air Force, the 3rd Carpathian Infantry Division, the 5th Kresowy Infantry Division, the 2nd Warsaw Armoured Division, two Grenadier Battalions, the 9th Carpathian Rifle Battalion, the 18th Rifle Battalion, the 1st Lancers Regiment, the Carpathian Lancers Regiment, the 3rd Field Regiment, the 10th Highland Regiment, the 1st Armoured Regiment, the 8th Rifle Regiment, the 9th Rifle Regiment, the 1st Field

---

5   Cieślewicz, *Diary of a Carpathian Soldier 1939–1947*, p.530.

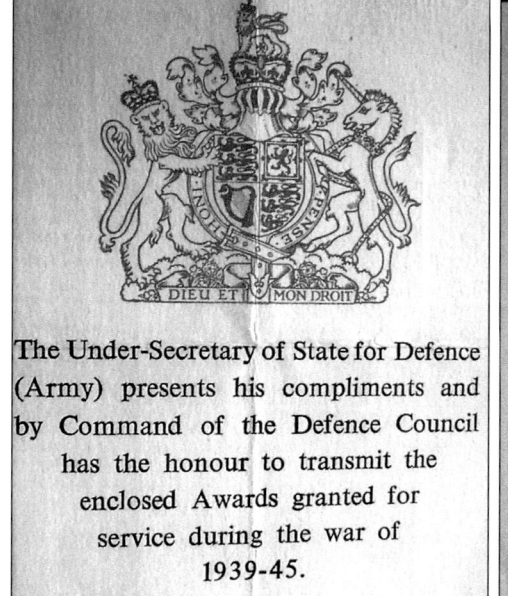

Members of the Polish Resettlement Corps were entitled to receive British service medals and awards. Individuals were presented with Notification of Awards cards.

Regiment, the 2nd Field Regiment, the 1st Parachute Regiment and the 10th Mounted Rifle Brigade amongst others.

At the end of the solemn event, Helena Sikorska, wife of the deceased Commander in Chief of the Polish Forces in the West, said,

> ' ... in the name of my husband may these colours remain under his care until they may be returned triumphantly to a real, free and complete Poland.'

19

The Command Structure

Under the 1940 Anglo-Polish Agreement, the Polish High Command had the authority to operate from British soil, whether this was undertaken in the United Kingdom or abroad. The command structure of Polish forces was typical for the wartime period, where different battalions accepted changing levels of responsibility as and when operations demanded. However, the Polish Resettlement Corps was a British formation and therefore had to have a new command structure based on King's Regulations, so this was put in place.

The Inspector General of the Polish Resettlement Corps was Major General Stanisław Kopański, who was based in the Corps' headquarters at 38 Egerton Gardens, London.

The relationship between Kopański and the British became an important one for he was sympathetic towards the Resettlement Programme and, probably more importantly, considered to be apolitical. General Anders, who could easily have been considered for the appointment, was tonally hostile to the programme and so was passed over as Commander.

Kopański was born on 19 May 1894[1] to a Polish family in St. Petersburg, Russia, and was the third child of Wincenty and Anna who had three other children. Kopański spent his early childhood on his maternal grandparents' estate in Kaunas but returned to St. Petersburg in 1902 to complete his studies. When he had reached secondary school age, he joined the Student Association for Self-Education, but his studies were interrupted by the outbreak of the First World War. However, as soon as he was old enough, he decided to pursue his interest in warfare and enrolled at the School of Artillery, St. Petersburg. He graduated on 21 December 1917 and was enlisted in the First Polish Army Group of the Russian Army.[2] When this formation was disbanded following the signing of the peace treaty between Russia and the Central Powers in March 1918, he took part in the Polish War of Independence and, following this campaign, enrolled at the University of Technology in Warsaw where he was awarded a degree in engineering on 27 June 1923. Following a brief posting to the 1st Mounted Artillery Battalion of the Polish Army, he was appointed to the Centre for Artillery Training in Toruń. His work here took him to the School of Artillery in Podgórze and later to the War Academy in France. Whilst there, he studied at the École Supérieure de Guerre, where he worked alongside officers well-versed in the latest thinking on the use of mechanised artillery in combat. Following a very successful stint in France, he returned to Poland where he accepted command of one of the battalions within the 6th Heavy Artillery Regiment in Lwów.[3] Following this posting he was promoted to the staff of the Department of Armoured Weapons in the Polish Ministry of Military Affairs, becoming second in command. During this time, when German-Polish relations were deteriorating fast, he was ordered to revamp Polish defence plans. Following spectacular German successes in September 1939, this work soon changed into planning for

---

1 George Jan Lerski, *Historical Dictionary of Poland* (Greenwood Press, 1996), p.265.
2 Lerski, *Historical Dictionary of Poland* (Greenwood Press, 1996), p.265.
3 Now Lviv in Ukraine.

Lieutenant General Stanisław Kopański – Inspector General of the Polish Resettlement Corps. (Courtesy of the Polish Library, POSK, London)

38 Egerton Gardens, London. Headquarters of the Polish Resettlement Corps.

retreat and evacuation. When the Soviet Union invaded eastern Poland on 17 September in agreement with Berlin, he evacuated to Romania alongside the High Command and some 60,000 men. Their destination was France, Poland's nearest ally in the West. As a result of his work in France during the 1920s, he found common language with French generals and on 2 April 1940 the Polish Government, which had also regrouped in France, appointed him commander of the Carpathian Rifle Brigade[4] being formed in the French protectorate of Homs in Syria. The formation was considered to be part of the Army of Levant. When France fell, Kopański transferred his brigade to British-held territory in Palestine rather than surrender to German forces. Promoted to the rank of Brigadier General, he saw action at Tobruk, Bardin, El Gazala, and Mechila. On 3 May 1942, the brigade was merged with 9th and 10th Infantry Divisions to form the 3rd Carpathian Rifle Brigade, which he commanded until July 1943. The brigade took part in the Italian campaign as part of the Polish Second Corps. In July he became Chief of Staff under General Klimecki and in 1944 was promoted to the rank of Major General. At the end of the war he did not return to communist Poland, preferring instead to take command of the Polish Resettlement Corps. He is buried at Northwood Cemetery, North London.

---

4   Later the Independent Carpathian Rifle Brigade.

THE COMMAND STRUCTURE 117

Table 13: Breakdown of Personnel and numbers in the service of the PRC Headquarters and the War Office in London

Unit	Nature of Work	Number ORs
PRC HQ	HQ of the Inspector General for PRC and PLF	54
Main Liquidation Committee	Responsible for the final liquidation of Records, Funds, Archives of the PLF, and registration of Births, Marriages, Deaths and Claims	143
12 Liquidation Units	Responsible for the winding up and disposal of Records, Documents, Equipment, Personal belongings of PLF who could not be located	370
PRC Records and Pay Office (Witley Camp)	Responsible for the payment of allowances to the PRC, the issue of family allowances and release benefits for those relegated to the reserve, discharged or emigrated. Officer in Charge was responsible for maintenance of all records as for relegation and discharge procedure.	728
PLF Records and Pay Office	Dealt entirely with all members of the PLF who had NOT joined the PRC or were ineligible to join.	171
Formation HQ – 5 Division Group Brigade	Organisation, administration, and maintenance of troops.	2,751
Foreign Despatch Centre and Repatriation Camps	Dealt with the collection and despatch of Poles to Poland and other European countries. Owing to differences in procedures for discharge for PLF and PRC – 2 Departments were set up.	201,213
Officer Training Units	Staff required for the administration of units formed for the holding of surplus officers.	1,265
Employed on War Department duties	Supply and transport, anti – squatter's guards, guards on dumps and stores. Duty with British Units. Clearing of ranges and administering Recalcitrant Camps.	3,017
On loan to civil Ministries	On loan to the Ministry of Labour	1,723
Dependants' Camps and Families Camps	Administration	1,300
Medical Units	Staff employed in medical establishments in all Home Commands	2,175
Workers' Hostels	Administration Staff for hostels until taken over by the National Services Hostels Cooperation	2,512
Base Units staff		2,466
Grand Total		19,089
PRC – Polish Resettlement Corps, ORs – Other Ranks, PLF – Polish Land Force		

There were nine departments in the PRC Headquarters in London:

1. The Overseas Travel Department, under the command of Lieutenant Jerzy Zaremba.
2. Polish Forces Archives, commanded by Sub Lieutenant Paweł Śliwa.
3. The Officer's Department, commanded by Lieutenant Henryk Piątkowski.
4. The Legal Department, commanded by Captain Bernard Szczepanik.
5. The Statistical Office, under the command of Lieutenant Zygmunt Celichowski.
6. The Records Department, commanded by Major Franciszek Derejewski.
7. The Catholic Mission, administered by Father Bronisław Michalski.
8. The Department for Other Faiths, administered by Brigadier Jerzy Sawa.
9. The Demobilisation Office, commanded by Lieutenant Tadeusz Majewski.[5]

The breakdown of personnel numbers employed in the administration of the Polish Resettlement Corps by the War Office demonstrates, quite starkly, how intensive the Polish Resettlement programme had become.[6]

The line of command of the Polish Resettlement Corps started with the PRC HQ in London and continued to Polish Divisional Group HQ in each Home Command, which worked alongside the Commander of the British Divisional HQ. Below the Divisional Group were Polish Brigade HQ Groups which were usually located in each PRC Service Camp. These worked alongside British District HQs.

The Naval wing was based on British Navy commands and sections.[7]

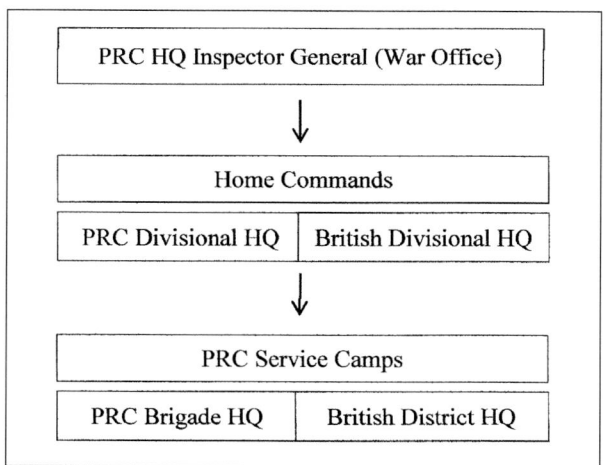

Figure 15: Command structure of the PRC Land forces.

---

5 TNA, WO 315/27, Administration matters regarding Polish Resettlement Corps, 1947–1949.
6 TNA, WO 315/27, Administration matters, 1947–1949.
7 TNA, WO 315/27, Administration matters, 1947–1949.

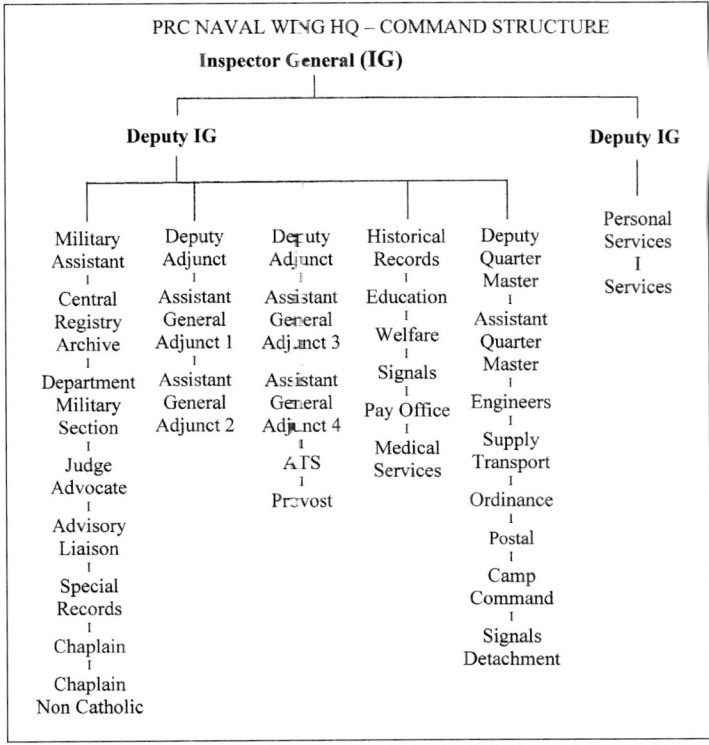

Figure 16a: The command structure of the Polish Resettlement Corps.

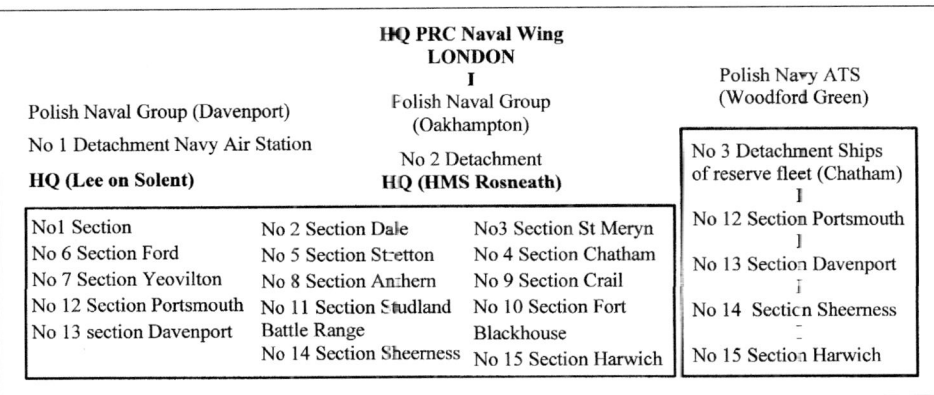

Figure 16b: Location of Polish Naval units.

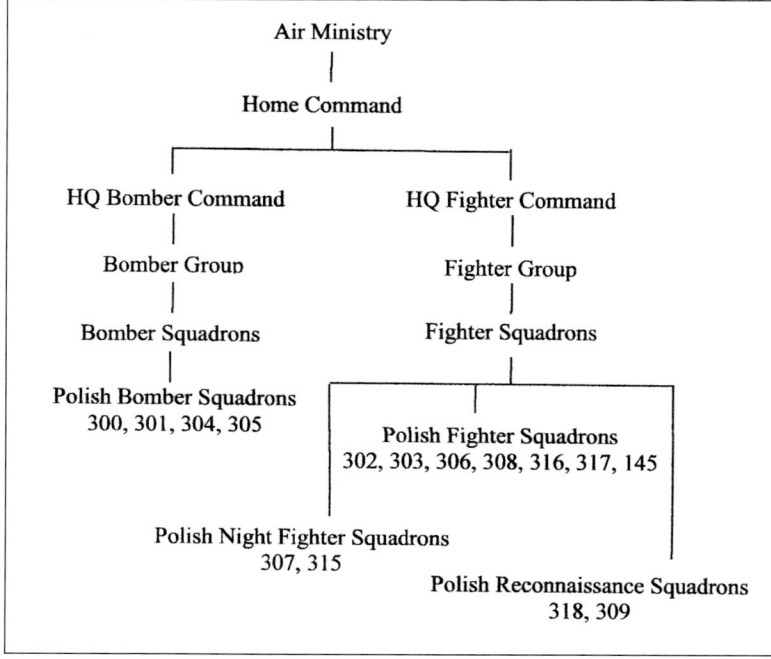

Figure 17: The Polish Air Force was embedded within the Royal Air Force and therefore in its command structure.

20

Health Services

When, in January 1946, the Polish Forces' Official Sub-Committee reviewed the situation regarding the arrival of the Poles, in order to determine the potential need for their healthcare, it came up with a figure of 200,000 people. It concluded that 95 percent of these would be military personnel and therefore be under the care of the War Office, Air Ministry or Admiralty accordingly, whilst the remaining 10,000 civilian dependants would fall under the care of the Interim Treasury Committee (ITC). The ITC, which was based at 40 Palace Gate, London, had inherited responsibility for Polish refugees (civilians) from the exiled Polish Government which had been disenfranchised in 1945. The objective of making such assessments was to ensure that the welfare of the Polish Resettlement Corps and its dependants did not place undue pressure on the country's medical services. To prevent this from happening, it was decided to bring Polish military hospitals to Britain and set them up in every Home Command where Polish troops were based.[1] This included specialist centres such as those for the treatment of tuberculosis and mental disorders as well as general hospitals. In Scottish Command, Number One Polish General Hospital was set up in Perth with a capacity for 900 beds. Number Two Polish General Hospital was established in Dupplin Castle with 195 beds and the small Polish General Hospital in Inverary with 98 Beds. Number Three Polish General Hospital was set up in Penley Camp with a capacity of 230 beds in Western Command, as was Number Four Polish General Hospital at Insoyed Park with 1,020 beds, together with Number 11 Polish General Hospital at Llarnech Panna Camp with 900 beds. Eastern Command received Number Six Polish General Hospital at Diddington with 300 beds including a maternity unit, whilst Southern Command received Number Five Polish General Hospital situated at Eveleigh Manor with 500 beds. Northern Command had Number Seven Polish General Hospital which was on two sites, one in the north of the command and the second in the south. These hospitals were accommodated on vacant military sites, which were used either by the Americans or Canadians during the War. Polish military doctors and nurses were also brought over to this country in order to man the establishments. The War Office made a special arrangement with the British Medical Association in order to place these personnel on a temporary register which allowed them to practise in Britain.

Mental services were also provided for those who were suffering with psychological trauma or psychiatric illness. Polish certifiable cases were passed to the Long Grove Hospital (Polish Wing) in Epsom, Surrey, which was the responsibility of the London County Council. The Polish section was staffed by Polish military psychiatrists and nurses who were also brought to Britain with the Polish forces. Cable Glen and York Villas in Sandgate, Kent, were psychiatric hospitals which provided treatment for 80 in-patients who were psychotic or post-psychotic cases. Schizophrenics and two epileptics were also among the residents in Sandgate. These patients were admitted from the Carstairs and Banstead Hospitals, Number

---

1 TNA, WO 315/13, Polish military hospitals. 1947–1948.

One, Four and 11 Polish Military Hospitals in Whitchurch. Out-patient clinics in London cared for personnel from the Polish Navy, Mercantile Marine and the Polish Air Force. Sixty percent of the patients were chronic cases requiring indefinite care. The patients at Castle Glen were the most vulnerable mental cases, and it was here that active intervention treatment was administered, including modified insulin treatment and electric convulsive therapy. Doctor Zakrewski was in charge of the unit and worked with a team of nursing sisters he had personally trained for this specialist role.[2] York Villa was the dormitory for more stable and trusted patients and, apart from specialising in occupational therapy, it had no other treatment function. Another 40 patients were accommodated at Elmstead Lodge in Chislehurst Kent, where treatment was mainly occupational therapy.

Five prenatal centres, each with 100 beds, were also established in the Home Commands. Polish General Hospital Number Six at Diddington, served Eastern Command; Hospital Number Three at Penley served Western Command; Hospital Number One at Taymouth Castle, Scottish Command; Hospital Number Seven, Northern Command and Hospital Number Six at Eveleigh served Sothern Command. The health care of dependants was the responsibility of the Interim Treasury Committee, which used one of the military hospitals donated to it by the War Office. The care was provided by fully trained Polish staff.

During 1949 the Polish Forces Official Committee spent time considering which civil authority should take these institutions over once the War Office relinquished its responsibilities and the Interim Treasury Committee was disbanded. It was decided that, in both cases, it should be the Ministry of Health for once a member of the Polish Resettlement Corps was demobilised and became a civilian, the War Office could not be expected to continue to be responsible. However, it was suggested that individuals could only be transferred into the care of a civilian department once they had left their War Department camp. Similarly, once the Interim Treasury Committee ceased to function, it seemed clear that responsibilities regarding Polish refugees should pass to the Ministry of Health. The Ministry was also earmarked to take control of all specialised units such as the tuberculosis hospitals, three homes for psychiatric patients and departments for neurotics as well as a number of convalescent homes. In order to maintain continuity of care, Polish military health workers were demobilised and transferred into the service of the Ministry of Health, a move which had been negotiated earlier with the British Medical Association.

Many of the hospitals were housed in aging military bases which were already showing signs of decay. Therefore the first action taken by the Ministry of Health on taking over responsibility was to carry out structural surveys on all establishments, and make improvements where necessary. Once these hospitals had been reclassified as civilian establishments, they could not remain part of the Home Commands, so they were passed to the newly created Regional Health Boards. Although the Ministry of Health accepted responsibility, it argued that it did not possess the correct expertise to do this immediately and therefore proposed interim measures which included the setting up of what it called temporary 'buffer bodies'. The Ministry argued that this could be done through an Omnibus Bill being added to the 1947 Polish Resettlement Act. It recommended that buffer bodies should be under the control of representatives from the Treasury, Ministry of Health, Ministry of Pensions, Ministry of Labour and, importantly, members of Polish staff who had previously worked for the Interim Treasury Committee. It was argued that

---

2 TNA, WO 315/14, Medical officers, pharmacists, dentists, and field ambulance officers who served in Polish Land Forces and Polish Resettlement Corps 1940-1949.

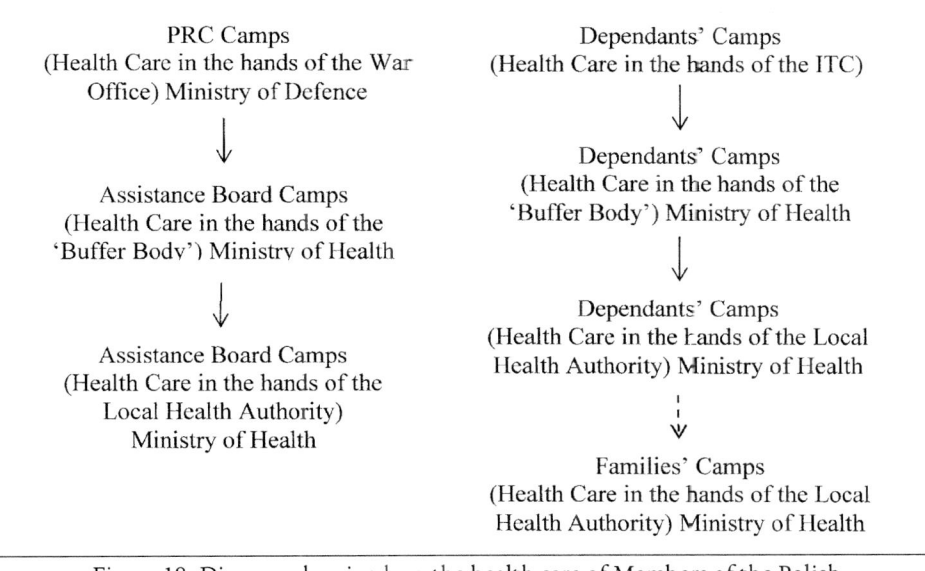

Figure 18: Diagram showing how the health care of Members of the Polish Resettlement Corps and dependants was integrated into national health services.

this approach had the advantage of employing Polish staff in 'the care of their own nationals', thus avoiding the placement of additional burdens on existing British medical services. It was also claimed that the presence of Polish speakers in the service of buffer bodies would ensure that communications between health staff and patients was as effective as possible. This arrangement lasted until the National Health Service came into existence in 1948. However, many Poles had obtained employment by then and, as a result, benefited from National Insurance privileges and the care provided by local health authorities.[3]

---

3   TNA, WO 315/15, Medical officers, pharmacists, dentists, and field ambulance officers who served in Polish Land Forces and Polish Resettlement Corps 1940-1949.

21

Vocational Training

The British Government's objective in establishing the Polish Resettlement Corps (PRC) was not only to dispose of the Polish forces under British Command, but also to ease the passage of Polish troops into civilian life in Britain. No one was under the illusion that this would not be fiendishly difficult but, even as early as 1946, the government was clear on one thing: no Pole was to be seen lounging about in unproductive idleness at the tax payer's expense. Consequently, a central part of the resettlement programme was to make Poles economically independent as fast as possible. However, persuading Poles to enrol in the Resettlement Corps brought with it other issues, for many of them believed that life as an 'alien' carried some serious disadvantages. Having been proud members of the victorious Allied Armies, they were now being asked to become 'second class citizens', hostages to the British Government and dependant on the goodwill and kindness of strangers. No wonder the War Office instructed all British personnel working with Poles always to be courteous and understanding lest they alienate them from enlisting which would allow the Polish problem to persist.

Ultimately, economic independence means employment and therefore, early on in the resettlement programme (1946), the War Office embarked on an extensive consultation programme with the Ministry of Labour, Trade Unions and Professional Associations about employing Poles. It was well understood at the time that agreement here would be vital if Polish resettlement was to run smoothly and demonstrate that Britain had honourably fulfilled her obligations to her ally. However, other obstacles existed which had to be overcome if meaningful objectives were to be achieved. For example, many of the soldiers lacked English-language skills and understood little of the British way of work. Many had had their education interrupted by the outbreak of war in 1939, and the training they had been receiving was in a Polish context, hardly a sound preparation for work in Britain. It is not surprising, therefore, that along with reuniting families, arranging accommodation, organising medicals and registering individuals, the War Office, in association with the Committee for the Education of Poles,[1] had to involve itself with arranging English-language classes and various vocational training programmes suitable for Poles. The first task was to recruit teachers and trainers[2] who could speak Polish. They would need to be supplied with suitable teaching materials especially prepared for use in the resettlement programme. The recruitment of 190 full-time teachers of English commenced in March 1946, and included some retired British Officers who were on the Register for Employment and were willing to take up such specialist work, even if it meant for a limited period[3]. Language classes prepared candidates for the Cambridge Proficiency Certificate in English at three ability levels: a beginner's level and an intermediate level, whilst the more fluent speakers sat the Advanced

---

1   Department of the Education Board.
2   TNA, WO 315/31, Disbandment of PRC (Polish Resettlement Corps): reports and statistics.
3   TNA, WO 315/31, Disbandment of PRC.

Army Test.⁴ Other language courses were also offered, for example, Spanish or Portuguese for those who had expressed an interest in settling in Argentina or Brazil. Individuals in the Polish Resettlement Corps were also recruited as tutors for programmes requiring a sound knowledge of Polish technical terminology.⁵ These individuals would have qualified in pre-war Poland, although their diplomas were not officially recognised in Britain until 1953.

Vocational training programmes were designed to prepare individuals for labour shortages that existed in the country; for example, in agriculture, mining, light engineering, building trades and land management. Courses designed for agricultural employment included the study of Rural Studies, Woodland Management, Animal Breeding, Horticulture and Farm Vehicle Maintenance which were usually staffed by tutors who had previously trained on army tanks during the War. The vehicle courses also attracted female students, particularly those women who had served in the transport divisions of the Polish ATS, as well as men for a qualification here allowed individuals to drive vehicles on public roads. Courses in horticulture were originally devised in response to national food shortages during the war, but were rewritten for use with the Poles. Resources used in these programmes included greenhouses for growing flowers, planting beds for herb cultivation and basic laboratories for the study of plant pathology.⁶ Those wishing to enter the building trades studied plumbing, carpentry, bricklaying, tiling, and electrical installation which included the physics of electric circuitry. Animal breeding courses included the study of inheritance where fast breeding fruit flies were bred under laboratory conditions, whilst plant propagation methods such as cutting, layering and grafting were studied in crop growing study modules. Programmes in bee keeping and honey manufacture were popular, as was grass growing and grazing management.⁷ Most of the vocational courses lasted six months and included practical work in the field as well as theory lessons in the classroom.

Despite all good intentions, there were some serious obstacles that had to be surmounted if the provision of such classes was to be wholly productive. One of them was the reluctance of many soldiers to take up the opportunity to study. This was an important issue for, although attendance on the training programmes was voluntary, classes needed a minimum number of students to enrol before they were allowed to run. No one was forced to attend classes and although this may have been good for motivation, because it meant that those presenting themselves in classes would be keen to learn, it was also the case that those not wanting to learn would constitute a large residue of untrained personnel who would be difficult to place in employment. It is difficult to ascertain why individuals did not take up the offer of further study or training, but it is possible to speculate that many of these Polish men and women were so traumatised by the war that concentrating on new learning in an alien environment was a step too far. Others may have believed that their stay in Britain was going to be temporary and therefore learning new skills for employment in the United Kingdom was unnecessary. The work offered those who refused to train was general labour, either in factories and the service industries or unskilled work in the building trades.

Some training programmes were bedevilled by underfunding and critical shortages. For example, many vehicle maintenance courses lacked heavy mechanised equipment to practise on, and those who acquired a vehicle found them to be old and obsolete. Tutors

---

4   TNA, WO 315/31, Disbandment of PRC.
5   TNA, WO 315/31, Disbandment of PRC.
6   TNA, WO 315/31, Disbandment of PRC.
7   TNA, WO 315/31, Disbandment of PRC.

> THE LONDON SCHOOL OF FOREIGN TRADE
> Limited by Guarantee
> Ref.No.338/52.
>
> Toynbee Hall,
> Commercial Street,
> London, E.1.
>
> June 12th, 1952.
>
> Dear Mr. [   ] ......
>
> With reference to your application for acceptance to this School I inform you that the entrance examination will be held on ...30.6.52 at ..11..a.m. at the above address. The nearest Underground Station is Aldgate East. You should go to the III floor of the new building where you will receive all instructions. Candidates should arrange to be here until 6 p.m.
> You should bring with you the documents concerning your general education, aliens certificate or other certificate with a photograph and the enclosed questionnaire, duly completed.
> Failure to attend the examination can only be excused in quite exceptional cases and will normally result in the candidate's name being removed from the list of prospective candidates.
>
> Yours faithfully,
>
> *(signature)*
> (Stefan Z. Szyszkowski)
> Principal

Officers in the PRC were encouraged to find training on their own. This letter from the London School of Foreign Trade informs an applicant of the examination he would need to sit before his application could be considered.

also reported that there was a shortage of spare parts which limited what could be learned in practical maintenance sessions. An inspection report on a woodland management course at Findo-Gast Camp in Scotland highlighted another common problem, a shortage of up to date textbooks. In fact the textbooks that were available were not only out of date, in short supply and in poor condition, but written in English which made them particularly unhelpful with Polish speakers. Furthermore, the report states, rather risibly, that 'the woods allocated for study were so deep that they could not be accessed by the students'. Other vocational courses were not so demanding of heavy machinery or expensive specialist equipment. For example, those in tailoring, sewing and cooking seemed well-resourced and proved to be very popular in PRC camps and hostels which stood near towns with thriving clothing manufacturing businesses.

It would be wrong, however, to suggest that only vocational training was provided for many younger members of the Polish Resettlement Corps, such as students who had arrived from the Polish Army cadet schools in the Middle East, and young officers were allowed to continue with academic studies. The Committee for the Education of Poles[8] arranged for study grants to be paid to those looking to enter higher education in Britain, although many had to travel to Ireland to complete their studies where pre-war Polish qualifications were readily recognised. For example, those who wanted to train as doctors sometimes completed their medical studies at Dublin University before returning to practise in Britain. Several British universities accepted Polish students with adequate English-language skills. Notable amongst these were the Polish University of Engineering and Technology in London, the Polish Faculty in Law in Oxford and the Polish School of Veterinary Science in Edinburgh.[9]

---

8   Department of the School Board.
9   Norman Davies, *Trail of Hope* (Oxford: Osprey Publishing, 2015), p.551.

Letter from the School of Foreign Trade regarding examination results.

The training and studying opportunities provided by the War Office would eventually lead to employment and were therefore an important step in the integration and assimilation of the members of the Polish Resettlement Corps into British society. Although many individuals did not avail themselves of the opportunities provided by the War Office and the Ministry of Labour, those that did could write on their CV that they had completed a government-approved course. This gave them a distinct advantage in the job market.

22

Employment

The number of Polish Resettlement Corps members successfully placed in employment was an important statistic, for it was used by the British Government to measure the success or otherwise of the resettlement programme. It was considered to be so important that the Attlee Government originally planned to call the Polish corps the 'Industrial Resettlement Corps' although this name was dropped in early planning. We have already seen the kind of limiting factors at play regarding employing Poles, but there were also political issues which had to be resolved. For example, it was decided that the work offered to Poles should be seen to be something more than the kind of work provided for German and Italian POWs[1] during the war. The view was that to do anything else would tarnish Britain's reputation as an honourable ally, and portray the displaced Polish forces as nothing better than prisoners. Another important decision was to ensure that it did not appear as if Poles were depriving British workers from making a living, something that would have offended public opinion. Consequently, the government trod very carefully when planning the resettlement programme, assuring trade unions and professional bodies that Polish men would not be given preferential treatment in the job market. Another factor the government had to manage very carefully was the scrutiny of a highly critical British press[2] which was ready to jump on unfair practices if it appeared that the Poles were receiving an unfair advantage. Paradoxically, however, criticism was also forthcoming from the Poles themselves, for whilst they waited for work, they complained that all they wanted was to get on with their lives but were 'under-employed', sitting around in unproductive idleness waiting for the opportunity of work to appear.'[3]

Other problems regarding the employment of the Poles were of a more practical nature. For example, many Polish Resettlement Camps stood in isolated locations where little or no public transport existed and this made travelling to potential employment problematic. The War Office's response was to encourage employers to provide transport, such as hired coaches or company lorries, for the journey to work. To help in solving transport problems, the War Office also began establishing workers' camps near centres of employment. However, no sooner had it solved one problem then another appeared. Married men taking advantage of the workers' camps were often required to leave their wives and children for long periods of time, something that contravened government advice which preferred it if families that had recently been reunited were not separated. Inevitably, such difficulties put a brake on the employment of Poles which had a knock on effect on the process of demobilisation and eventual assimilation. Consequently, the War Office repeatedly reminded Polish soldiers that they retained the right to emigrate or repatriate at Britain's expense at any time during the resettlement process.

The whole procedure for placing Poles in work had to be carefully choreographed for,

---

1   Prisoners of War.
2   By and large 'print press'.
3   Nanke, *Cena Bycia Innym*, p.156.

> THE WAR OFFICE,
> LONDON, S.W.1.
>
> 15th. September, 1948.
>
> POLISH/ 4713./1 (M.S.2.B.)
>
> Sir,
>
> I am directed to inform you that, in view of your absorption into industry, you will relinquish your commission in the Polish Resettlement Corps with effect from **14th. June, 1948.**
>
> I am, Sir,
> Your obedient Servant,
>
> Major General
> Military Secretary.
>
> Second Lieutenant. F.J. Szuta,
> 4. The Grove,
> Edgware,
> MIDDSX.
>
> Copy to:- Officer i/c. P.R.C. Records.

Once a member of the PRC accepted employment in the private sector, he was notified that his army pay would be withdrawn.

if it was too fast, the machinery for resettlement could easily become overwhelmed and, in extreme cases, grind to a halt or, if it was too slow, the government would leave itself open to the accusation that it was allowing Poles to lounge about in unproductive idleness. In the final analysis, government action during the resettlement programme had to be carefully balanced between preparing Polish soldiers for work and ensuring that openings for them in the job market were available.

Enlistment into the Polish Resettlement Corps furnished Poles with a right to be placed on the Register for Employment. This meant that the War Office was contracted to assist individuals with finding suitable, appropriate work. Once a good match between an individual's skills and the demands of a placement was found, employment would commence with a probationary period lasting approximately six months.

During the period the employer would pay wages and military remuneration would cease. At the same time, the individual would be relegated to the Reserve (ORs)[4] or be placed on the Unemployed List in case of officers. The relegation was recorded by the War

---

4 Other Ranks.

Office statistical section once it was informed by the local Ministry of Labour office that a successful placement had been made, and that the wages and conditions of employment were not less favourable than those for a British worker in a similar capacity. It also had to be shown that attempts had been made to ensure that no suitable British labour was available before the placement was completed. If it was deemed by both parties (the individual and the employer) that the probation period had been successful the position was made permanent and full demobilisation from the PRC followed. In the case of officers, the individual would apply for the relinquishing of his commission. From this point onwards the individual was considered as have left the military and a Certificate of Registration would be issued. However, if the probation period was considered to be unsuccessful, the individual was taken off the Reserve register and returned to his unit. This would also mean that the individual would be placed back on the Labour Exchange's register and the process would begin again. During 1946 to 1947 the numbers on the Register for Employment grew rapidly.[5]

Table 14: Registration for Employment by the Ministry of Labour up to 17 May 1947

	Up to 30 Years of Age				Over 30 Years of Age			
	Men		Women		Men		Women	
	Army/RAF	Army/RAF	Army/RAF	Army/RAF	Army/RAF	Army/RAF	Army/RAF	Army/RAF
Officers	1,477	449	92	6	7,034	1,036	132	19
ORs	38,466	3,634	1,139	444	26,926	3,080	684	139
Total	39,943	4,083	1,231	450	33,960	4,116	816	158
Grand Total	84,759							

Table 15: Fluency in English of Poles Registered in the PRC

	Men		Women	
	Army	RAF	Army	RAF
Fluent	15,864	7,267	307	214
Broken/None	58,039	932	1,740	394
Total	73,903	8,199	2,047	608

Source: TNA, T 236/1369, Polish resettlement employment policy, 1946–1948.

It was on 1 September 1946 that the Ministry of Labour and National Service began consulting with trade unions and local employers about the likelihood of them accepting Poles in the job market. Invariably it took a series of meetings to agree on the potential number of employment opportunities that could be made available, the rates of pay and working conditions under which Poles could be employed. When this information had been

---

5   TNA, T 236/1369, Polish resettlement employment policy, 1946–1948.

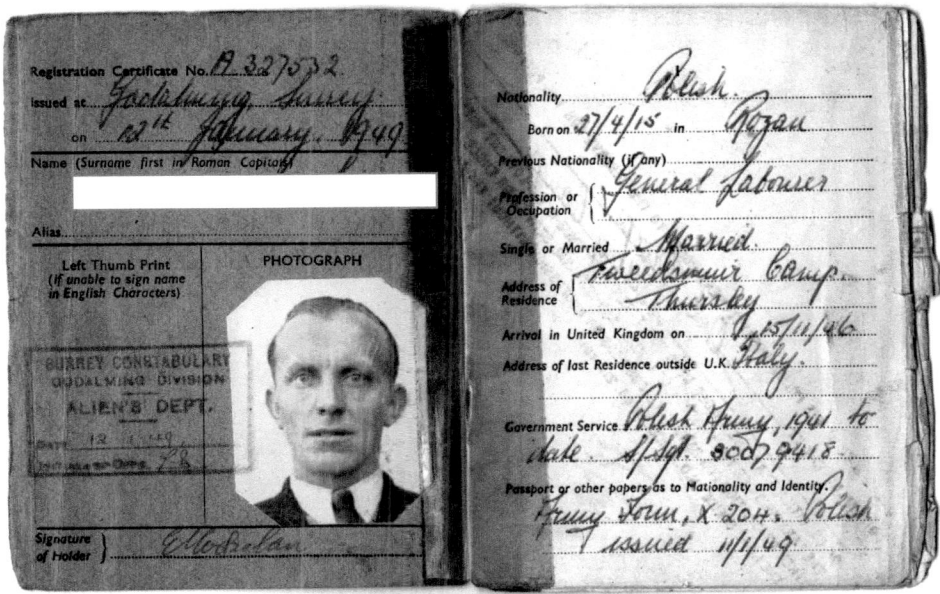

A Certificate of Registration was issued to members of the PRC on demobilisation. At this stage he/she would be considered a civilian.

agreed, it was transmitted to London where it was collated with other regions into national agreements. The major industries canvassed in 1946 included Building and Civil Engineering, Agriculture, Forestry, Coal Mining, Textiles, Hotel and Catering Brick Making, Iron and Steel, General Engineering and Allied Industries. Once national agreements were published, potential employers were expected to supply local offices of the Ministry of Labour with lists of job vacancies. The rate of placement was recorded diligently and discussed regularly at Cabinet level and in the House of Commons in order to reassure ministers and members of Parliament that things were going well with the resettlement programme. By May 1947, the War Office reported that officer placements were running at an all-time high with 1,700 per week being made, and that about 17,000 had already been found work.[6] However, the rate of placements fluctuated and hovered around 1,000 per week. By 1948, 80,000 rank and file men had been placed in work successfully.

Members of the Polish Resettlement Corps were employed in forestry in two ways, either as gang labour or as individual workers. In the former case employees were sent to work in squads, irrespective of their professional qualifications. They received a small supplement to their normal army pay or at most a pittance.[7] Those who were employed as individuals were relegated to the Reserve in the normal way and received the going rate for the work from the employer. The Ministry of Labour preferred it if the men were employed as individuals as this was in accordance with the pledge made by His Majesty's Government to the members of the Polish Resettlement Corps. The Forestry Commission argued that gang labour was used because there was a lack of accommodation, and was a temporarily measure whilst workers' camps were being prepared However, the Ministry of Labour expressed concern

6 TNA, T 236/1369, Polish resettlement employment policy, 1946–1948.
7 TNA, T 236/1369, Polish resettlement employment policy, 1946–1948.

Table 16: Distribution in industries which had absorbed more than 400 PRC Members

Industry	Army	RAF	Total
Building	8,541	363	8,904
Agriculture, Horticulture and Forestry	7,959	211	8,170
Coal Mining	7,283	10	7,293
Catering, Hotel etc.	5,675	439	6,114
National Government Service	4,986	107	5,093
Bricks and Firework Goods	3,062	57	3,119
Civil Engineering (Contracting)	2,931	66	2,997
General Engineering	1,672	635	2,307
Woollen Industries	1,929	41	1,970
Iron and Steel	1,767	49	1,816
Cotton Spinning	1,334	98	1,432
Professional Services	1,647	124	1,771
Distributive Trades	1,231	236	1,467
Transport	837	497	1,134
Chemical Manufacturing	1,282	65	1,347
Rail	1,602	215	1,817
Domestic Service	1,198	86	1,284
Tailoring	1,083	81	1,164
Local Government Services	978	36	1,014
Quarrying and Mining	861	15	876
Utilities Supplies	792	50	842
Bread, Biscuit and Flour	805	53	858
Metal Industries	816	72	888
Timber	697	44	741
Non Ferrous Metal mining	687	30	717
Rayon, Nylon Waving	394	312	706
Cotton Weaving	594	56	650
Rayon Nylon Production	527	87	614
China Earthenware	605	10	615
Smelting and Rolling	580	27	607
Cobbling	417	92	509
Furniture Making	406	159	565
Sea Transport	444	9	453

that the sight of gangs of Poles working in forests created a very poor impression with local communities, and insisted that this method of employment was not allowed to continue.

Despite Polish men having to report to local employment offices in order to obtain employment, some sectors recruited directly from the Corps. For example, staff from the Ministry of Agriculture visited resettlement service camps in order to publicise the benefits of working in agriculture, and recruited those who had shown an interest, by-passing the local employment office. In a similar way the National Coal Board sent out 'ambassadors' to PRC Camps in coalmining regions in order to showcase the virtues of working in the mining industry. This approach, argued the Coal Board, enabled potential workers to approach the Board on an individual basis to discuss their personal plans. However, there were instances where formal procedures broke down altogether. In May 1947, for example, the Ministry of Labour received reports that staff in some of its labour offices were disregarding Poles who had presented themselves for work. Since the Ministry did not want to appear as failing in its duty, it reprimanded staff and demanded that greater vigilance was exercised. The Kingston-upon-Thames office was singled out for particular criticism, as was the office in Winchester.[8] In reply, staff at the Kingston office argued that they had not received any information on the employment of Polish workers and therefore did not know what to do with them when they turned up for interview. However, when they were asked to examine their files again, the information miraculously surfaced. Since such events would have been detrimental to important statistics on the success of the Resettlement Programme, the Ministry of Labour insisted that such things should not be repeated. In areas where employment was not available, PRC personnel were loaned out to private employers in order to supplement their workforce engaged on 'national reconstruction projects'. Employers engaging men under this scheme had to pay the War Office at the appropriate rate of pay, whilst the men continued receiving their military salary. It is difficult to estimate how far Polish workers were still employed in the industries in which they were first placed, but there seems to be no evidence to suggest an abnormal turnover of Polish labour.

Those who appeared to be rejecting work for no good reason had to appear before an Anglo-Polish tribunal where an explanation for refusal had to be presented. Those who failed to do this adequately were threatened with a dishonourable discharge and the loss of benefits. If refusals to accept work were done on medical grounds, medical certificates and doctors' notes had to be provided.

As the resettlement programmes continued, it soon became evident that placing older and disabled personnel into jobs was proving difficult. In order not to slow the run down of the Resettlement Corps, it was decided to offer such individuals clerical work, despite their poor language skills and the presence of strong British competition for the work. Disabled members of the Polish Resettlement Corps, who were entitled to benefits from the provisions of the Disabled Person's Employment Act, were also difficult to place in employment and so were given light work in sheltered occupations in the REMPLOY factory in Lancashire. Another trend identified by the War Office during the resettlement programme detected that many Polish officers considered themselves far too important to undertake 'ordinary casual work'. A cynical saying circulating in officers' clubs illustrated this attitude well,

When we were in Russian captivity, the Soviets said, 'you are the enemies of the Soviet

---

8   TNA, T 236/1369, Polish resettlement employment policy, 1946–1948.

The Polish workforce was made up of ex-members of the Polish Resettlement Corps. Employment offered to Poles was as unskilled labour, irrespective of their Polish qualifications.

people and so you will work in our mines'. Now you in Britain are saying to us, 'you are our friends and so you will work for us in our mines'.[9]

With the date for disbandment of the Resettlement Corps fast approaching, scheduled to take place in September 1949, the War Office devised two new strategies to unblock the logjam concerning the employment of Polish officers. One was a five point action plan which included the demobilisation of officers of 50 years of age and older (about 2,500 in number) immediately. Under Section 2(i)(b) of the Polish Resettlement Act, it was decided to remove them from War Office registers and pass them into the care of the Assistance Board. The War Office advised the Board to establish special accommodation for this category of men. Disabled officers, those with one limb or one eye or similar degree of permanent disablement, who were able to work (about 200 in number) were demobilised and retrained for employment by the Ministry of Labour. Those unable to work were given rights under the Disabled Person's Act 1944 and were made the responsibility of the Ministry of Pensions. Regarding incurables and what the War Office called 'mentals' (about 60 in number) were accepted to remain on 'permanent charge' to the British Government. The responsibility for this category of men, under Section Four of the Resettlement Act, was passed to the Ministry of Health. 'Bad characters', that is those officers with poor army records, were treated as *persona non grata* and earmarked for deportation, although this was rarely enacted. The officers who were generally suitable for work were offered further vocational training and encouraged to avail themselves of the Polish Officers' Resettlement Scheme (also known as the Carrot Scheme)[10] which was the second strategy. It included six new initiatives: Scheme I was to encourage officers to relinquish their commissions with a grant or gratuity and 112 days' pay. This scheme was designed for those who wanted to set up in business or work for themselves; however, they would have needed to be in possession of the Cambridge Lower Certificate in English to qualify. Scheme II was intended for married officers with wives in the United Kingdom, and designed to encourage officers to apply for

---

9   Nanke, *Cena Bycia Innym*, p.156.
10 TNA, WO 315/33, PRC Officers.

An advertisement placed in the Polish Press in Britain on behalf of the National Coal Board. The caption reads 'BECOME A MINER'.

relegation with 112 days' pay, but they were required to make contributions towards the support of their wives. Scheme III was little more than leave on probation. This scheme was designed to encourage individual initiative and to help the genuine trier. Applicants had to be in the possession of an employer's certificate which guaranteed that an employer was willing to take the applicant on permanently after a period of probation. The employer would pay the officer a wage but only if he left his Polish resettlement camp. An officer accepting these conditions was issued with civilian clothes. Scheme IV was leave for technical study and enabled the officer to attend a vocational course at his own expense. Such courses were distinct from those organised by the Committee for the Education of Poles in Great Britain and entitled the officer to 180 days' leave and an appropriate supernumerary rate of pay. On completing the course, the officer could apply to his unit commander who would put him on the Unemployment List. After three months paid employment, the officer could apply to relinquish his commission whereupon he would receive his war gratuity which was paid into the officer's Post Office Savings bank account. Scheme V required the officer to attend a War Office approved course designed for officers and paid for by the War Office. After completing the course, the officer could apply to relinquish his commission and receive his gratuity. Scheme VI consisted of persuading an individual to repatriate to Poland. An officer taking advantage of this option would be eligible to receive a war gratuity and a marriage allowance if he was married which would be increased to 112 days' allowance if his wife travelled with him. Any officer who refused to take advantage of any of these new measures was threatened with court martial.

Naval wing members of the Polish Resettlement Corps could apply for employment on British mercantile ships. Any applicant would have to be medically fit (A1) with good eye sight for sea-going service. It was also necessary to have a good command of the English language. The recruitment process followed a precise procedure which started with an application form being sent to the officer in charge of the individual's unit. The officer in charge would check the application form and decide on the suitability of the applicant. If it was decided that the application could be supported, he would contact the Port Liaison Officer who would in turn contact the local Port Labour Office and the local office of the Shipping Federation. The Shipping Federation would arrange to interview the applicant and would inform the Port Liaison Officer, via the Port Labour Office, of the time and place of the interview. If it was deemed that the individual was suitable for employment, an offer of a position on a British ship was made. The Port Labour Office would then embark on an investigation to ascertain whether any British labour was available for the post. If it was proved that there was none, the office would initiate the discharge procedure whilst at the same time informing the Port Liaison Officer of its decision. At this stage, the applicant would be informed that his application had been successful and discharge papers would be drawn up. If an applicant failed his interview he would return to his unit. The approval of the Shipping Federation meant that the applicant would be placed on a ship after discharge. The final step saw the applicant undergo a full medical examination. If an applicant applied for work on a foreign ship, the same procedure was followed but without the interview.

23

British Protests

Despite the British Government's attempt to give the Polish Resettlement Programme low visibility, it was unable to prevent news of the Poles taking up work dripping into the popular press. Regardless of the attempt to unite British and Polish workers under one common banner of 'rebuilding post-war Britain', it was soon evident that the Resettlement Programme was on a collision course with the views of many elements in British society. This manifested itself with strident lobbying of the Foreign Office calling for a change in policy. As early as August 1946, even before the first Polish troops set foot on British soil, protests began to land on Ernest Bevin's[1] desk. On 28 August 1946, for example, Mr E. Knight wrote to the Foreign Secretary giving the result of a straw poll he had conducted which showed that the majority of British people were opposed to the resettlement of Polish troops in Britain.[2] At about the same time (24 August 1946) a letter arrived from the Amalgamated Engineering Union.[3]

> Dear Sir, I have been instructed by the members of the above branch to send the following resolution. We the members of the above branch strongly condemn the action of the government in letting 200,000 Poles come to this country on the reconstruction programme. It must not be overlooked that these Poles had strong fascist elements and thus fought against the Allies during war time. This type are a danger to the peoples of Britain and the world, and it is our strong opinion that these Poles be sent back to Poland to help in reconstructing their own war scarred country. The Branch Secretary of the Ruislip Branch[4]

The reply was soon in coming,

> Mr Bevin, who is in Paris, has asked me to reply to your letter on behalf of the Amalgamated Engineering Union about the demobilisation in this country of the Polish Armed Forces under British Command. Many thousands of men in the Polish Armed Forces have already returned to Poland. His Majesty's Government are of the view that it is the duty of these men to go back and take part in the work of national reconstruction in all cases where they can safely do so. Nevertheless, His Majesty's Government are not prepared to bring any compulsion to bear to force these brave men to return against their will. It still remains open to any member of the Polish Armed Forces to return. The object of the Polish Resettlement Corps which is to be formed shortly is to resettle these men into civilian life either here or abroad.

---

1 Foreign Secretary.
2 TNA, FO 371/56513, Resettlement of members of the Polish Armed Forces in the United Kingdom, Code 55, File 308 (papers 7827–8384),1946.
3 TNA, FO 371/56513, Code 55, File 308 (papers 7827–8384), 1946.
4 TNA, FO 371/56513, Code 55, File 308 (papers 7827–8384), 1946.

On 27 August 1946 the Kirkcaldy Trade Council wrote to the Foreign Secretary,

Dear Sir, I have been instructed by the above council to send you the following resolution: this trade council strongly protests against the importation of Polish Forces from Italy. Many of these men fought on behalf of Hitlerism and as such have no place in our democratic society. Furthermore, many of our fellow workers are without work and the influx can only aggravate the situation. We demand that the Foreign Secretary compel those men to return to their country where they will be welcomed if they are prepared to toil in the reconstruction of Poland.
Yours faithfully, J. Johnson

The Foreign Office replied on 6 September.

Dear Mr Johnson, Mr Bevin has asked me to reply to your letter of 20 August on behalf of the Kirkcaldy Trades Council about the Polish Forces under British Command. Many thousands of Polish servicemen have already returned to Poland. His Majesty's Government are of the view that it is their duty to go back to Poland and to take part in the work of national reconstruction there in all cases where they can safely do so. Nevertheless, His Majesty's Government are not prepared to bring any compulsion to bear to force these brave men to return against their will. It still remains open to any member of the Polish Armed Forces who wishes to return. With regard to the Council's statement that many members of the Polish Armed Forces fought on behalf of Hitlerism, the positon is as follows: of the 109,600 troops lately in Italy and the Middle East, 80,000 have neither fought for nor been associated with the Germans in any way. Of the remainder, about 22,000, have been either captured from or deserted from the German Forces into which they had been forcibly conscripted through no fault of their own and have since fought in battle on the Allied side. The remaining 6,000 were recruited into the Polish Armed Forces between the end of hostilities in Italy and the end of the war, many having been held as prisoners by the Germans.[5]

The Manchester and Salford Trades Council sent the following letter to Ernest Bevin on 27 August 1946:

Dear Sir, On behalf of the above Trades Council I have been instructed to forward to you a copy of a resolution passed by our delegates meeting held on 21 August 1946 as attached. Trusting for your earnest consideration: This meeting of the Manchester and Salford Trades Council condemns the decision to permit the settlement in Britain and the Empire of 16,000 Poles from General Anders' Army. That 53,000 of them should have been captured by the British Forces in North-West Europe alone disproves their claim to have been our Allies. Whilst having sympathy with any genuine anti-fascist who may wish to settle in British life may be serious and they may be fertile material for a fascist group, now dormant in this country. We demand that this policy be abandoned and all immigrants be treated on their individual merit.

---

5   TNA, FO 371/56513, Code 55, File 308 (papers 7827–8384), 1946.

A letter in a similar vein was sent by the London Trades Council, Bedford Row, London;[6]

This London Trades Council emphatically protest against the decision of the government to admit this country and allow to take employment, members of Anders' Army, many of whom fought actively with the Nazi Army against British and Allied troops. We request the government to rescind their decision and immediately disband the Anders' Army officer corps, allow the Polish Government (in Warsaw) free access to those troops with a view to explaining the policy of the Polish Government and their desire that all Poles return to Poland to help reconstruct their own country.

The Foreign Office replied as follows,

Sir, I am directed by Mr Secretary Bevin to reply to your letter of 3 September forwarding a resolution of the delegates of the London Trades Council about the demobilisation in this country of the Polish Armed Forces under British Command. The Polish Forces under British Command fought gallantly on the Allied side during the war in Africa, Italy and North West Europe. The resolution suggests that many members of General Anders' army fought actively with the Nazi Army. In fact, of the 100,000 Polish troops lately in the Middle East and Italy, over 800,000 neither fought with nor were ever associated with the Germans. Of the remainder, about 22,000, were either captured from or deserted from the German Forces into which they had been forcibly conscripted against their will. The remaining 6,000 were enlisted into the Allied Forces after the conclusion of the war in Italy, many having been kept prisoner until being released by the Germans. His Majesty's Government are of the view that they have obligations to these troops which must be fulfilled. It is with this object that the Polish Resettlement Corps is now being formed in this country. It is a purely transitional and provisional expedient designed with the unmilitary object of passing its members into civilian life as quickly as possible. Although it is necessary, for administration reasons, to retain the services in this Corps, it will be under effective British discipline and control. His Majesty's Government have made it quite clear to the men concerned that it is their duty to return home to assist in the reconstruction of their country and full publicity is given to any statement of the Polish Provisional Government which are likely to contribute to this end. Furthermore, we have at all stages kept the Polish Provisional Government informed about the machinery we are setting up for the demobilisation and resettlement of these men and we have considered carefully all representations which we have received on this subject from the Polish Provisional Government. Signed R. M. A. Hankey

On the 24 August 1946 the Bretton Branch of the Amalgamated Engineering Union wrote to Mr Bevin regarding accommodation shortages,[7]

Dear Sir and Brother, At the request of my fellow members of the above branch, I am writing to you to protest about the unfair treatment of our brothers and sisters, who finding themselves without a home of their own, took over part of a vacant

---

6   TNA, FO 371/56513, Code 55, File 308 (papers 7827–8384), 1946.
7   TNA, FO 371/56513, Code 55, File 308 (papers 7827–8384), 1946.

army camp as a means of temporary accommodation – we are now informed that they were ejected from same in order that Polish refugees can be found refuge. We are also informed that some of these same refugees were at some time enemies of the Allies. If these facts are true, my colleagues do not hesitate to express their wholehearted disapproval of such action. I request you to take the necessary steps to see that incidents of this nature are not repeated any further, that if enemies of our recent past are among them, that they should be returned to their own countries as soon as it is possible. We are convinced that in writing to you we can rely upon your full cooperation and that this matter will receive your immediate attention. Signed, I. M. Tudor

Mr Bevin replied through his Private Secretary, John Hencker,

Dear Mr Tudor, Mr Bevin has asked me to reply to your letter of 27 August on behalf of the Bretton Branch of the Amalgamated Engineering Union about the alleged removal of British civilians from an army camp of which they had taken possession. I am to state that certain military camps in this country have been recently vacated and are to be used as accommodation for the members of the Polish Forces under British Command who are now being demobilised. These troops fought gallantly on the Allied side during the war in Africa, Italy and North West Europe. His Majesty's Government feel an obligation to these brave men and in order to fulfil it are embodying them into a Polish Resettlement Corps, the object of which will be to either resettle them here or abroad, as quickly as possible. At the same time it is the view of the His Majesty's Government that they go home and every assistance will be given them to do so. Many, however, do not feel able to return to Poland and His Majesty's Government are not prepared to bring any compulsion to bear on them to do so against their will. The accommodation which these troops, who are not refugees, will occupy consist of hutted camps which have been left vacant by the demobilisation of our own soldiers.

The following is a letter from the Kilmarnock Local Trades Council.[8]

Dear Sir, Kilmarnock Local Trades Council protest very emphatically against the decision of the Foreign Office to settle 160,000 Poles in Scotland when demobbed from General Anders' Army. We contend that Scotland is totally unable to absorb any addition to her population, as her economic position is already most difficult and the present and the future holds many problems which will have to be solved before full employment can be provided for the people of Scotland. We suggest that there is more need of their labour in Poland today. Trusting this matter will be reconsidered.

The Foreign Office replied as follows;

The troops which are being brought to the United Kingdom will be distributed throughout England and Scotland the majority being stationed in England. The total increase in the number of Polish troops in Scotland will only be about 6,000. As regards

---

8 TNA, FO 317/56513 Resettlement of members of the Polish Armed Forces in the United Kingdom. Code 55 File 308 (papers 7827–8384).

the council's fears that their presence will cause unemployment there can be no doubt that this country is at present short of manpower to fulfil our worldwide commitments and to produce the exports by which we live. Such unemployment there is at present is due to the peculiar conditions of the change over from a war economy to peacetime conditions rather than to the shortage of jobs. His Majesty's Government are satisfied that it will be possible to employ the proposed Polish Resettlement Corps in such a way that it will not compete with British labour to the disadvantage of the latter. This whole aspect of the matter has of course been carefully considered and care has been taken to proceed in close consultation with the Trade Unions Congress who have promised their cooperation. Further the Resettlement Corps is a purely provisional and transitional expedient and it is probable that a large proportion of its members will eventually return to Poland. If they do not return to Poland they may decide to emigrate to other countries willing to receive them.[9]

Some protests were in the form of petitions as the example below which was posted to the Foreign Office on 20 June 1946:

We the undersigned, wish to bring your attention our objections to the scheme which the government has in hand concerning the settlement of Polish troops in Britain. It is estimated that the first group will number 160,000 plus their families. If the British people allow this to happen it will in time probably lead to more and larger numbers of Poles entering Britain. We must bear in mind that these foreigners are going to occupy areas which British soldiers have fought for giving up their country for up to seven years of their lives (in many cases their wives). We are told that the Poles have done good work in this war, we admit that, but Britain seems to have overlooked the fact that the Poles have done some very bad work. It is forgotten that many of General Anders' Polish troops have fought with the German Army, and that many British troops lost their lives in Italy at the hands of these Poles. It was for their own benefits that they did good work in this war and it was on their behalf that Britain entered the war which has robbed the people of seven years of their lives and robbed Britain of thousands of young lives. The Poles have received far more from Britain than any other nation, isn't that sufficient, must the British people nurse Poles for the rest of their lives? Must we give them the food, homes and jobs which so many of our people need? The Government tells us it isn't possible to release our own troops more quickly owing to employment difficulties and the housing shortage, yet it is their intention to bring Polish troops to Britain, as civilians, as quickly as possible. If homes and jobs can't be found quickly enough for returning British troops, how and why can they be found for Poles? If the Poles had any sense of patriotism surely they would expect to return to Poland. We were under the impression that men who fought for and beside their country's enemy were looked upon as traitors as were the British Free Corps in Germany. We can't afford to overlook the possibility that, in time to come, the influx of Poles into Britain is likely to cause a political and social upheaval for they will find it very difficult indeed to accustom themselves to our social system and they have a different outlook with regards politics. They are also a race with a peculiar temperament with

---

9   TNA, FO 371/56513, Code 55, File 208 (papers 7827–8384), 1946.

ideas of their own regarding justice. We feel we can't emphasise strongly enough how decidedly unwelcome the Poles will be in Britain.

If such sentiment held sway, the government's objective to settle the Poles in Britain would have been derailed. Protests also appeared in the popular Press.[10] A headline, referring to a speech made at the 1946 TUC Meeting in Brighton, which Prime Minister Attlee had attended, read 'Scotland Will Eject Arrogant Poles'.

> The Poles are the most unpopular visitors Scotland ever had, and they strut about like the arrogant fascists they are. If the government does not put the Poles out of Scotland, the people of Scotland will be required to do it. This part of a bitter attack made on Polish soldiers by Mr C.E. McKerro at the TUC Conference in Brighton today, when criticism was made of the admittance of 160,000 Poles into Britain for resettlement. On a card vote, a resolution moving the reference back of the section of the General Council's Report on the employment of Poles in Britain was defeated by 3,300,000 votes to 2,416,000 ... In Scotland the Poles have made themselves the most unpopular visitors we have ever had, he declared. They strut about like arrogant fascists they are, well fed, well clothed, better clothed, indeed, than our British lads. In Scotland you see them with more briefcases than you will see in Brighton here this week. They swan around wearing their Hitler decorations as if they owned the place ... They have attempted to break up working class labour meetings and they spoil posters and advertisements of working class meetings ... If this government does not put the Poles out of Scotland the people of Scotland will be required to do it ... People in my part of Scotland started to do it on one occasion. A fight broke out in the town in which I work. The Poles marched to their camp and brought out bayonets. A lot of people were taken to hospital. The British troops, most of them English lads, returned to their camp and brought machine guns. Had it not been for the good officers of the police, there would have been a massacre in that town that night.

There were also protests against the resettlement of Poles made on religious grounds. Mr J.G. Watt of the Ergemont Duke Schomberg Temperance Orange Lodge No. 486, Wallasley, Cheshire, wrote to Captain A. E. Marples MP, on the 20 August 1946.

> Dear Sir, At the recent monthly meeting of the Duke Schomberg Temperance Loyal Orange Lodge No. 486, the attached resolutions were unanimously passed and I was instructed to forward copies to you requesting your immediate and favourable action. Attached Resolution 2: This meeting deplored the decision of Her Majesty's Government to settle Polish troops and civilians in Great Britain believing this to be a further step in campaigning against the liberties of England and the protestant religion, which we as Orangemen are pledged to maintain.

However, it should be remembered that not all letters to the Foreign Office were negatively disposed to the Poles. The Glasgow Branch of the Scottish–Polish Society wrote to the Foreign Office in the following manner;

---

10 TNA, FO 371/56513, Code 55, File 308 (papers 7827–8384), 1946.

Dear Sir, The Glasgow Branch of the Scottish-Polish Society have asked me to send you a note of their congratulations on your speech in the recent parliamentary debate on Poland. They wish to assure you that contrary to statements by communists and other supporters of Russian policy, the majority of people in Scotland are friendly disposed towards the government policy in relation to Polish affairs and Polish soldiers in Great Britain. Signed, the Chairman

Perhaps the government should have anticipated the difficulties it would face with the Resettlement Programme, since a Gallop Poll on 1 July 1946[11] had shown that 56 percent of the population was against the initiative (75 percent in Scotland). However, the protests emanating from the British community about the formation of the Polish Resettlement Corps were based as much on the misunderstanding of political matters concerning Poland in 1945, as on the perfectly understandable sentiment regarding the sudden influx of a large number of foreign personnel of one nationality into the country. Few appreciated, for example, that the displaced Poles were invited to settle in Britain after becoming stranded in the West on account of the Iron Curtain, which in effect was allowed to be erected by Allied policy.

A large number of the letters landing on Bevin's desk were essentially letters of protest and expressed sentiments completely opposed to the resettlement programme. Although the senders had a right to express their views, it is regrettable that the justifications for these views were ill-informed and founded on misconceptions. For example, the belief that the Poles were not returning to Poland because they were attempting to avoid hard toil and wanted an 'easy ride' at Britain's expense was a complete misunderstanding of the political situation on the continent. Other letters, which depicted the Polish Forces as a 'Fascist formation', were also incorrect. It is true that some Poles from German occupied Poland were forcibly conscripted into the *Wehrmacht* under threat of death and later joined the Polish forces in the West when Germany capitulated, but this does not mean that they were fascists. These and other false impressions could easily have been corrected by the dissemination of accurate information and the decision not to can only be explained by the suggestion that Attlee's government did not want draw unnecessary attention to the existence of the resettlement programme unless it was absolutely necessary.

---

11   *Trzecia Dywizja Strzelców Karpackich. Tom I*, (Londyn: 3 DSK, 1978), p.169.

24

Security Concerns

It was inevitable that the transfer of displaced Polish forces to Britain between 1946 and 1949 as part of the Resettlement Programme would bring to the country individuals with varying attitudes, political views and disappointments about Poland's treatment in 1945. The Home Office was so concerned about the influx that it instructed MI5 to produce a report outlining the potential risk to national security of so many foreigners of one nationality arriving in the country. It was particularly perturbed by the employment of Poles from the Resettlement Programme in sensitive industries, and the risk that some of them may get involved in political activities against British interests. After all, disenfranchised Polish authorities in Britain after the war had made it known that their objectives were to counteract the intelligence activity of institutions of communist Poland, such as the Ministry of Public Security, and prepare for the re-establishment of an émigré armed force to serve the needs of international organisations which could help in freeing Poland; for example, the United Nations. The secret services were also instructed to monitor whether money earmarked for the Resettlement Corps was being used by Poles in Britain to finance anti-communist activities in Poland, and devise strategies to mitigate any dangers that may arise from such activity.[1] When MI5 reported back, it complained that all it had to go on were 'scant and difficult to access' Polish records brought to Britain with the Polish forces, and so recommended that it would be prudent to view all Poles in Britain as a potential danger to national security. The reason given for this view was that many of them appeared to be harbouring negative feelings towards Britain following the Yalta Conference. The report also cautioned 'that the longer the Poles were employed in sensitive work in Britain, the more time foreign agents would have to make contact with them and open clandestine relations'.[2] However, it clarified that the danger did not necessarily come from what Poles might learn from their work but more 'from the contacts they were likely to meet in their work'.[3] It therefore recommended that care be exercised when considering Poles for employment in sensitive work, and that a list of Poles working in such areas be periodically sent to the Joint Intelligence Sub-Committee for scrutiny. The Ministry of Supplies also insisted that it be fully informed about Polish workers so that information could be shared amongst other departments.

In another part of the report, MI5 warned that the Poles were prone to 'collecting information' which could easily be sold to the highest bidder, including a foreign power. Whilst acknowledging that the Poles would provide the least likely field for the recruitment of agents, either by the Warsaw regime or by other Eastern European states, MI5 was fearful that they were open to blackmail from threats that could be made against their families still living in Poland. As the secret services could not guarantee the loyalty of Polish

---

1 TNA, KV 4/286 Polish Resettlement Corps, Jan 01–Dec 31, 1946.
2 TNA, KV 4/286 Polish Resettlement Corps, Jan 01–Dec 31, 1946.
3 TNA, KV 4/286 Polish Resettlement Corps, Jan 01–Dec 31, 1946.

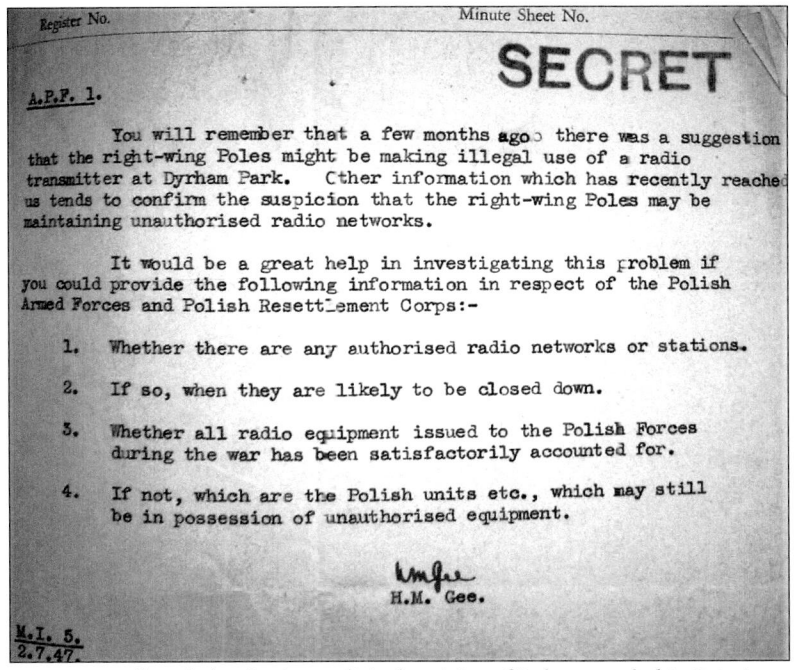

Note on alleged clandestine political activity of Poles resettled in Britain.

personnel, the Air Ministry decided not to employ any Pole in its research and development department.[4]

Following the release of the report, it was decided to monitor the whereabouts and activities of all Poles in the country using Britain's constabulary. For instance, no Polish person could accept new employment or move house without first registering the change with the local police.[5] Polish records were also regularly scrutinised in order to monitor an individual's political allegiances and the likelihood of secret information being passed to a power which might be considered hostile to Britain. Another concern was whether members of the Resettlement Corps would be tempted to act as agents for Catholic powers such as Spain, South America or the French right wing.

Similar concerns embraced organisations which were being established by Poles in Britain. Their apparent desire to continue campaigning for Polish independence forced the British authorities to monitor their activities as well in order to assess if their operations had any security implications. Communications between Polish organisations in this country and resistance groups operating in Poland were regularly intercepted and analysed. This action provided information on which anti-communist resistance groups were still active in Poland and whether they were in communication with Poles in the West.

Particular attention was given to Freedom and Independence (*Wolność i Niepodległość – WiN*), the Polish Organisation (*Polska Organizacia – OP*), and the National Armed Forces (*Narodowe Siły Zbrojne – NSZ*). The Freedom and Independence organisation was described as having been formed by ex-members of the wartime underground Home Army

---

4   TNA, KV 4/286, Polish Resettlement Corps, Jan 01–Dec 31, 1946.
5   TNA, KV 4/286, Polish Resettlement Corps, Jan 01–Dec 31, 1946.

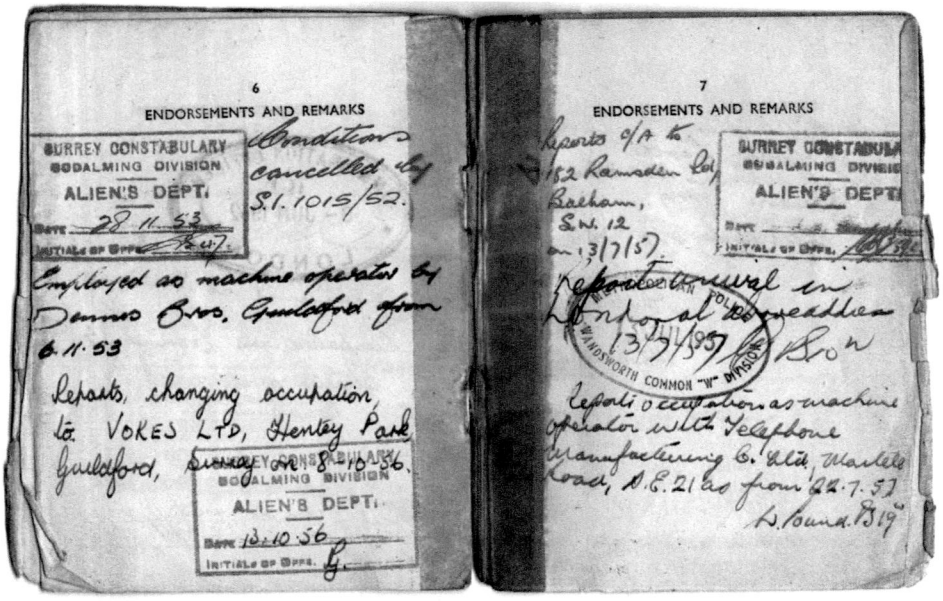

Endorsements and remarks recorded by the Police on the employment and movements of Poles in Britain.

(*Armia Krajowa – AK*) whilst the National Armed Forces was considered to be the fighting wing of the National Democrats and the Radical National Democrat Party, formed in 1944. The movement refused to subordinate itself to the Home Army and had its headquarters in Regensburg, Germany, in the American Zone of occupation and was suspected of having close links with General Anders. MI5 found little information on the Polish Organisation although London considered it to be a political counterpart to the National Armed Forces. According to British intelligence, all these clandestine groups had one objective in mind; to put political power back in the hands of an anti-Soviet government. British security authorities were particularly concerned with the Polish objective of securing the existence of a rear émigré military force on British soil for a future confrontation with the Soviet Union and to exploit the Polish Resettlement Corps for the purpose. This aim was contrary to the reasons why Britain had established the Corps.

Clandestine groups in Britain were also monitored in order to ascertain to what degree they were supporting the underground groups in Poland. The Council of Political Groups, for example, was formed in Britain during 1946 by younger members of the Polish diaspora who were allegedly associated with Władysław Raczkiewicz, the ex-President exiled in London. Independence and Democracy (*NiD*)[6] was established in February 1945 and was another group operating from Britain. Its members were trying to establish a centre of resistance for anti-communist activity in the hope of destabilising Soviet power.[7] Members of this organisation included ex-ministers, National Democratic Party leaders, *Piłsudskiites*,[8] former members of the Home Army and Polish generals in the Middle East. MI5 paid

---

6   *Niepodległość i Demokracja*.
7   See the Yalta Agreement.
8   Political and Military figures who worked closely with Marshal Piłsudski.

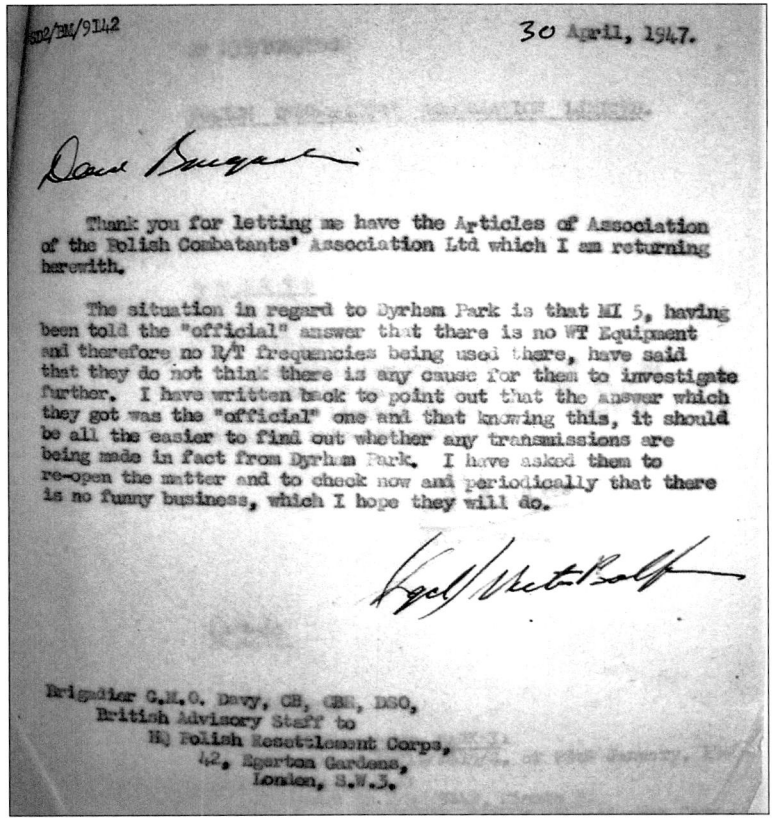

A letter from the Security Services concerning alleged
clandestine Polish broadcasts from Britain.

particular attention to the *Piłsudskite* faction as many had been senior staff officers in the Polish forces under British Command during the war, and were believed to have a strong sway over Polish soldiers now in the Resettlement Corps. The security services also expressed concern about seemingly innocent organisation such as Polish ex-combatant groups. For example, the leaders of The Polish Ex-Combatant Association (SPK)[9] (loosely based on the British Legion) was called upon by Homeland Security to explain what its mission statement was and its reason for existing. The governing body replied in writing:

> The Polish ex-Combatant Association is a voluntary organisation for mutual aid, it has no political character whatsoever and resembles in its fundamentals the English organisation for ex-soldiers, the British Legion'. The Polish Navy Association was also questioned and explained that its aim was to take care of the welfare needs of Polish ex-sailors and their families. It explained that it was predominantly concerned with 'cultural matters' and in 'assisting its members in pursuance of their studies, thus contributing to the upkeep of their morale ... ' The Association intends to collaborate

9   *Stowarzyszenie Polskich Kombatantów*

closely with the Polish Resettlement Corps (Naval wing).

A related concern was the fear that the communist regime in Warsaw may have infiltrated the Corps with agents who were prepared to spy on behalf of Moscow.

In its final conclusion, MI5 published the following recommendations regarding the Polish Resettlement Corps:

1. No encouragement to be made for the formation or continuance of large Polish organisations or institutions in the United Kingdom such as might cause embarrassment to the British Government by means of open or clandestine opposition to the Warsaw Government on a large scale,
2. To disperse the Poles as widely as possible throughout the body politic and avoid aggregation of Poles who could prove difficult to assimilate,
3. To prevent the former London Government acting as an unofficial government of the Polish community in Britain,
4. To prevent large Polish communities forming in Britain,
5. Not to employ Poles in government departments,
6. To make additional routine checks on Poles in addition to checks already carried out by MI5 and MI6 on Polish records,
7. That staff officers and all important appointments be subject to additional checks by the security services.[10]

---

10   TNA, KV 4/286, Polish Resettlement Corps, Jan 01–Dec 31, 1946.

25

Special Needs

By mid-1948, the Polish Resettlement Programme was going as well as could be expected, especially regarding the settlement of young, fit, healthy personnel. Provisions were being targeted well and the transfer of Polish forces to Britain was continuing smoothly. However, certain classes of individuals were proving difficult to resettle. For example, it was discovered that middle aged, ill or infirm personnel required special consideration if their resettlement was to be successful. Consequently, a ruling was made to demobilise them immediately on arrival in Britain and place them under the care of the Assistance Board and the Department of Health and Pensions. Difficult cases amongst the dependants, identified as 'abandoned orphans' or 'separated wives', were also placed under the care of the Assistance Board. Finally there were those who were suffering from post-traumatic stress disorder (PTSD) exacerbated by 'ambivalent loss' which could even result in suicide. For example, one individual wrote to the Assistance Board asking it to contact his family living in Kutno, near the Polish city of Łódź, to inform it that he 'could not live any longer.'[1] The number of suicides among ex-members of the Polish forces is difficult to estimate for records regarding this category of people were not retained, but is estimated to be approximate to 0.6 percent of the diaspora.

Individuals who found themselves in severe hardship could write to the Assistance Board to obtain extra help by filling in a pro forma obtained from their hostel warden. The warden was permitted to help fill in the form for those with a poor grasp of English, though he was not allowed to give advice. The completed forms were passed to the local Assistance Board Office for consideration. If the request was for special payment money to be made, it was paid out of the local office's hardship fund.

The following is an extract from a Warden's report made on behalf of a 'dependant wife';

> Arrived at Eastmoor Polish Hostel on 29.4.1949. December 1940 deported to Germany to do compulsory work. Her first husband was killed 1939. October 1947, arrived in the United Kingdom. January 1948, remarried. Husband working in the mines and he is an ex-member of the PRC. Regina is an expectant mother.[2]

During the War, Regina was a widow and worked as a slave for the Germans. Her official classification at the end of the war would have been Displaced Person (DP) under the protection of the United Nations Relief and Rehabilitation Administration (UNRAA). Once she had remarried and became a dependant of a member of the Polish Resettlement Corps, she became entitled to help under the Polish Resettlement Act 1947 and could seek assistance from the hardship fund.

Orphans were accommodated in National Assistant Board orphanages. One such orphan wrote to the National Assistance Board in 1948 seeking pocket money:

---

1   TNA, T 236/1369, Polish resettlement employment policy, 1946–1948.
2   TNA, T 236/1369, Polish resettlement employment policy, 1946–1948.

I arrived from Africa[3] to England 15/8/1948. Up to 3/9/1948 I stayed at Daglingsworth Camp. On the 3/9/1948 I was moved to Springhall. During this period I have not received any pocket money although I received clothing. I have applied to go to school and I am waiting for a reply.[4]

On the 3 May 1949, an inspection took place at a National Assistance Board Hostel near York which demonstrates how vigilant the monitoring of special cases was. The inspector, Miss Dingle, contacted the warden informing him that during her visit she observed a Polish man suffering from a diseased spine who, she thought, would never work again. Although she acknowledged that the man had 'already been in York Hospital for X-ray treatment' she expressed the view that this individual should not be living in an ordinary hostel and should be transferred to a Ministry of Pensions Hospital or a Board's Special Hostel.[5] Miss Dingle was reassured by the warden that he was aware of the special nature of the case, and that the Polish gentleman would be re-entering York County Hospital on 23 May 1949 for further treatment.

Mikołaj (Nicholas), also an ex-member of the Polish Resettlement Corps, was suffering from 'mobile amnesia'.[6] This individual was absenting himself from his hostel during meal times and bed times. The warden of the hostel wrote to the Local Office of the National Assistance Board about the problem. The warden reported that the person had said, 'in his mental confusion' that he was seeking his own accommodation and a doctor. Local office informed the Warden to arrange special treatment forthwith.

The following is a typical personal history sent to the Department of Pensions;

Left Russia 1942. Joined the Polish Army 1942, transferred to Persia, Iraq, Egypt and Palestine. Discharged from army 1944. Stationed in Palestine until leaving for this country. On arrival no pension recommended. Wife was also in Palestine from 1942 until 1945. Neither was employed. Language, Polish only. Wife ditto. Education 6th Grade, wife 7th Grade. Arrived in Britain on 10/1/48. No money since arrival. Clothing met at Wheaton Aston Camp.[7]

Not all letters, however, received by local offices of the National Assistance Board concerned hardship cases. One ex-serviceman wrote to his local office to inform it that he wished to set up a boot and shoe repair shop at his hostel. During his interview, he confirmed that he had successfully obtained a Home Office permit to work in Britain but required a licence from the Board of Trade to set up in business. Following his interview, the applicant was registered with the Board of Trade, but the Assistance Board was reminded that that he should not be paid his pocket money whilst he was trading.

There are many examples of individual requests for help in the archives, but perhaps the most important assistance was that provided for Polish organisations by the Polish

---

3   During the War Polish children who had been freed from Soviet captivity were placed in British safe havens in countries of the Commonwealth pending a return to Poland. After Yalta, a return was not possible for them.
4   TNA, T 236/1369, Polish resettlement employment policy, 1946–1948.
5   TNA, T 236/1369, Polish resettlement employment policy, 1946–1948.
6   TNA, T 236/1369, Polish resettlement employment policy, 1946–1948.
7   TNA, T 236/1369, Polish resettlement employment policy, 1946–1948.

Resettlement Trust. The press was not allowed to report on the Trust in case its existence resulted in anger and protests from the general public which was also in need during the period of wartime austerity.

The Trust was set up by the Attlee government in 1946 under the stewardship of a Board of Governors, and was chaired by the Head of Central Advisory Staff to the PRC, Major General MacLeod.[8] Also on the Board was the Inspector General of the Polish Resettlement Corps, General Kopański.[9] Much of the Trust's money came from the National Services Fund, which was receiving large rebates from the reduction of NAAFI operations. The mission statement of the Trust stated that its purpose was to provide assistance for Polish relief institutions, societies and associations which would help in the process of resettlement. To access the Fund, an organisation would need to make an appeal at the Trust's offices. The request would then be discussed at a special meeting and, if approved, money would be released from the Fund. This would either be in the form of a loan, in which case the terms of repayment would have been attached, or a grant which would require the recipient to produce a quarterly report on how the money had been spent. In 1948 the Trust held £30,000 in its current account for distribution, which it did by allocating £17,000 as loans and £10,000 as grants. £3,000 was put into reserve. By 1949 its account was topped up to £65,000 and apportioned into three lots of £12,500 and scheduled to be released in January 1949, July 1949 and January 1950. The remaining amount, £27,500, was held back for release in July 1950. The Trust's accounts stood at £45,000 and fell to £25,000 in 1951. The total income of the Trust between 1948 and 1951 amounted to £165,000,[10] although it was not the case that all the money was allocated, in which case it was invested. The Trust's Statement of Investments for 1953 provides an indication of the investment pattern.

Table 17: The Trust's Statement of Investments for 1953	
On deposit at short notice at London clearing rate	£18,428.13.0
On deposit with Post Office Savings Bank @ 2.5 percent	£500.0.0
Purchase of 2,500 Defence Bonds @ 2.5 percent	£2,500.0.0
Purchase of 25,000 Treasury Bonds @ 1.74 percent	£25,402.13.6
Purchase of 31,000 National War Bonds @ 2.5 percent 1949/1950	£31,422.14.1
Purchase of 31,000 National War Bonds @ 2.5 percent 1951/53	£31,995.18.5
Polish Soldiers Assistance Fund	£48,900.0.0
Cheque Book	£10.0.0
Balance at Lloyds Bank account	£6,084.11.0
Source: The National Archives of the UK (TNA):WO315/42	

The Trust's accounts are of particular interest, for not only do they provide information on the amounts of money it was dealing with, but who was benefiting from payments. It is apparent, for example, that extensive assistance was provided for community projects and

---

8 TNA, WO 315/42, Transfer and Disposal of PRC Funds.
9 TNA, WO 315/42, Transfer and Disposal.
10 TNA, WO 315/42, Transfer and Disposal.

Table 18: Names of Polish causes receiving money from the Polish Resettlement Trust

Amount Provided	Cause
£9,000	Setting workshops on, farming and gardening
£9,000	Assistance Fund for soldiers, widows and orphans
£1,000	Inspector of Welfare
£1,000	Help for the disabled
£2,000	Polish Families Relief Association
£200	British Joint Committee for Polish Affairs
£48,900	Polish Soldiers Assistance Fund
£6,000	Penrhos Camp for the Aged
£6,000	Workshops for Farming etc.
£801	Federation of Poles in Great Britain
£1,500	Association of Polish Agriculture
£2,500	Polish Club in Manchester
£1,100	Union of Polish Craftsmen and Workers' in Great Britain
£375	Anglo-Polish Society
£500	Anglo-Polish Review
£400	Polish Farmers' Association
£60	Polish Protestant Association
£240	Polish Council for Physical Training and Sport
£600	Union of Polish Invalids and Disabled Association
£150	Veritas Foundation
£120	Society of Polish Engineers
£200	Fisheries School, Aberdeen
£400	Polish Boy Scouts and Girl Guides
£400	Central Administration of Federation of Poles in Great Britain
£200	Polish Theatrical Bureau
£120	Polish Ex-Combatants' Association (Employment Bureau)
£200	Information Services
£170	Sports Clubs
£100	Polish Women's Association in Great Britain
£300	Union of Polish Craftsmen and Workers' Association (Bristol)
£200	Union of Polish Craftsmen and Workers' Association (Cambridge)
£200	Polish Military Families Relief Fund
£70	Association of Friends of Polish Children
£200	Anglo-Polish Society
£100	Relief Society for Poles
£53	Polish Invalid Trust
£250	Polish-Jewish Ex-Combatant Association
£100	Regiment of Polish Lancers
£160	Secretariat of the Polish Regimental Association
£400	Protestant and Orthodox Centre
£1,000	Polish Club House (Cardiff)

Source: *The National Archives (TNA): WO 315/42; Transfer and Disposal of PRC Funds*

social initiatives which were considered particularly useful in helping Polish integration. However, it is also telling that no money was given for political activity. Such groups are distinctly absent from the list of beneficiaries.

Table 18 covers the period 1947 to 1951 and is not comprehensive:

Most of the amounts in table 18 were provided as grants but those given as loans had to be repaid to an agreed timetable. Interest free loans were provided for causes that had the potential to make a specific contribution to the Resettlement Programme. Loans that had been paid off were recycled and used for fresh appeals arriving at the Trust's offices.

The intention of providing money for workshops in farming and gardening was to enable Polish individuals to become self-sufficient in growing food during periods of shortage. Money was also spent on skill development, the provision of equipment and specialist gardening tools such as tractors and ploughs. For example, the Lark Agricultural Association was provided with agricultural tools having been established by 40 ex-members of the Polish Resettlement Corps who had banded together to establish a farming community near Peterborough. Each member had bought four acres of agricultural land which was combined into one large farm.[11] Another interesting beneficiary of the Fund was the Polish Families Relief Association, which was manufacturing luxury goods of Polish design for a ready market amongst Polish communities in the United States. The Board concluded that the scheme was highly commendable and had the potential of earning much needed US dollars.[12] The Polish ex-Combatants' Association received financial help since it maintained a job-finding bureau and a repository of information for job seekers. It was considered to be a most useful agency, dealing with Poles who could not speak enough English to cope with the administration at the Labour Exchange. It was also noted for assisting 17 Polish sports clubs which provided teams for competitive games, whose members, through lack of experience, were not yet proficient enough to join local British clubs. Grants were also made available for the Polish Actors' Association, the Polish Judges' Association and a number of Polish choirs up and down the country. The printing and distribution of Polish sheet music was also financed, being of cultural and recreational value. The Union of Polish Craftsmen and Workers in Great Britain was also offered help, because it successfully argued that it would never be able to become self-supporting without aid. Many Polish workers belonging to this union were also required to enrol in British associations. For every shilling it received, the union had to hand over seven (old) pence to the appropriate British union and so could never become self-financing. During 1948 it had handed over £1,760 and a further £400 during the first quarter of 1949. It was then agreed that a grant of £1,100 should be made available for the Polish union.

However, there were some notable refusals for financial help. For example, the Polish Institute and Sikorski Museum in London had failed to secure assistance for not providing a comprehensive business plan. This was also the case with the Polish Fisheries Association for not providing enough information.[13] An appeal by the Polish YMCA was also turned down as, surprisingly, the association was considered to be outside the remit of the Resettlement Fund's charter. In some cases, money was retracted after being approved. For example, a £6,000 grant was withdrawn from the Polish Club in Newcastle, as local British citizens had paid the amount to the club from voluntary donations.

---

11 TNA, WO 315/42, Transfer and Disposal.
12 TNA, WO 315/42, Transfer and Disposal.
13 TNA, WO 315/42, Transfer and Disposal.

Polish Institute and Sikorski Museum, Prince's Gate, London.

Part III

The Rundown of the Polish Resettlement Corps and its Legacy

Right, as the world goes, is only a question between equals in power, while the strong do what they can do and the weak suffer what they must.

(Thucydides, Peloponnesian War, V, 89)

26

Termination of Service

In April 1948, the War Office made an appeal to all remaining members of the Resettlement Corps who had not yet accepted work to do all in their power to assist the various government departments working on their behalf. This was an attempt to persuade the Poles not to be too demanding about the kind of employment they were being offered as their vacillations were threatening to derail the War Office's deadline date for the closure of the Resettlement Corps. Termination of service in the Polish Resettlement Corps usually took place for four reasons; absorption into civilian employment (the most common reason), the completion of the two year service contract, disciplinary transgression or a decision to repatriate or emigrate. Typical transgressions involving Polish officers were poor, unbecoming conduct, inefficiency or unsuitability. Other ranks, who were serving under Kings Regulations paragraph 390, could have their service terminated early if they were improperly enlisted, made false claims on their attestation, had lied about their age during enlistment or had been convicted of a felony.

Disciplinary procedures used in the PRC were the same as in the British Army, except that Polish officers worked alongside British officers throughout the process. Disciplinary action would start with an arrest and a warning being issued to attend the Orderly Room. In the meantime, the senior warrant officer or NCO was informed of the arrest and proceeded to write a charge report. The report had to be worded in such a way as to disclose some act, neglect or conduct which constituted an offence under the Army Act, for example: insubordinate language to an officer, drunk on billet or improper conduct in barracks. When the charge report was complete, the commanding officer would draw up a list of witnesses. When all the paperwork was satisfactorily complete, the accused was marched before the officer flanked by an escort. If, after questioning, the accused was found not guilty, the soldier was marched off and the charges were dropped; if it was decided that a soldier had a case to answer, disciplinary action followed which could include a dishonourable discharge for serious cases. Whatever the final decision, a note of the outcome was placed in the individual's records.[1] Female officers could also have their service in the ATS terminated early for family reasons, which usually meant reuniting with husbands, getting married or falling pregnant.

Discharge on completion of the service contract occurred after two years (one year for older officers). Since this could occur before employment had been found, such an individual would have to find work by themselves. In order to support these individuals, special dispersal centres were set up which were run by the War Office in conjunction with the National Assistance Board. The centres were managed by British officers assisted by staff from the Assistance Board, and were organised in such a way as to provide advice and information about local work opportunities and social amenities. If necessary, a monetary allowance was provided for hardship cases but only when the individual had left his

---

1 TNA, WO 315/21, Invalids, disabled and category E other ranks, 1943–1950.

PRC camp. It was thought that this policy would encourage self-reliance and accelerate assimilation into the British community.

On the day of discharge, a British officer would arrive at the discharge centre, set up an interview room and a discharge panel which was comprised of him, an interpreter and a representative from the Ministry of Labour and National Service. After being discharged, the individual was not credited with any pay allowance but was entitled for a one off war gratuity, civilian clothes or, in the case of female personnel, cash in lieu. As well as civilian clothes being issued, a one way travel warrant was provided to a destination of the individual's choosing. If at any time during the discharge process an individual expressed the desire to leave the country, normal repatriation or emigration procedures would apply. The discharge procedure for personnel of the PRC (Air wing) followed a similar pattern except clearance certificates were issued prior to final termination of service. Once discharge procedures had been completed, final pay, war gratuity, civilian clothing and, in the case of a WAAF in the Polish Resettlement Section, 50 clothing coupons and a railway warrant were issued.[2]

The future employment status of ex-members of the Polish Resettlement Corps discharged because their two year contract had run its course was the same as those individuals who had been discharged because they had accepted employment. As with other members of the Corps, they were registered with the local police as aliens although they were not subject to any requirement under the Aliens Order in the matter of employment. They were, however, subject to the same employment restrictions imposed by the Control of Employment Order on those who were discharged from the PRC to secure a job. This in fact meant that they were treated as long term aliens.

The discharge of men in Category E also took place through the dispersal centres.[3] Individuals who had disabilities, but were able to carry out some kind of work, were given information on local job opportunities suitable for them before being allowed to leave, but those who were considered unable to hold down a job were provided with continued hostel accommodation. The policy regarding those who required more than six months in-patient hospital treatment was to discharge them once they had become strong enough to care for themselves. All personnel classified as Category E were entitled to apply for disability pensions if they could provide suitable medical evidence such as medical cards and assessments. Once formalities at the discharge centres had been completed, the individuals were considered to be civilian, furnished with a 'Notice of Relegation' and instructed to report to the police for registration. On registration they were issued with a 'Police Registration Certificate' which was endorsed as follows;

> Released from the Polish Resettlement Corps by _____ on condition that the holder does not take or continue in employment without the permission of the Ministry of Labour and National Service or engage in any other occupation for reward and or business or profession without the permission of the Home Office [4]

All personnel relegated from the Corps under these and other conditions, except for disciplinary, were treated as persons upon whose stay in the United Kingdom no conditions had been imposed.

---

2 TNA, WO 315/21, Invalids, disabled and category E other ranks, 1943–1950.
3 TNA, WO 315/21, Invalids, disabled and category E other ranks, 1943–1950.
4 TNA, WO 315/21, Invalids, disabled and category E other ranks, 1943–1950.

Discharge Certificate from the Polish Resettlement Corps.

The paper trail for relegation began with a note from the Ministry of Labour and National Service informing PRC Records Office that a member of the Polish Resettlement Corps had been discharged. This would result in the issue of a National Registration Identity Card which was exchanged for the individual's Alien Identity Certificate and a pamphlet called 'General Instructions for Relegation'. At this point, any pay or emolument from the War Office ceased to be paid. However, if a sum of money remained to the credit of an individual in his/her regimental cash account, it was paid to the individual without delay. They were given a grant in lieu of 21 days' pay and a marriage allowance for family men. This money was issued by the Regimental Paymaster Army Pay Office of the Polish Resettlement Corps and, in the event of recall to the unit, a similar grant was deducted from the war gratuity payable. On discharge, the war gratuity was paid at the same rate and under the same conditions as for British personnel except that 'reasonable service' was defined as 'that service with the Polish Forces under British command during the period 1 June 1940 to 15 August 1946'. No service was reckonable in the case of Poles who entered the Polish Forces after 31 May 1945. The rank for the purpose of the gratuity was that corresponding to the Polish rank held on 15 August 1946. On discharge, Polish personnel were not allowed to wear military uniform, except where specially authorised.

PODANIE O ZWOLNIENIE Z POLSKIEGO KORPUSU
PRZYSPOSOBIENIA I ROZMIESZCZENIA
WZGL. Z POLSKIEJ SEKCJI PRZYSPOSOBIENIA I ROZMIESZCZENIA

Szef Biura Ewidencyjnego PKPR,
Witley, Surrey.

Numer/ .... /Stopień/............ ..../Nazwisko/................ /Inicjały/

Application for Discharge from the Polish Resettlement Corps.

Table 19: Clothing issued or retained by PRC Personnel on Relegation to Reserve		
Male		Female
Hat or Cap	1	No civilian clothing was issued, but a cash allowance and clothing coupons were allowed – the same as for British ATS personnel.
Jacket	1	
Trousers	1	
Or Suit as available	1	
Shirt	1	
Collar	1	
Tie	1	

Table 20: Scale of Military Clothing retained by PRC Personnel on Discharge

Male			
Head Dress	1	Towels Hand	2
Battle Dress	1	Vests Woollen	2
Boots Pair	2	Brushes Hair	1
Great Coat	1	Brushes Tooth	1
Jersey Pullover	1	Brush Shaving	1
Shirts Khaki	2	Razor Safety	1
Cao, Comforter	1	Holdall	1
Draws (Woollen/ Cellular)	2 of either	Laces Spare Pair	1
Gloves Knitted pair	-	Hair Comb	1
Sock Worsted Pairs	3	Cap Badge	1
Identity Disc	1 set	Title Set	1 set
Female			
Service Dress	1	Vests	3
Boots/Shoes Pairs	1	Stockings Pairs	2
Shoes Canvas Pairs	1	Towels	2
Jersey	1	Gloves Knitted Pairs	1
Shirts	2	Kit Bag	1
Collars	4	Cleaning/Toiletries	1 Set
Ties	2	Cap Badges/Titles	1 Set
Studs	2	Identity Discs	1 Set
Belts/Corsets	2	Pyjamas	2
Belts/Sanitary	1	Caps/ATS	1
Brassieres	3	Slung Satchel	1
Knickers	3	Panties	3

27

Rundown – Personnel

> The Polish Resettlement Corps will be essentially a transitional arrangement designed to facilitate the transition from military to civilian life.[1]

The Resettlement Corps was a temporary British Army formation established as a holding unit for the Polish forces who were going to be resettled in Britain. Unlike British personnel, the discharge of Polish forces comprised two stages: stage one was the transfer of Polish personnel into the British Army (the PRC) followed by stage two, final demobilisation. This procedure was designed to slow the passage from military to civilian life and provide an opportunity to adjust to a life in exile. Paradoxically, although it was the government's policy not to rush the demobilisation of the Poles, it was also the intention to disband the Resettlement Corps as quickly as possible. Continued existence of the Corps was seen to be confusing the general public who were asking, 'Why aren't the Poles going home?' Trade unions, despite having agreed to accept Polish workers, were also protesting that the Poles were taking British jobs, housing and resources. Consequently, no longer had the Polish Resettlement Corps been established than the government began planning for its disbandment and closure, scheduled to take place in September 1949. The Polish Resettlement Corps Liquidation Committee was founded in June 1947 and was to oversee the disposal of Polish forces in Britain. The strength of the Corps rose rapidly between 1946 and 1947 as Poles were transferred to Britain, but fell markedly between 1947 and 1949 because of demobilisation through voluntary repatriation, emigration or employment in Great Britain. Eventually, the responsibilities of the Liquidation Committee were taken over by the Liquidation Section of the HQ of the Polish Resettlement Corps in London where six teams were formed for the purpose: an Advisory/Liaison Department manned by two majors and one civilian clerk; an Advisory/Liaison Department manned by one general; a coordinating section manned by one major, one captain and two civilian clerks; a Legal Department, with one major; Medical Services, with one colonel, one civilian clerk and one captain; a Welfare Department with one major and one clerk, and finally a General Department to deal with other Polish matters, manned by one major and one clerk.[2] Once the Polish Resettlement Corps was finally disbanded on 30 September 1949, any outstanding issues became the responsibility of the Aftermath Liaison Section at the War Office, which began work on 1 October 1949. Its main duty was to administer and collaborate with appropriate branches of the War Office in order to finally disband the Corps, including the closure of officers' clubs, auxiliaries, army and air force units and all Polish records and archives. It was also responsible for the disposal of any equipment or furniture which had been used by Polish military and political authorities.[3] When, on 30

---

1   Hansard Vol 420 No 106, 22 May 1946, Ernest Bevin.
2   TNA, WO 315/27, Administration matters, 1947–1949.
3   TNA, WO 315/34, PRC, Aftermath Liaison Section.

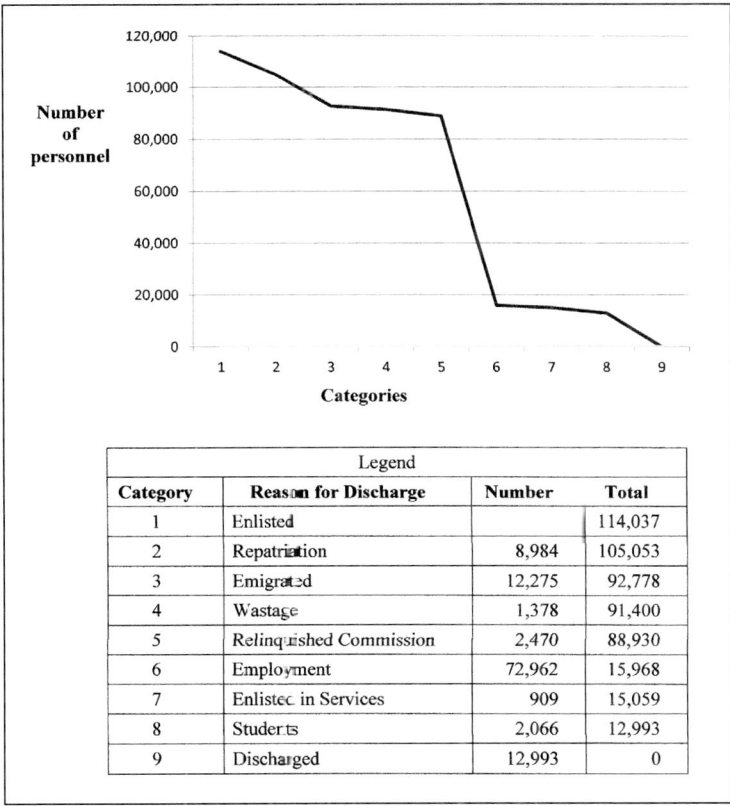

Figure 19: Breakdown of PRC personnel versus reasons for discharge. (Global figures adapted from War Office data for February 1951.)

June 1950, the Section itself was finally disbanded, it signalled the formal end of the British commitment.

According to the War Office, 7.8 percent of the Resettlement Corps repatriated to Poland whilst 10.7 percent emigrated to other countries.[4] This left 81.5 percent of those enlisting resettling in Britain. Statistics for these individuals indicates that by far the main reason for discharge was successful placement in employment. The next reason for discharge was the successful completion of the two year service contracts with the PRC, even if employment had not yet been found for such individuals. The contracts, which were timed to finish after the official closure date of the Resettlement Corps, were backdated and terminated early so that the Corps could be disbanded on schedule (30 September 1949). If backdating was not possible, the contracts were taken over by the National Assistance Boards which acted as agent for the War Office and allowed to run their course. The Assistance Board was authorised to make ex-gratia payments equivalent to Resettlement Corps pay and allowances, as well as arrange emigration or repatriation at War Office expense.

---

4   TNA, WO 315/27, Administration matters, 1947–1949.

Discharge from the Polish Resettlement Corps took place when a member of the Corps accepted employment in the private sector, or a PRC Contract of Service had lapsed, whichever was the sooner. This document was issued when the contract with the PRC had been completed.

The War Office authorised the discharge of senior officers of the Polish Resettlement Corps between the years 1948 and 1949. Lieutenant General Kopański, Inspector General of the Polish Resettlement Corps, for example, was discharged on 5 September 1949 at the age of 56. General Duch on 25 October 1948 at the age of 52, General Maczek on 12 September 1948 at the age of 56, Major General Wiśniowski on 12 February 1949 at the age of 53, General Rudnicki on 12 February 1949 at 52 and General Sulik on 22 February 1949 at the age of 55.[5] The Chancellor of the Exchequer authorised the payment of pensions for Polish service chiefs which were paid under the authority of 'Extra Regulations'. General Anders was awarded a pension of £100 per month, Admiral Świrski, £75 per month and General Rudnicki, £75 per month.

As the strength of the Corps declined, the Polish group headquarters in each Home Commands were run down and transferred to Western Command which took over sole responsibility for the Polish Resettlement Corps. The first Polish group HQ to close was in Scottish Command, followed by North East Command and then Southern Command. In March 1948, Polish Resettlement Corps HQ responsibilities in London were amalgamated with the Polish Forces Directorate at the War Office, and then transferred to Western Command where they were reorganised to become the senior HQ of the Corps. At this

---

5   TNA, WO 315/34, Aftermath Liaison Section.

point in time, the Officer in Charge of Western Command became the Administrator for Polish Forces. He was assisted by HQ BAS Unit PRC Western Command and based at Witley Camp in Surrey. Remaining branches at the War Office, for example, the Liaison Section, assumed responsibility for Polish matters in London. On 1 October 1949, when the Senior Polish Resettlement Corps HQ was disbanded, the management of Polish affairs was taken over by the Aftermath Liaison Section at the War Office.[6]

---

6   TNA, WO 315/35, Aftermath Liaison Section.

28

Rundown – Records and Archives

When the Polish Army under British Command was transferred to Britain, it was inevitable that it would bring with it all its records, diaries and archives. These documents were not standardised because of the numerous problems with communication between units and the exiled Polish Government in London during the War. This meant that many were improvised as Polish formations were being formed outside Poland. The War Office referred to them as 'Polish Forces' Records' and they remained separate until they were merged with PRC records at the Polish Records Office at Witley Camp, Surrey.[1] In 1946, the National Government of National Unity in Warsaw requested the return of the Forces' Records, arguing that they belonged to Polish authorities and should not be of any interest to London. The difficulty facing the Foreign Office, however, was that by this time they were part of the PRC Records and earmarked for disposal. The Foreign Office sought advice from Treasury solicitors on the matter who reported that all documents at Witley were public records and therefore the property of His Majesty. In order to avoid any confusion between London and Warsaw, all records held at Witley were reclassified as 'Late PRC Records' and retained in the country.

Many of the records were destroyed in the early 1950s[2] according to a schedule devised by the War Office. Headquarter files, war diaries which were to be used in the official history of the War 1939–1945, nominal rolls, individual histories such as attestations, promotions and appointments, as well as medical categories, which were to be used by the Pensions Office, and character assessments in release books were to be retained. An English translation of the Polish 2nd Corps diaries, Volume II, was sent to the Ministry of Information at the War Office for publication and, because some of the formations had served in 21 Army Group with the Canadians, across the Atlantic to official Canadian archives. The destruction of files could only begin after September 1949 and then only if strict conditions were satisfied. Other files were destroyed according to a timetable. For example, obsolete card indexes could be destroyed immediately. Copies of returns rendered to the War Office at half yearly or longer intervals could be destroyed after one year, whilst those rendered at intervals shorter than half yearly, could be destroyed after six months. Daily casualty returns were destroyed after two months whilst weekly strength returns and distribution and nominal rolls of officers were destroyed after one month. Nominal rolls of other ranks (ORs) were destroyed after one year, as was correspondence of a routine or temporary nature. Circulars and memoranda received by PRC units from the War Office could be destroyed after three years. Mobilisation schemes and the register of letters received and dispatched by the War Office were destroyed after two years. Letter books containing copies of outgoing letters were destroyed after three years. Receipts for soldiers' documents were destroyed immediately, but those not returned to individuals were destroyed after two years. Books of receipts for effects were destroyed after six years. Records of the proceedings

---

1   TNA, WO 315/29, PRC, Enlistment, Employment.
2   TNA, WO 315/30, PRC, Unemployment, Discharge, Disbandment.

of promotional boards were destroyed after three years, as were attendance registers and shadow promotions. Personal files of civilianised personnel who had worked for the PRC Records Office were destroyed after two years upon leaving employment. Medal issue records were destroyed after 10 years. Individual receipts for medals were destroyed after one year, as were applications for medals in respect of non-effective soldiers and applications for the Defence Medal. Applications for other campaign stars were destroyed after one year although records of issue of medals were preserved. Documentation referring to emigration and repatriation was also destroyed. Notifications of Dates of Embarkation were destroyed after five years, as were repatriation returns, alien certificates, notifications by Home Office of Grant of Naturalisation and registers of assumed names. Records relating to the proceedings of Polish Military Courts of Honour were destroyed after three years as were pay cards, demobilisation certificates of the Polish Land Forces and records of personnel who were not enrolled into the Polish Resettlement Corps. Registration cards and questionnaires from Polish Records, verifications of former ranks in the Polish forces were also destroyed after three years. Private record cards handed in for custody and not yet claimed were destroyed after 10 years. Account documents of the Polish Land Forces (1940–1949) who had been stationed in the Middle East, Italy, France, the UK and BAOR were destroyed after 30 years. However, some individual service records still survive.

During 1948, the Polish Government in Warsaw approached the British authorities stating that it believed Poles in Great Britain were in the possessions of archives, books and museum exhibits which had been spirited out of Poland during the chaotic evacuation of the country in 1939. In the opinion of Warsaw, these items were the property of Polish museums, libraries and institutions and should therefore be returned immediately. Responding to the Polish request, the Foreign Office made enquiries and found that part of these artefacts were in the possession of the Sikorski Institute in London, whilst the bulk was stored in the Polish Resettlement Corps Military Museum in Scotland. It confirmed that most of the items had been collated by exiled Polish forces and comprised of military and historical documents, together with artefacts of a sentimental value which had been accumulated in the Middle East. Following Warsaw's enquiry, the Administrator of Polish Forces (APF) was instructed to compile an itinerary of the content, excluding the material being held at the Sikorski Institute which was considered to be a purely civil organisation and therefore outside the remit of the War Office. When the surveying team arrived in Scotland and met Lieutenant Domański, the Curator of the 2nd Polish Corps Museum, it found some 150 items, including antique saddles, stable implements, bandoliers, power flasks, ammunition boxes, gloves and epaulettes dating back to 1819. The collection also included Polish medieval helmets, armaments, prints, lithographs and paintings which had been catalogued before storage. After inspecting the documentation presented by Lieutenant Domański, the APF inspectors were satisfied that the items stored at the museum had been purchased or donated legally, and were rightly considered to belong to the exiled Polish diaspora.

One complication was the discovery of a private collection of artefacts which appeared be the property of the Krasiński family and their heirs. The original Krasiński Museum was a well-known collection in pre-war Poland and, as the heirs were believed to be residing in Britain, the APF enquired of their whereabouts in order to obtain further instructions regarding their disposal. The hope was that the family would donate the collection to the Sikorski Institute in London. The inspectors were also intrigued by a horde of valuables lodged at the museum, including such things as gold chains, gold sovereigns and money.

On return to London, it was later discovered that before the outbreak of the war, perhaps in 1938, the Polish Government had set up a fund called the 'Fund for National Defence' to which citizens were invited to donate in order to bolster the country's war chest which was eventually placed at the entire disposal of the Commander-in-Chief of the army. People sent gold rings, paintings, watches and other curios which were realised and the proceeds used for the purpose of funding Polish resistance. Included among the items was a nobleman's embroidered belt and a tapestry chair covered with the initials of Stanislaw August, King of Poland (1732–1798). These valuables were brought to Britain as the Poles retreated via Dakar and Marseilles. In its final report the APF informed the Home Office that, in early 1942, General Sikorski, the Polish Prime Minister exiled in London, had ordered that the artefacts be passed to the museum at Banknoch House for safe-keeping while he organised a commission to liquidate the assets. Captain Katski signed a receipt for the valuables when they arrived in Scotland, a copy of which was presented to the APF inspectors. The final report on the inspection established that there were some 4,900 coins and 2,500 foreign coins at Banknoch House, and some 20,000 campaign photographs preserved at Gask House. Major Blomfield (BAS to PRC) concluded that he had found nothing which could interest the Warsaw Government. Much of this material was then passed to the Sikorski Institute, London, with a small number of items being passed to the Marian Fathers at Fawley Court, Berkshire, where a small museum was established. The survey team also reported that it had made a snap check of a small number of boxes, but had found nothing which could 'even remotely concern Warsaw'. A document was also found stating the fact that a small collection of valuable coins was donated to St. Andrews University in July 1942 as a thank you for the assistance given to Polish students by the university.

In order to reassure Warsaw that nothing was being hidden from the Polish Government, the Foreign Office proposed that its representatives should visit the museum and go through the material 'properly and scientifically'. Meanwhile, to ensure that nothing was illicitly removed or concealed from the collection, it recommended that all documents and stores be frozen. It also requested that British staff be put into the museum alongside the Polish personnel serving there. On receipt of the report, the Home Office replied that it had no objection to the proposals but expressed concern about finding British staff as there was a shortage of spare personnel. It also noted that, when the PRC was disbanded, it would be necessary to replace the Polish Resettlement Corps staff at the museum with civilians, perhaps from the Ministry of Works, if there was a desire to prolong the life of the museum. The APF reminded the Home Office that the Poles intended to put a small civilian staff in on 15 July which was approved as long as the Poles remained under British supervision. Eventually, the museum was closed and its contents transferred to the Sikorski Museum in London, although the whereabouts of the material, which formed part of the Marian Fathers' collection is unknown.

29

Rundown – The Resettlement Corps

Not all records relating to the rundown of the Polish Resettlement Corps survive but, from the ones that have been located, it appears that the majority of PRC units were disbanded between 1948 and 1950. The pattern of disposal was determined by the rate of discharge for employment, although the War Office's policy of disbanding the Resettlement Corps by September 1949 was also a key factor.[1] The last Polish facility to close was the Records Office which was still operating in June 1950, although it was relocated from Witley to Droitwich.[2] The staff at Witley, who did not wish to transfer to Droitwich with the records, were discharged in March 1950. Some of the earliest facilities to be closed were hospitals. For example, Number One PRC Hospital was closed on the 1 November 1947 and Number Two PRC Hospital was disbanded on 1 July in the same year. Others were taken over, either by the Ministry of Pensions or by the Ministry of Health, and were staffed by civilian Polish medical personnel discharged from the Corps. PRC hospitals that cared for invalid patients fell under the Disabled Soldiers' Scheme. Vocational training centres and the pool of English Language instructors were disbanded between December 1947 and August 1949. There were 4,465 technical instructors employed on the Resettlement Programme who were gradually dismissed as their contribution to the programme reduced.

The year 1948 was by far the busiest period for the disposal of Polish Resettlement Units. In Scottish Command, the process began with the closure of the Convalescence Depot at Quebec Camp, Inverary, which took place on 15 April 1948. In May of the same year, the Instructional Company in Glasgow and the Number 11 Officers' Holding Unit was disbanded. The Light Aid Detachment of the Resettlement Corps, based in West Lothian, was closed on the 31st. The month of June was particularly busy for Scottish Command. Number Three Pre-Vocational Training Centre at Thurfhille Camp, Number One Special Investigative Branch in Glasgow, Four Provost Company at Mansfield Park, Perthshire, Number One Military Archives and Museum at Charlesfield Lodge, Number Eight Recalcitrant Camp at Banff Airfield, 1st Corps Military Bureau in Glasgow, Number One Mobile Dental Trailer based at Ross and Cromarty, the Corps Dental Laboratory and Group Three Military Registrar Staff were all closed. The Base Units disbanded during June were 101, 102, 103 and 107. Base Units 100 and 104 were disbanded in May whilst 105, was disbanded in September. 1948 was also a very busy time in Eastern Command where many closures were also taking place. Base Units 332 and 311 closed in February, Number Four Pre-Vocational Training Centre at Bedge Hill, Sussex, closed on 16 May closely followed by the closure of Number 30 Officers' Holding Unit on 19 June. Number Three PRC Company was disbanded on 1 June as was Number Three SIB Unit. Base Unit 310 at Woodland Park Camp, Buckinghamshire, was closed on 3 July, whilst Base Unit Number 32 at Blinford Camp, Sussex, was disbanded on 2 August. In September the Polish

---

1   TNA, WO 315/30, PRC, Unemployment, Discharge, Disbandment.
2   TNA, WO 315/34, PRC, Aftermath Liaison Section.

Resettlement Corps HQ Medical Camp and Number Six General Hospital, located at Diddington, Huntingdonshire, were also closed.

Northern Command saw many Polish Resettlement Units close in 1949; however, the first unit was the Number Two British Military Hospital in Lincoln, which was disbanded on 7 April 1947. Following the closure of this military hospital there followed a lull in disposals. Approximately a year later, on 14 April 1948, Number 21 Officers' Holding Unit was shut down at Duncombe Park, followed two months later by the Polish Medical Corps HQ at Sand Hutton Hill, closing on 1 June. Seven days later on 7 June, Number Three Wing British Military Hospital in York was closed. Closures continued into 1949 with the disposal of Base Units Number Two, Three, Four, Five, 200 and 201. Northern Command Polish Group HQ in York was closed on 7 July 1949.

As Western Command inherited responsibility for the Polish Resettlement Corps from London HQ and Polish Group HQs in other Home Commands, the disbanding of Resettlement Corps Units in this Command were some of the last to take place. However, one of the first units to be disbanded here was the pool of Instructors in English which occurred on 31st August, together with the Provost Section of the Resettlement Corps and the 460 Provost Company which was disbanded in Cheshire. The rundown continued with the closure of the Light Aid Detachment and 403 Medical Section on 10 September. The disposal of the Polish Resettlement Corps Special Investigation Section Numbers Four and Five followed on 25 September. On 30 September Base Unit 411 was closed, followed closely by the disbanding of the British Advisory Staff PRC on 31 October. The Western Command Advisory team was disbanded on 30 November.

The disposal of PRC equipment and specialist facilities became a contentious issue when the Polish Government in Warsaw requested that they be transferred to Poland. Decisions regarding the disposal of stationary, office furniture, desks, filing cabinets, typewriters, medical equipment such as syringes, scissors and bandages, and catering equipment such as ovens, kitchen utensils and bowls, collectively called 'Equipment P', were complicated by the fact that the material possessed varying status and therefore ownership. To simplify the disposal process the War Office identified three categories of equipment. One category included equipment spirited out of Poland in 1939 which had found its way to Britain. It was considered to be the property of the Second Republic of Poland and, although it no longer existed, the artefacts were not considered to be owned by Warsaw. The second category was the equipment that the British Government had provided the Poles under the authority of the Anglo-Polish Agreement signed in 1939 and 1940 and designated to remain in Britain. The final category comprised donations made to the exiled Polish Government in London by Polish communities in other countries, such as the United States. The policy of His Majesty's Government was to resist the return of any donated equipment, for example medical tools, dental utensils and an ambulance donated by the people of Chicago, for it was given to benefit the exiled Polish community in the country which was destined to continue under the Resettlement Programme. Other material was scheduled to be used in the vocational training of Polish personnel in Britain and play an important role in assimilating Poles in the country. Lieutenant General Kopański[3] supported this position, arguing that these items were not returnable[4] as they could only be disposed of once surplus to requirement which would be a long time in the future. He added that in any case the

---

3   Inspector General of the Polish Resettlement Corps.
4   TNA, WO 315/26, Polish equipment: administration and disposal 1946–1952.

equipment belonged to the Republic of Poland and not People's Poland. The Aftermath Liaison Section of the War Office decided that the correct thing to do on the matter was to pass any equipment in the possession of the Polish Resettlement Corps to the Polish civilian organisations establishing themselves to serve the displaced Poles. It recommended that it should be transferred to an appointed plenipotentiary,[5] such as the Polish ex-Combatant Association (SPK) or the Federation of Poles in Great Britain. In fact the War Office persuaded the Federation to become the licensee for all equipment.[6]

---

5 TNA, WO 315/26, Polish equipment.
6 TNA, WO 315/26, Polish equipment.

30

Polish Resettlement Corps – Final Report

The Polish Resettlement Corps was formed on 1 June 1946 as a transient expedient designed to dispose of Polish Allied forces who had refused repatriation on account of the Iron Curtain. The formation of the Corps was designed to place the Poles under British military law and then facilitate their demobilisation and settlement in the country. The decision to resettle Polish troops in Britain after the war was to be the country's first attempt at organising a mass immigration programme, and was expected to take until 30 September 1949 to complete. The political decision to enter these uncharted waters was the fact that the country had a formal agreement of mutual assistance with Poland, and to diffuse international pressure coming from such countries such as the Soviet Union which was repeatedly asking for the disposal of protesting Polish forces who were 'threatening peace in Europe'. Communist authorities in Yugoslavia were also writing to the Secretary General of the United Nations enquiring why the Polish 2nd Corps was still stationed in north Italy and not being disbanded. Belgrade believed that the continued existence of Polish formations on the country's northern border constituted a military threat to Yugoslavia,[1] and reported that some units had already been seen moving towards the Yugoslav border whilst not wearing any Polish insignia. The Poles were also accused of recruiting and arming anti–communist 'terrorists' who were crossing the border under the slogan 'Yugoslav Fighters against Communism'. The memorandum ended with a request that the United Nations act urgently against the 'illegal formations'. Italian communists also protested about the Poles, fearing that their presence would influence the communist vote in forthcoming Italian elections. With pressure growing regarding the Polish forces who were apparently languishing aimlessly in southern Europe, it became only a matter of time until London felt it had to respond.

We have seen that the first attempt to dispose of these forces was to encourage them to repatriate at Britain's expense. However, when this policy failed, it was then decided to finance passage for every Polish soldier who wanted to emigrate to a country other than Poland or Britain. This plan also had limited success and so the final solution was to resettle them in Britain, which entailed inviting approximately 200,000 men of the Polish forces to travel to this country. If truth be told, His Majesty's Government was reluctant to approve such a policy because such a programme would inevitably put pressure on the nation's resources, and dismay public opinion which was slow in understanding the reasons behind the resettlement of the Poles. But Britain had little choice in the matter, apart from marching the Poles under bayonet into the hands of communist authorities in Poland, just as it had done with Cossack (Ukrainian) refugees and Soviet authorities, condemning them to certain death.[2]

News that Polish forces under British command would be invited to settle in Britain had to be carefully managed, for not only were many MPs unconvinced of the wisdom of

---

1 *Dziennik Polski I Dziennik Żołnierza, Rok 3 Numer 63*, 14 March 1946.
2 Charles Williams, *Harold Macmillan*, (Phoenix Publishers, 2009), p.175.

the policy, but it was far from certain that the general public would countenance the idea. In order to allay people's fears, Prime Minister Attlee reassured the British population that the Poles would not remain in the country for long as they would be encouraged to repatriate, or to emigrate, just soon as they arrived. However, the encouragement was not as productive as was hoped, and it dawned on the government that it would be necessary to give the Polish soldiers permanent resident status in the country.

Resettlement in Britain began with enrolment into the Polish Resettlement Corps which took place between autumn 1946 and winter 1948. The final count of Poles joining the Corps numbered 114,000 which included 15,000 Polish officers, 92,000 men and 5,500 female personnel. Among these were 16,500 Polish airmen and a few airwomen who enlisted in the Air Wing of the Corps. 30,000 dependants of the members of the Polish Resettlement Corps, who had spent the war in British safe havens, were also brought to Britain during late 1947 and early 1948. This humanitarian act was a response to information coming from the refugee camps that officers of the communist regime in Warsaw were arriving to take Polish citizens back to Poland something that alarmed the Polish troops.

Approximately 21,000 of the total of 114,000 personnel of the Corps eventually emigrated or returned to Poland. 900 members of the Corps enrolled in Britain's Services and 2,000 students were discharged to continue their studies in Britain. During its existence, the Corps also lost some 3,000 personnel through other losses (death) which left approximately 90,000 in the United Kingdom for whom resources for satisfactory settlement, including meaningful employment had to be found. Release from the Resettlement Corps was gradual, lasting approximately four years with 800 being released in 1946, 53,000 in 1947 and 24,000 in 1948. This left about 14,000 men awaiting release at the beginning of 1949 when the Resettlement Corps was scheduled to be disbanded. As the date for disbandment approached, the Ministry of Labour put into place special measures to help older men and high ranking officers into employment. The measures varied from crude insistence that the men accept work without being too choosey, to pressurising employers to play a fuller part in the resettlement programme. Although the initiative proved helpful, approximately 2,000 men were still awaiting placement on 30 September when the Corps was finally disbanded. The War Office agreed to continue paying these men after that date until their terms of service expired, or until they had found employment for themselves, whichever came first. Of the individuals who were discharged on termination of their Service Contract, the majority found work either on discharge or shortly after.

There were particular difficulties in resettling infirm and disabled personnel, many of whom had special requirements and were unable to hold down a job. Despite these difficulties, the Ministry of Labour professed that the resettlement programme had been a huge success, despite the fact that 1,600 demobilised troops were still living in hostels being run by the National Assistance Board in 1949.

The War Office was extremely proud of the successes of the resettlement programme and, despite early concerns about its feasibility, congratulated itself in 1949 on the way it had fulfilled the requirements the Government had placed before it. The War Office announced enthusiastically that the problem of Polish resettlement had been solved to the general satisfaction of the Poles themselves, who had cooperated in every possible way (in spite of there being a great number of hard cases and resistance in the British community), and government departments which had worked diligently throughout. The War Office proudly announced 'The Poles have thus now been settled'. However, the government knew that discharging the Poles from the Resettlement Corps into employment hardly constituted real settlement, for wellbeing is more than just bread and water. People's innate motivations also include the need for safety, belonging and the maintenance of self-esteem. Discharge from the PRC for the Poles was just the beginning of a long, hard road to spiritual integration and assimilation into British society. The Ministry of Labour was also worried about what would happen if at any time there was a serious trade recession and the Poles got pushed out of employment first. It reported that it would monitor the situation closely, and promised to watch relations between Polish and British workers until it was certain that they were not being discriminated against. The following statistics were presented to summarize the situation regarding the winding up of the Resettlement Corps.

Table 21: Global Numbers – 30.09.1949			
	PRC	PRC(RAF)	Total
Repatriation	8,542	442	8,984
Emigrated	10,861	1,414	12,275
Wastage	1,338	40	1,378
Relinquished Commission	1,928	542	2,470
Resettlement in Employment	67,607	5,355	72,962
Enlisted in British Services	405	504	909
Students	1,599	467	2,066
Discharged	10,867	2,126	12,993
Totals	**103,147**	**10,890**	**114,037**

Table 22: Number of Emigrants PRC, Polish Forces, Civilians – 11 June 1949					
	Services	Men	Women	Juveniles	Total
All Countries	17,153	1,412	1,873	1,127	21,565

Table 23: Number of Emigrants PRC, Polish Forces, Civilians – 3 September 1949					
	Services	Men	Women	Juveniles	Total
All Countries	17,254	1,695	2,005	1,209	22,163

Table 24: Strength and Distribution PRC – 11 June 1949

	Men				Women				Total
	Officers		ORs		Officers		ORs		
	Army/Navy	RAF	Army/Navy	RAF	Army/Navy	RAF	Army/Navy	RAF	
Enrolled in PRC	14,471	1,861	83,915	8,150	919	45	3,842	834	114,037
Repatriation after enrolment	1,255	68	7,046	338	60		161	34	8,962
Emigrated after enrolment	1,928	317	8,410	1,051	123	2	310	43	12,184
Wastage	1,853	9	547	31	127	24	366	518	3,475
To Reserve									
Employment or own business	2,639	425	61,735	4,787	355	10	2,736	133	72,820
As Students	566	79	959	350	11	3	63	35	2,066
Into Services	6	91	393	411		1		1	909
Discharge on expiry of service	3,710	832	2,917	1,141	89	5	117	70	8,881
Progress in run down	11,957	1,821	82,013	8,109	765	45	3,753	834	109,297
Awaiting resettlement	2,514	40	1,902	41	154		89		4,740
Total awaiting resettlement registered with MOD	2,200	15	1,703	36	141		111		4,210
Discharged from Reserve after three months	2,737	257	58,856	2,364	311		2,230		66,755

Table 25: Strength and distribution PRC – 3 September 1949

	Men				Women				Total
	Officers		ORs		Officers		ORs		
	Army/Navy	RAF	Army/Navy	RAF	Army/Navy	RAF	Army/Navy	RAF	
Enrolled in PRC	14,471	1,861	83,915	8,150	919	45	3,842	834	114,037
Repatriation after enrolment	1,267	68	7,056	340	60		162	34	8,984
Emigrated after enrolment	1,968	317	8,447	1,056	125	2	321	43	12,275
Wastage	1,963	9	732	31	148	24	423	518	3,848
To Reserve									
Employment or own business	2,691	425	61,828	4,787	356	10	2,732	133	72,962
As Students	566	79	959	350	11	3	63	35	2,066
Into Services	6	91	399	411		1		1	909
Discharge on expiry of service	5,750	872	3,743	1,179	210	5	127	70	11,956
Progress in run down	14,211	1,861	83,161	8,150	910	45	3,828	834	113,000
Awaiting resettlement	260		754		9		14		1,037
Total awaiting resettlement registered with MOD	74		353		2				429
Discharged from Reserve after three months	3,256	257	62,405	2,364	366		2,681		74,329

Table 26: Provisional number of personnel due to complete their period of service during 1949–1950

	Men				Women				Total
	Officers		ORs		Officers		ORs		
	Army/Navy	RAF	Army/Navy	RAF	Army/Navy	RAF	Army/Navy	RAF	
1949									
August	19		30		2		2		53
September	96		194		3		6		299
October	21		161				3		185
November	20		179				2		185
December	4		86		1				91
1950									
January	26		63				1		90
February	26		52		2				80
March	41		52						93
April	35								35
May	5				2				7
June									0
July									0

Table 27: Number of discharges affected by expiry of service

	Men				Women				Total
	Officers		ORs		Officers		ORs		
	Army/Navy	RAF	Army/Navy	RAF	Army/Navy	RAF	Army/Navy	RAF	
1948									
28 Sept	577		133		5				715
16 Oct	1,218		422		5		6		1,651
27 Nov	1,721	79	749	339	5	1	16	18	2,928
1949									
22 Jan	1,791	532	1,213	796	6	5	32	47	4,422
19 Feb	1,891	649	1,609	803	6	5	38	47	5,048
16 Apr	2,474	809	2,457	1,119	25	5	81	68	7,038
14 May	3,044	831	2,731	1,136	46	5	98	70	7,961
11 Jan	3,710	832	2,917	1,141	89	5	117	70	8,881
9 Jul	4,080	858	3,107	1,154	113	5	123	70	9,510
6 Aug	4,526	872	3,185	1,179	167	5	124	70	10,128
3 Sept	5,950	872	3,743	1,179	210	5	127	70	11,956

Table 28: Poles in Great Britain in groups according to source of income*

	Number	percent	Employed	percent	Maintained by Head of Family	percent	Maintained By Treasury	percent
Ex-Polish Forces including PRC and PRC(RAF)	96,200	100	78,400	82.5	–	–	17,800	17.5
Families and Dependants	38,500	100	14,500	37.6	14,900	38.6	9,100	23.8

*Estimates, *The National Archives (TNA): WO 315/51*

Table 29: Distribution in industries in which more than 400 Poles had been placed

Industry	Army	RAF	Total
Building	8,541	363	8,904
Agriculture etc.	7,959	211	8,170
Coal Mining	No breakdown		7,293
Catering, Hostels	6,575	439	6,114
National Government Services	4,986	107	5,093
Brick/Fireclay Work	3,062	57	3,119
Civil Engineering	2,931	66	2,997
General Engineering	1,672	635	2,307
Woollen Industries	1,929	41	1,970
Iron & Steel	1,767	49	1,816
Cotton Spinning	1,334	98	1,432
Professional Services	1,647	124	1,771
Distribution	1,231	236	1,467
Motor Vehicles/Aircraft	837	497	1,134
Chemical Manufacturing	1,282	65	1,147
Rail	1,602	215	1,817
Domestic Service	1,198	86	1,284
Tailoring	1,083	81	1,164
Local Government services	978	36	1,014
Quarrying & Mining	861	15	876
Utilities	792	50	842
Bread, Biscuit, Flour	805	53	858
Metal Industries	816	72	888
Timber	697	44	741
Mining	687	30	717
Rayon, Nylon, Weaving	394	312	706
Cotton Weaving	594	56	650
Rayon, Nylon Products	527	87	614
China, Earthenware	305	10	615
Smelting, Rolling	580	27	607
Cobblers	417	92	509
Furniture makers	406	159	565
Other Food Industries	550	54	604
Sea Transport	444	9	453

Consultation in 1946 between the British Government and industries likely to absorb appreciable numbers of the Polish Resettlement Corps resulted in national agreements being formulated in 40 industries and occupations. These arrangements proved to be pivotal in ensuring that Polish workers entered British industry in circumstances likely to lead to permanent social assimilation. The Poles, keen to rebuild their lives and eke out an existence in exile, adapted quickly to working alongside British colleagues. Their reputation as conscientious workers soon grew to impress employers and resulted in mutual respect growing amongst the workforce. Consequently, no abnormal turnover of Polish labour was detected. A number of ex-members of the Corps, particularly those who had married British women – who helped them to understand the British way of work – set themselves up in business. Typical businesses included jewellery shops, food shops and light manufacturing companies.

The Final Report on the Polish Resettlement Corps, however, also acknowledged the fact that the Ministry of Labour and National Service had found great difficulty in placing Polish men with families, older members of the Corps (particularly older officers) and unfit or disabled personnel in to employment. Perhaps this should have been anticipated, for family men were naturally reluctant to leave their dependants in order to find work, and disabled men were in some cases unemployable. On the other hand, younger officers adapted quickly to working in Britain, although the work they accepted was very different from what they would have expected in their own country. One former officer, for example, who had commanded an airborne brigade at Arnhem,[3] 'took a job as a humble factory worker'.[4] The Ministry of Pensions was responsible for the long term sick and disabled although the Disabled Persons' Employment Corporation found them light work in sheltered employment such as at the Remploy factory in Lancashire for those who could hold down a job.

The Report on Polish 'estates',[5] which now were under the management of the National Assistance Board, describes that they were demolished once they had been vacated by the Poles. Their demolition was immediate for fear of squatters moving in. The procedure of demolition was helped by the fact that many of the structures used to build bases were prefabricated and easily dismantled. Wooden structures, such as the Yukon barracks, were often bulldozed, burned and buried whilst the Nissen huts were unbolted and recycled. Camps which originally stood on requisitioned land were either demolished by the War Office or by the landowner who had received financial support from the War Office for the task.

---

3 Operation Market Garden.
4 *The New European*, J. Snelling, *How Britain Embraced its friendly Polish Invasion (the first time round)*, (8–14 July 2016).
5 Originally Service Camps for the Resettlement Corps.

31

Life in Families' Camps

Although the intention of the Government was to encourage a quick and smooth absorption of the displaced Poles into British society, in reality the process proved to be far more difficult than anticipated. In fact the process was so challenging, that many demobilised Polish personnel and their families were still living in Assistance Board estates until the late 1950s, some 15 years after the War. The barriers to rapid assimilation were physical as well as psychological. The physical obstacles are perhaps simple to understand, for many of the Polish hostels stood in isolated localities which more often than not, also meant social isolation. No English person had any need to enter the estates except on business, which was rare, and there were few reasons for Polish people to leave the confines of their estates (camps) until, that is, men gained employment or children entered the education system. Most Poles had also arrived in Britain with little money, and had to wait until enough had been saved for a deposit on a house, or a down payment for a Local Authority dwelling outside the camp system. However, to continue living in Assistance Board hostels and housing estates indefinitely was not an option, and therefore British authorities put gentle pressure on the Poles to depart and seek accommodation in the wider community.

The psychological barriers to assimilation were far more complex although their influence was no less profound. As in many exiled groups, the Poles believed that their displacement was temporary and that all they had to do was endure until the West realised that the occupation of central Europe by the Red Army was unacceptable. Many individuals even predicted a Third World War which would push the Soviet occupiers out of central Europe, freeing their Polish homeland. In fact, when the Korean War erupted in 1950, many believed that it was the beginning of the end of their exile but, when stalemate was reached on the Korean peninsula, they soon realised that their stay in the West would be longer than they had predicted and they had better get on with integration.

Two types of Polish families lived in the families' camps; those who had been reunited on arrival in Britain and those established in Britain after the war. Family members[1] and dependants[2] of reunited families would have spent the war in British safe-havens such as those in southern Rhodesia (now Zimbabwe), Mozambique and India.[3] On arrival, they were registered under the 1920 Aliens Act pending reunion with their menfolk (Polish soldiers displaced to this country). The diaspora was considered to be 'stateless' as their Polish citizenship had been taken away from them by the communist regime in Warsaw for not repatriating. This meant that their only option, if they wanted to gain citizenship, was to become naturalised in Britain. Polish children born in this country, on the other hand, were given British citizenship automatically on the strength of being born in the

---

1 Members of the nuclear family.
2 Members of the extended family.
3 British safe-havens were set up for Polish civilians who were outside of Poland whose menfolk were in the Polish Army under British command.

United Kingdom. Data from the National Statistical Office shows that the number of Polish individuals seeking naturalisation increased significantly in the late 1960s, when travel abroad became an option and passports were required. This even allowed some to travel behind the Iron Curtain to visit their long lost family members still living in Poland. According to Jeżewski,[4] approximately six percent of the Poles had obtained naturalisation in 1951 which increased to 11 percent by 1955. In the event that an individual wished to travel before naturalisation, a British travel document could be issued but it did not provide the traveller with the protection of Britain's diplomatic or consular representatives abroad.

When a couple arrived at a families' camp, they were met by the Assistance Board's warden and taken to their accommodation. They had little choice, as space was scarce. The accommodation would have been prepared for them and furnished with utility furniture which had been manufactured during the austerity years of the war. The furniture provided for the community was renewed with a fresh coat of varnish and, where appropriate, a set of decorative handles. The War Office insisted that the accommodation made available for the Poles was to be markedly superior to that used for POWs during the war. Although many of the dwellings were of crude construction, they were nevertheless perfectly serviceable and comfortable.

As in the wider community, the principle of 'make do and mend' also applied to Polish families but they were also issued with food coupons and clothing tokens. Special clothes, such as for weddings and christenings, were usually made from remnant material skilfully sewn by a member of the community with tailoring skills. Otherwise, they were bought after a period of saving. The same was true of children's clothes. If the accommodation became drab, it was refreshed with paint and pictures on the wall.

Invariably, a small garden would have been created near the dwellings occupied by the Poles, where vegetable growing and limited livestock rearing could be undertaken. Many individuals kept chickens and geese which provided them with fresh eggs and poultry meat as well as down feathers for pillows and duvets. Much of the food eaten by the families would have been grown in these gardens; however, specialist food, such as ice cream or bread and butter, was bought from the nearest village shop or from the local greengrocer who delivered to the estates on a daily basis. If the camp stood near woodland, families would also forage for mushrooms. The Poles were very adept at finding edible varieties and could spot fruiting bodies growing in the ground at some distance. After drying, mushrooms were used to season dishes and soups. Some items, such as women's stockings, books and make–up were sometimes bought from a door-to-door salesman who would turn up with a suitcase full of goods. Of course the Poles were unaware that these transactions probably contributed to the black market.

Children born to ex-members of the PRC before the inauguration of the National Health Service (NHS) were delivered in Polish military hospitals run by the War Office, such as the one at Diddington Camp in Cambridgeshire. These hospitals were staffed by Polish personnel who had previously served in the Polish Army during the war and were recruited into the Polish Resettlement Corps alongside the troops. After the establishment of the National Health Service (NHS), children were delivered in local public hospitals under the authority of the Resettlement Act 1947. The inauguration of the NHS often saved Polish women from travelling long distances to the nearest military hospital during

---

4 B. Jeżewski, *Rocznik Polonii Zagranicznej*, 1953, p.17.

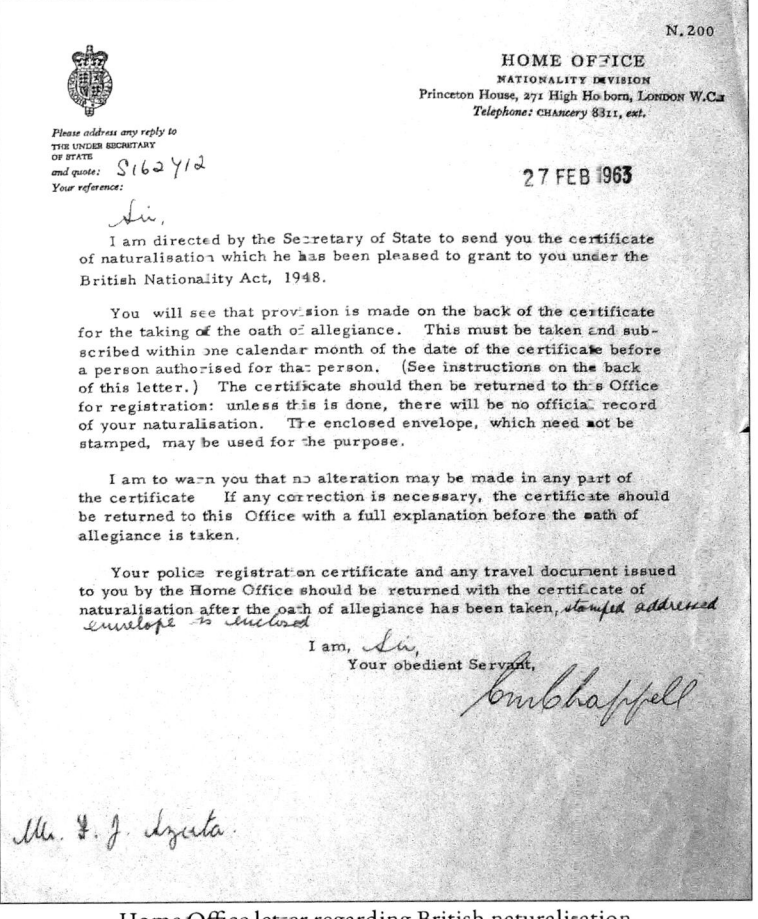

Home Office letter regarding British naturalisation.

pregnancy, which was invariably located some distance from their homes.

Much time in the camps was spent in controlling the spread of infectious diseases with disinfectants and liquefied DDT[5] (trade name FLIT). Fumigation operations saw wives spraying chemicals under beds, in corners of rooms and over curtains until this activity ceased when these products were banned for being too dangerous. 'Aspro', the trade name of aspirin, was commonly used to control pain, fever and inflammation. After the start of the NHS, the communities were provided with a doctor and district nurses.

Polish children entered the school system just like any other child in the country. Invariably they were at a distinct disadvantage in class because of their poor grasp of the English language. No Polish child spoke English at home, unless they lived in a mixed family, and were, therefore, some four years behind in their language development compared to their British classmates. Education authorities distributed Polish children amongst schools in their area so that no one institution would be overburdened with a large influx of pupils

---

5   Dichlorodiphenyltrichloroethane.

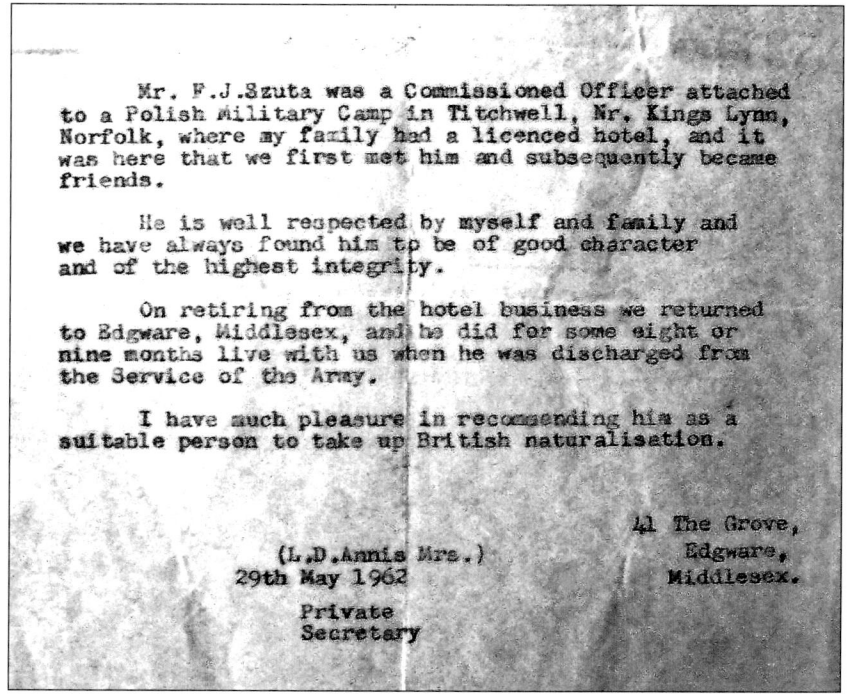

Character reference for naturalisation applicant.

with language difficulties. Some education authorities employed retired primary school teachers to provide remedial language classes, although this usually occurred in schools which were in bigger towns. Learning the English language started in earnest when children entered the British school system at five years of age. Usually, Polish children did well in subjects such as mathematics, art, physical education and crafts where language skills were not so important. Formal schooling usually began in pre-school nurseries in hostels staffed by Polish teachers who had qualified in Poland before the war. The curriculum was delivered in the Polish language and included subjects rarely related to British history and culture which did little to help with integration and assimilation.

Very few families in the camps/hostels possessed a television and those who did were often joined by others to view programmes. The transmission of the Coronation of Elizabeth II was well attended, probably more from curiosity than any deep patriotic feelings. However, radios were common although transmissions in the Polish language were scarce. Some listened to Radio Free Europe and Vatican City broadcasts in the Polish language. No Polish language transmissions from communist Poland were sought and, in any case, they were often blocked by the West during the Cold War. There was also a lack of printed material in the camps. Any that did exist was usually published by the Polish Catholic Mission of Great Britain and covered religious and social topics.[6] Hard news was usually found in the Polish *Daily Newspaper*,[7] published in London. The newspaper was first published in 1940 and was amalgamated with the *Soldiers Daily* in 1944, which was

---

6   For example, *Gazeta Niedzielna*.
7   *Dziennik Polski*.

Naturalisation Certificate: naturalisation was sought when travel abroad was contemplated and a British passport was required.

produced in Scotland during the war for Polish troops stationed there. Perhaps the more important events for families in the camps were the collective activities which involved the whole community. Most communities established drama groups, sports clubs and choirs in their hostels and it was not surprising that they were well attended as there was a feeling of reassurance in numbers. Performances in the hostels' theatres celebrated religious and national events in the Polish calendar and were the staple diet of presentations at the time.

As the Polish communities in the resettlement programme were predominantly of military origin, it was perhaps inevitable that they would establish ex-combatant associations. As these associations sprang up spontaneously as grass root initiatives, a regional coordinating authority was not established until later. However, as soon it was realised that some kind of overarching management structure was required for these groups, the national Polish ex-Combatant Association (SPK) was established which was based in London. Other national organisations were formed to serve the diaspora such as the Union of Polish Craftsman and Workers Association, the Polish Theatrical Bureau and the Polish University Abroad (PUNO). As the child population grew, both in size and age, Polish Saturday Schools were established, as were youth clubs and scout groups. This development saw the young being schooled in the British tradition during weekdays and the Polish tradition at the weekend,

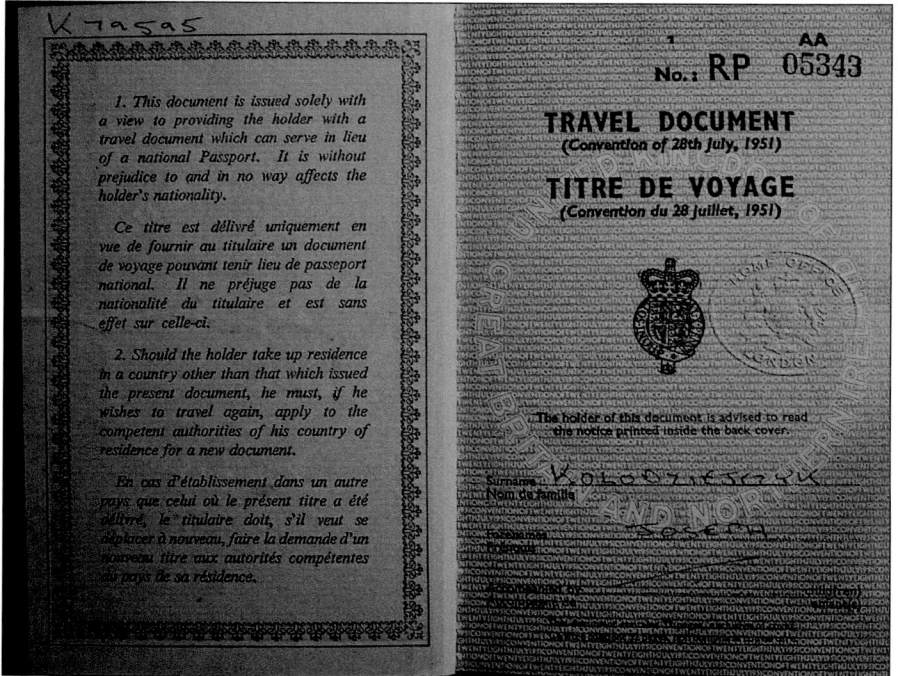

Travel Documents were issued by the Home Office for 'Alien' individuals who had not yet obtained naturalisation, but needed to travel abroad. The holders could travel to countries other than Poland, although without the protection of British diplomatic or consular services.

resulting in what might be called 'cultural hybridisation'. This allowed children to choose the best from both traditions and prosper. It also resulted in many children understanding the British way of life far better than their parents ever did, which resulted in youngsters filling in official forms and translating official letters for them.

Many of the barracks and Nissen huts in camps possessed a basic level of insulation, and so temperatures fluctuated wildly. In the summer they were very hot whilst in winter time they were extremely cold. Heating in the barracks was provided using coal-burning stoves erected during the building phase, or from portable Valor paraffin burners brought in by the Assistance Board. If the barracks were not supplied with running water, inhabitants were obliged to fill a bucket using a standpipe in the camp and bringing it inside for use. Ablutions often took place in the camp's communal shower and bathing facilities, originally built for the military. Many comprised of rows of cast iron baths and showers with wooden duckboards. Privacy was achieved using heavy tarpaulin curtains slung from a sturdy frame. As with the washing facility, laundry was carried out in a centralised complex comprising large earthenware sinks and hot running water. Drying rooms were also available but labour-saving devices, such as washboards and mangles, were rare. Lavatories were situated in latrines which may have stood some distance from the barracks and so, during the dark nights of winter, people would have to trek to toilets in total darkness following a single beam of light from their handheld torch.

Cultural life in the resettlement camps revolved around the community centre and the chapel. The community centre (*świetlica*) was usually located in what would have been the NAFFI and was furnished with easy chairs, a piano and a bar. Invariably, the walls were adorned with pictures of important Polish national figures such as Marshal Piłsudski and General Anders, although pride of place would be reserved for the emblem of the homeland, a Polish Eagle displayed on a red background.

Although communities in the resettlement camps were transitory, they were stable enough to allow for the establishment of close friendships, some lasting well beyond the camp system. Friendship was not only a way of finding some security in an 'alien landscape' but provided a way of sharing thoughts and plans for the future. The displaced diaspora faced many difficulties and important questions that needed answering. For example, where to settle after leaving the hostels, where to find new employment to replace the work provided through the Polish Resettlement Corps and how to secure a permanent home for the family. These decisions were taken without any deep understanding of the options or opportunities available and invariably such choices were nothing more than a leap in the dark. The demolition of barracks occurred as soon as families left, a policy employed to prevent squatters moving in. The pace of dismantling the camps/hostels was determined by the rate of departures which could condemn those remaining to live in partially demolished estates.

32

Triumph and Tragedy

The formation of the Polish Resettlement Corps in 1946 was at the same time a triumph and a tragedy. It was a triumph because Britain, in deep post-war austerity, managed with engineering precision to relocate and demobilise some 150,000 Polish troops and resettle them with their dependants in the United Kingdom.

The whole endeavour, which was costly, politically sensitive and based on the premise that progress could only be maintained if action was based on process, was completed by September 1949. Polish soldiers, airmen and seamen had to be strongly but sensitively encouraged to enlist in the Polish Resettlement Corps as enlistment could have easily been seen as a metaphor for national humiliation and Allied betrayal. Consequently, the War Office, not wanting the 'Polish problem' to fester any longer, went on a charm offensive, arguing that the future of the men lay in the Resettlement Corps where a fresh start in Britain awaited. In the final analysis the success of the resettlement programme was impressive, for once in the country no Polish serviceman or woman lived in destitution, hunger or abandonment. The War Office went out of its way to encourage successful assimilation first, by providing individuals of varying rank, age and ability with training followed by employment. However, the resettlement of a foreign army, albeit an allied one, required British authorities to manipulate public opinion in such a way as to prevent the emergence of anti-Polish feeling. Many people at the time had failed to grasp the necessity and justification for resettling the Poles in the country, which resulted in the misguided chatter that the Poles had turned their backs on their own homeland only to exploit Britain's economic opportunities, and to take unfair advantage of the British people's welcoming attitude towards the displaced. Whenever the Government was challenged about its motives, it energetically defended itself with clarification and explanation. Thankfully for the government and, indeed, the displaced Poles, public opinion eventually grew to understand the situation concerning the political difficulties in eastern Europe, allowing some to find enough courage to accept their new Polish neighbours. The resettlement programme was also a great success on a humanitarian level, for it offered a group of displaced people a fresh opportunity to distil their feelings and redeem their lives; an opportunity which was eventually grasped with both hands. The resettlement programme was also a triumph at diplomatic level, for the successful demobilisation of Polish Allied Forces under British command successfully diffused the rows brewing over the Yalta Conference and the apparent injustices committed on the Poles in 1945.

While the establishment of the Polish Resettlement Corps can be described as a remarkable triumph, it can also be seen, particularly by friends of Poland, as a sad and tragic episode. In the light of the rubric of the Atlantic Charter and Britain's stated war aims, the Poles should have been furnished with the freedom to choose the kind of government they wanted to live under and to return to a free homeland; after all these were the absolutes they had been fighting for throughout the war. So it should not be a surprise that, while London rejoiced at the end of conflict in Europe with the tolling of church bells, street

Ex-member of the Polish Resettlement Corps settles down to family life in Britain.

parties, triumphant back slapping, dancing in the squares and royal waves from the balcony of Buckingham Palace, Poles in the West sulked and brooded. Not only did the Polish political and military elite fail to secure their country's integrity and esteem, but the country's Allies had allowed the promises made to them in binding agreements to be forgotten and discarded. To many members in Polish Forces under British command, the Polish Resettlement Corps could have been no more than a metaphor for failure and betrayal. No wonder feelings of despondency and disbelief stalked the Resettlement Camps where victory for the Poles was a bitter sweet conclusion to the war. Rarely in history had an army slogged its way around so many bloody battlefields, achieved victory and then felt unable to return home. Furthermore, it was unprecedented in history for one ally to annexe the territory of another and then claim to have the right to impose its own political will on the people. This is exactly what the Soviet Union was doing to Poland in 1945. These were the realities that faced the Polish soldier under British command at the end of the war. It would be interesting to consider what the British would have done in similar circumstances.

Perversely, the more the Poles protested about their perceived betrayal, the more vulnerable they became. It was a turbulent and bewildering backdrop to the life changing decisions the Poles were facing at the time; whether to stay in exile or return to a Soviet-dominated homeland, the very regime which five years earlier had arrested and tormented them? The decision was agonising, for although Britain promised the Poles bread and water, Poland gave them a mother and father. Who was to help them in this dilemma now that trust in leaders, who had failed so utterly during the War, was at such low ebb? Of course British authorities understood these issues so proceeded cautiously and carefully attempted to speed up social integration where certainty was readily available.

The objective of members of the Corps was to enter British society as confident, independent and self-assured individuals. This was a tall order, for it necessitated the rebuilding of self-esteem and self-assurance in the unfamiliar context of exile. It is not surprising that different people took varying amounts of time to make decisions about their future plans, resulting in a stuttered and staggered exodus from the camp system. The first task of resettlement was to construct a new and viable personal identity in an alien context which could not be done by simply forgetting the past, but by editing memories and concentrating on the future. This required dismantling their Polish identity established during childhood in Poland, and rebuilding it using Polish elements in conjunction with British components. However, during the early stages of resettlement, where ignorance of British culture was at its highest, this was well nigh impossible to do, and so initially identity was based on collective experience in the Second World War. During this time, Polishness, the Catholic Church and ex-combatant associations proved vital. For example, events in the Christian calendar were enthusiastically celebrated according to Polish traditions. During Corpus Christi, for example, the community built open air field altars just as they had done in the army. These served as focal points for prayer during a procession. Each altar had its own theme and character, and was dedicated to a particular Polish Saint or holy event in the Catholic calendar such as the Blessed Virgin Mary, Queen of Poland, or Saint Stanisław, the country's patron saint. During worship, appeals were made to the saints to help in freeing the homeland and facilitating a return home. Also Christmas was celebrated on 6 December, St. Nicholas' Day when presents were distributed – the norm in parts of mainland Europe – and continued with an evening vigil meal on 24 December. According to tradition, the vigil meal started when the first star appeared in the heavens and consisted of 12 dishes in honour of the 12 disciples. Easter was also celebrated in the Polish way where food to be eaten on Easter Sunday was first blessed on Easter Saturday in the Resettlement Camp's Chapel. During such celebrations, children were dressed in national costumes and Polish songs and dances were enjoyed. The communities were also spiritually affiliated to local English parishes where marriages, baptisms and First Holy Communions were entered in Parish records.

What is being described here, of course, is the building of identity on nostalgia which is a typical human response to turbulent and uncertain times. As with every exiled group, the displaced Polish soldiers desperately clung onto their heritage, particularly during the early stages of resettlement. However, building identity solely on nostalgic memory has its limitations, for such memories are not mere recollections but often reinterpretations of the past with little relevance to reality. Memories of pre-war Poland in people's minds were often romanticised, glamorised and, above all, individualised. Eventually, using the past to build identity had to be superseded by issues related to the present and personal goals relevant to surviving in Britain. This subtle change in motivation (which had to take place if assimilation was to be successful) occurred as confidence and understanding of the host community improved; however, the consequence of re-examining cultural reference points pulled the diaspora in two directions and saw those who were unprepared to dilute their Polish identity almost completely at one end of a continuum, and those resisting any dilution at all at the other. Those who were prepared to relinquish their Polish identity emphasised their Englishness energetically, although the anglicisation of surnames was rare. The desire to pursue personal goals saw the desire to exit the camp system grow. There were two psychological forces acting on the inhabitants of the resettlement camps; the push of authorities reminding the Poles that the camps were a temporary arrangement and the pull of various attractive opportunities prevalent in the wider community. Gradually, the

As the Poles grew in confidence in their new homes, and resources were accumulating, they started their own institutions and cultural centres. This is the front of Polish Cultural Institute in London. It was built using donations, bequeaths, and gifts.

haemorrhaging of individuals departing the resettlement camps and hostels meant that it became difficult to consider those left behind as a community. People left in search of work and a permanent home for their continued existence which invariably meant finding homes near existing Polish Catholic parishes. It was perhaps inevitable that Polish individuals, given the freedom to decide where to live, would choose to live amongst their own kind and saw Polish parishes grow into substantial communities. Children were also growing up and their education and future employment needed consideration. The necessity to educate children, and to assess where they stood the best chance of finding good work, convinced many Polish families that their future existed outside the camp system. The Polish exodus from the camps and hostels was the second and final evacuation of these wartime bases, allowing them to be finally dismantled and demolished.

We have already seen how the Resettlement Camps, in which the Poles were temporarily housed on their arrival, provided for physiological needs, offering shelter, warmth and security. However, these camps also served on the psychological and emotional level, often becoming a surrogate nation for a disorientated people dispirited by the betrayal of moral absolutes such as loyalty and honour. All had accepted exile without really knowing what this meant in a British context, and so the Polish Resettlement Corps provided them with a way of making sense of their new existence. They had to recalibrate their lives where things they had taken for granted had lost their innocence, and questions such as, 'How should I live now?' and 'What is the point of my life?' required answers. They also knew that they would be unable to make any further contribution to their own nation, something that disappointed them greatly. However, the pace of assimilation into British society was not only determined by the gallant provisions of the resettlement programme but by the age and personality of the Poles themselves. Research confirms that younger members of the displaced Polish forces were some of the first to realise, and take advantage of, the opportunities available in the host community. However, it is also the case that the response to exile is mediated by personality and temperament. For example, much depended on whether the person was extravert, agreeable, neurotic or open. A neurotic individual was more likely to be anxious about dealing with displacement, and therefore more vulnerable to hesitation and even mental illness which ended with suicide whilst, if neuroticism was mild, the individual would be calmer and therefore more able to cope with the challenges of resettlement. Also an open personality tends to be creative and imaginative which placed such an individual in a good position to manage uncertainty – a positive trait in exile. The timid and reserved, on the other hand, took longer to reflect on their future and were some of the last to leave the security of their resettlement camps.

The Polish diaspora, invited to Britain between 1946 and 1949 as a result of the war, was primarily a military settlement founded on common experience in the Second World War. It was, therefore, perhaps inevitable that it would establish self-help groups based on the camp system and ex-combatant associations. For example, the Polish Airforce Association was formed in July 1945 and the Polish ex-Combatant Association (SPK)[1] in 1946. The SPK grew to be the second largest veterans' association in Britain after the Royal British Legion. The national (later international) Association continues providing welfare, cultural and social support for ex-members of the Polish Resettlement Corps to this very day. Initially, the structure of the Association was based on local organisations but, when the camp system was dismantled, its structure was altered to reflect geographical districts where centres of civilian Poles had emerged. Twelve districts were identified, such as those in Glasgow, Manchester, Sheffield, Bedford and London. In December 1962, Her Majesty's Government provided the Association with an annual grant to enable it to pursue its mission statement: this included solving the problems associated with the future of the Polish Armed Forces in the West, counteracting communist propaganda and defining the role of the Polish Resettlement Corps from the Polish perspective. Between 1963 and 1973, the Association received £845,000 which allowed for 3,000 veterans to be supported, some on a permanent basis. Eventually, the Association extended its operations to cover the Polish Saturday School System, parish choirs, music ensembles, traditional dance troupes and sports clubs (see below).

Tables 30–1 to 30–12 SPK Branches in 2000 – brackets denote number of members in 1995, 'CH' denotes whether the branch had a Club House. All tables adapted from *'The Polish Ex-Combatant Association in Great Britain 1946–2003'*, author Dr Andrzej Suchcitz.

Tables 30–1: SPK Branches in 2000 – Region 1	
Branch Number	
179	Blackpool (22)
180	Preston (90) CH

1　*Stowarzyszenie Polskich Kombatantów.*

TRIUMPH AND TRAGEDY

183	Blackburn (132) CH
251	Chorley (52) CH
268	Liverpool (21)
488	Lancaster (48)

Table 30–2: SPK Branches in 2000 – Region 2	
Branch Number	
413	Leeds (110)
416	Keighley (46)
417	Halifax (41) CH
440	Huddersfield (102) CH
451	Bradford (300) CH

Table 30–3: SPK Branches in 2000 – Region 3	
Branch Number	
181	Manchester (350) CH
189	Todmorden (10) CH
201	Northwich (26)
220	Penrhos (48)
231	Ashton-under-Lyne (18)
232	Oldham (42) CH
240	Rochdale (37) CH
246	Bury (39)
270	Merseyside (65)
469	Wrexham/Penley (55)
479	Crewe (58)

Table 30–4: SPK Branches in 2000 – Region 4

Branch Number	
415	Chesterfield (40) CH
418	Lincoln (77) CH
439	Sheffield (315) CH
441	Doncaster (35)
445	Rotherham (27)
499	Scunthorpe (81) CH

Table 30–5: SPK Branches in 2000 – Region 5

Branch Number	
382	Loughborough (44)
407	Mansfield (70) CH
431	Leicester (116) CH
432	Derby (140)
465	Nottingham (105)

Table 30–6: SPK Branches in 2000 – Region 6

Branch Number	
182	Telford (35)
215	Kidderminster (97) CH
225	Birmingham (180)
236	Worcester (64) CH
239	Wolverhampton (101)
242	Stafford (72)
252	Stoke-on-Trent (60)
301	Rugby (56) CH
399	Coventry (58) CH

Table 30-7: SPK Branches in 2000 – Region 7

Branch Number	
108	Ipswich (53)
274	Peterborough (120) CH
293	Wellingborough (32) CH
296	Cambridge (56)
302	Bedford (63)
319	Witham (22)
364	Luton (335) CH

Table 30-9: SPK Branches in 2000 – Region 9

Branch Number	
340	Cheltenham (50)
342	Bristol (158) CH
365	Bridgwater (18) CH
378	Dursley (27)
380	Trowbridge (48)
475	Cardiff (67)

Table 30-10: SPK Branches in 2000 – Region 10

Branch Number	
115	Amersham (78) CH
192	Slough (111)
200	Aylesbury (22)
286	High Wycombe (71)
334	Swindon (204) CH
344	Oxford (71) CH
386	Reading (94)

Table 30-11: SPK Branches in 2000 – Region 11

Branch Number	
25	Edinburgh (117) CH
27	Aberdeen (34)
28	Perth (52) CH
36	Falkirk (168) CH
50	Kirkcaldy (200) CH
60	Dundee (50) CH
105	Glasgow (148) CH

Table 30-12:.SPK Branches in 2000 – Region 12

Branch Number	
4	London, Ealing (93)
11	London Central (136)
30	London (80)
106	London Provost (45)
107	Godalming/Horsham (56)
112	London, Enfield (33)
113	Paratrooper and 1st Armoured Division (122)
114	London (Scouts) (25)
118	London Hove (54)
123	London South (199)
309	Southampton (50)
316	London (Women's Service) (40)

Today, many of the ex-members of the Polish Resettlement Corps have been laid to rest in British soil. They did not return to Poland, even when their country had finally obtained independence and freedom in the late 1980s, some 40 years after the end of the war. For many of them who were still alive, it was too late to return for their identity had grown to be deeply rooted and reshaped by Britain's culture. Many of these veterans had lived in Britain far longer than in Poland but, nevertheless, they continued to consider themselves as Poles in exile rather than British citizens of Polish extraction.

Epilogue

The establishment of the Polish Resettlement Corps, which became the tipping point for the future lives of Polish soldiers, was a temporary expedient designed to solve the problems caused by Polish forces under British command after refusing to stand down on account of the decisions taken at the Teheran and Yalta Conferences. For the men in these forces, the placing of their country firmly behind the Iron Curtain in 1945 was a political and military betrayal. They were dismayed by the fact that it was not their enemies who had rendered them stateless, but their allies. The intransigent Poles, as British authorities eventually came to call them, had to be disposed of in order to prevent them from becoming an unwelcome beacon of Polish protest. However, two questions remained: firstly, could anything have been done differently, rather than resettle these forces in Britain; and secondly, could the resettlement programme have been improved?

From government records it appears that the options open to British authorities regarding the protesting Polish Allied Forces were limited. Perhaps the most obvious solution would have been to *force* the Poles to stand down and return home – after all they were under British operational command. This course of action was not pursued as it would probably have meant some form of military coercion, which would have been unsightly and therefore unacceptable to London. Moreover, the episode concerning the repatriation[1] of the XV SS Cossack Cavalry Corps to the Soviet Union in May 1945 had embarrassed the British government and precipitated a torrent of disapproval. The British had forcibly herded the Cossacks across the Russian zonal border in Germany where they were immediately executed by the Red Army.[2] This British operation was later considered to be one of the darkest stains on the country's wartime history.[3] Following this unsavoury event, the British felt they could not risk further damage to Britain's reputation and so settled on persuading the Poles to accept their invitation. The initial attempt to dispose of the Poles through repatriation, paid for by His Majesty's Government, and provide generous gratuity payments for service with the Allies did not work. The communist authorities in Warsaw decided not to accept these Polish soldiers, fearing that the arrival of such a large anti-communist contingent would destabilise the fledgling regime in the Polish capital. Subsequently, London was informed that Polish forces under British command were no longer considered to be Polish formations, so Warsaw signalled that it would not concern itself with their demobilisation any more. In any case, it soon became clear that Polish soldiers would not accept living in a homeland under Soviet domination, the very regime that had arrested and tormented them in 1940. The second attempt to dispose of the Poles was to pay for their emigration to countries other than Poland and Britain. Support was sought from both Commonwealth and Roman Catholic countries, but problems soon materialised when Australia and Canada announced that they were only interested in young, single, healthy individuals suited for general labour, and New Zealand only wanted Polish orphans. However, a sizeable number eventually settled in South America.

---

1 Operation Keelhaul.
2 David Stafford, Endgame 1945, Little Brown Books, 2007 London, p.431.
3 Williams, *Harold Macmillan*, Phoenix Publishers 2009, p.173.

Plaque at 51 New Cavendish Road, London.

Sign outside the Polish Social and Cultural Association, Hammersmith, London.

Another option could have been to push the Red Army back into the Soviet Union using further military action, and so open the road for Polish repatriation to an independent Poland. This option, although seriously considered by Churchill in 1945, was soon rejected when America explained that her forces were still embroiled in war with Japan where Soviet help might still be needed, especially if the Manhattan Project failed. Alternatively, the peace conferences could have been postponed until all the fighting had stopped, which would have strengthened Churchill's hand during negotiations with Stalin. There were two reasons why decisions on post-war Europe were taken so quickly, even before the end of the war in the Far East. Firstly, the Americans feared that the power vacuum, which was certain to develop on Germany's surrender, would be filled by the Russians; and, secondly, that the Red Army might continue its advance into Western Europe if not checked by a formal agreement. As 'political space' appeared in central Europe, the Americans moved rapidly to occupy it using speedy negotiations on where the geopolitical demarcation lines should be set. In a desperate attempt to reach an agreement with Moscow, Western Allies were even prepared to compromise on a number of their primary war aims, such as the independence of Poland and other European countries. It seems that Britain, having a Pact of Mutual Assistance with pre-war Poland, had no other option but to resettle the Poles in the United Kingdom. The Resettlement Programme was a creative initiative, unprecedented in Britain's history, for it

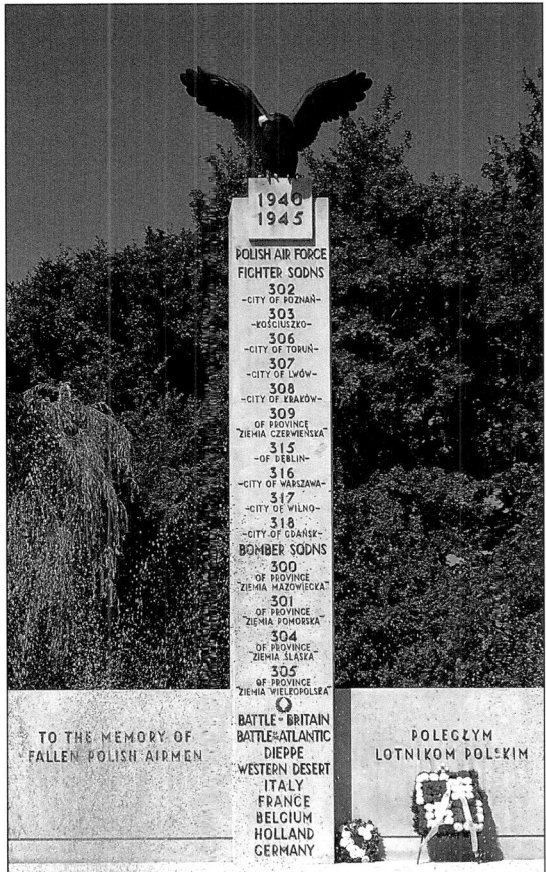
Monument to the Polish Airforce, London.

allowed a foreign sovereign army to be demobilised on British soil for the first time.

On the question of whether things could have been done differently in the resettlement programme, it is true that not all had gone well with the initiative. For example, preparing the Poles for a life in exile through the provision of training, education and employment, soon became problematic. This is because trade union and professional bodies, as well as the British public, were not convinced that the resettlement programme was an unavoidable national necessity. Also, reports from the training centres employed in the Training Programme suggested that some of the study courses were underfunded and used out of date teaching material and equipment. Such situations militated against meaningful training and had, as a result, significant implications for the employability of the displaced Poles. However, despite such difficulties, government agencies successfully managed to place the majority of Poles into work – something which has to be acknowledged and lauded.

The process of integrating and assimilating Poles into Britain also proved to be far more complex than at first envisaged, and it is a moot point whether true integration had ever taken place. Attitudes, together with human emotions, are very resistant to change, even when it seems to be the most rational thing to do. The situation was probably exacerbated

Part of the remembrance Wall in London dedicated to the
Polish Airmen who fought in the Battle of Britain.

Plaque on the Rubens Hotel, London.

Rubens Hotel, London Headquarters of General Sikorski during the Second World War.

by the government's failure to explain effectively the reasons behind the resettlement programme, presumably fearing a public backlash against the policy On the other hand, if the British Government had been more forthcoming in providing information regarding the resettlement programme, perhaps it could have prevented the spread of prejudice and objections being voiced against it. Integration was also compromised by the decision to accommodate Poles in small, isolated enclaves throughout the country in an attempt to prevent the emergence of Polish ghettos.

Encouraging the Poles to assimilate into British society, whilst urging the British to be receptive to their new neighbours, was so difficult that success in this area was very elusive. Assimilation is more than merely mimicking the host culture, and just because a Polish veteran went to have a pint at the local pub did not necessarily mean that he was successfully accepted by the host community. Assimilation also required Poles to sacrifice part of their Polish identity, modifying it using British cultural components, which many were loathe to do – either fearing being called a traitor to the cause by their compatriots, or believing that such a recalibration was a step too far, especially when feelings of loss and fear predominated.

Another important question is whether the establishment of Polish organisations, such as the Polish Cultural Institute and the Polish Airforce Association helped the process of

They did not return to Poland even when their country had finally obtained independence and freedom in the late 1980s, some forty years after the end of the War. For many of them it was too late to return, since their personal identity had grown to be deeply rooted and reshaped by Britain's culture. Many of these veterans had lived in Britain for much longer than in Poland; nevertheless, they continued to consider themselves as Poles in exile rather than British citizens of Polish extraction. This is a general view of the cemetery at Gunnersbury showing the graves of ex-Polish Resettlement Corps personnel.

assimilation, or contributed to continued division.

The British government certainly found itself on the horns of a dilemma for, whilst wanting to demonstrate its respect for the Poles and their war effort, at the same time it wanted them to discard their pre-war identities and integrate. Perhaps the National Assistance Board, who took over the management of the resettlement camps after demobilisation, could have organised social events where the two communities had a chance to mix and get to know each other better; something which would certainly have helped the process of Polish assimilation. Familiarity breeds understanding and hopefully acceptance. Some unfortunate mistakes were made by the government which, if avoided, could have helped the situation. One mistake was its failure to invite the Polish forces to take part in the Victory Parade in London during June 1946.[4] Not only was this decision taken by the Poles as the true reflection of Britain's attitude towards them, but it also made them feel like second class citizens, especially when all other allied formations, including the Soviet Union's, were represented at the event. However, perhaps the construction up and down the country of war memorials dedicated to the Polish forces goes some way in correcting the

---

4   Nanke, *Cena Bycia Innym*, p.202.

political errors committed by the British. However, not everything was a disaster; the way British authorities dealt with ill, infirm or unstable Polish personnel was very commendable. Every effort was made to ensure that their special requirements were satisfactorily catered for.

It is easy to criticize in hindsight, but it has to be acknowledged that, despite some of the most challenging conditions prevailing in post-war Britain, the Polish Resettlement Corps 1946–1949, was a success on so many levels. Above all, it gave the displaced, dispossessed and psychologically shattered salvation and peace and, perhaps most importantly, human dignity. On this score, Britain did not let her ally down, and saw her discharging her responsibility to these men in an honourable way.

Bibliography

Government Documents

The National Archives of the UK (TNA): AST 18, Assistance Board and successors: Polish Resettlement, Registered Files (PR and PLH Series).

The National Archives of the UK (TNA): AST 18/43, Women and children resident in maternity units in Polish Hostels: claims against Ministry of Health for maintenance.

The National Archives of the UK (TNA): AST 18/101, Assistance Board and successors: Files dealing with problems arising out of the administration of the Polish Resettlement Act 1947 by the Assistance Board, the National Assistance Board and the Supplementary Benefits Commission.

The National Archives of the UK (TNA): AST 18/115, Admission of refugee Poles from East Africa.

The National Archives of the UK (TNA): AST 18 ref: PRO 57/703, National Service Hostels Corporation: files and papers.

The National Archives of the UK (TNA): FO 371/56513, Resettlement of members of the Polish Armed Forces in the United Kingdom, Code 55, File 308 (papers 7827–8384), 1946.

The National Archives of the UK (TNA): HO 213/1235, Recalcitrant Poles: use of deportation orders, 1947–1948.

The National Archives of the UK (TNA): KV 4/286, Polish Resettlement Corps, Policy for the absorption and control of Polish Forces in the UK, 1946 Jan 01–1946 Dec 31.

The National Archives of the UK (TNA): MH 76/645, Health Service.

The National Archives of the UK (TNA): OF 91, Emigration Policy.

The National Archives of the UK (TNA): T 236/1369, Employment Policy, 1946–1948.

The National Archives of the UK (TNA): T 236/1370, Polish Resettlement, 1950.

The National Archives of the UK (TNA): WO 315/13, Polish military hospitals, 1947–1948.

The National Archives of the UK (TNA): WO 315/4, Cipher telegrams October–November 1945 Repatriation to Poland.

The National Archives of the UK (TNA): WO 315/9, Polish Resettlement Section, Polish Resettlement Corps.

The National Archives of the UK (TNA): WO 315/14, Medical officers, pharmacists, dentists, and field ambulance officers who served in Polish Land Forces and Polish Resettlement Corps 1940-1949.

The National Archives of the UK (TNA): WO 315/18/11, Polish Military Mission in France.

The National Archives of the UK (TNA): WO 315/28, The 'Carrot Scheme' PRC Officers, Appointments and Nominal Roles.

The National Archives of the UK (TNA): WO 315/29, PRC, Enlistment, Employment.

The National Archives of the UK (TNA): WO 315/30, PRC, Unemployment, Discharge, Disbandment.

The National Archives of the UK (TNA): WO 315/31, Disbandment of PRC (Polish Resettlement Corps): reports and statistics.

The National Archives of the UK (TNA): WO 315/33, PRC Officers.

The National Archives of the UK (TNA): WO 315/34, PRC, Aftermath Liaison Section.
The National Archives of the UK (TNA): WO 315/35, PRC, Aftermath Liaison Section.
The National Archives of the UK (TNA): WO 315/36, Polish Forces Official Committee.
The National Archives of the UK (TNA): WO 315/37, Polish Forces Official Committee.
The National Archives of the UK (TNA): WO 315/38, Information Bulletins, Political Information Bulletins.
The National Archives of the UK (TNA): WO 315/39, Medals.
The National Archives of the UK (TNA): WO 315/40, Home Army, ex POWs.
The National Archives of the UK (TNA): WO 315/41, Polish Soldiers' Assistance Fund.
The National Archives of the UK (TNA) WO 315/42, Transfer and Disposal of PRC Funds.
The National Archives of the UK (TNA) WO 315/43, Transfer and Disposal of PRC Funds.
The National Archives of the UK (TNA): WO 315/44, Deceased and Missing Personnel.
The National Archives of the UK (TNA): WO315/45, Employment of Civilians Refugees and Military Families.
The National Archives of the UK (TNA): WO 315/46, Civilian Camps in Italy, Evacuation from USSR.
The National Archives of the UK (TNA): WO 315/47, Polish Land Forces, Legal Matters.
The National Archives of the UK (TNA): WO 315/48, PRC, Legal Matters.
The National Archives of the UK (TNA): WO 315/49, Laying Up of Colours.
The National Archives of the UK (TNA): WO 315/50, Policy statements, messages, telegrams, minutes of meetings.
The National Archives of the UK (TNA): WO 315/52, Repatriation, Emigration Enlistments.
The National Archives of the UK (TNA): WO 315/53, Polish Institutions in the UK and Middle East.
The National Archives of the UK (TNA): WO 315/54, Anglo-Polish Agreement Concerning Credit.
The National Archives of the UK (TNA): WO 315/55, Finance.
The National Archives of the UK (TNA): WO 315/56, War Gratuities, Release Benefits, Compensation.
The National Archives of the UK (TNA): WO 315/61, Historical Background.
The National Archives of the UK (TNA): WO 315/62, Historical Background.
The National Archives of the UK (TNA): WO 315/63, Anglo-Polish Agreement, VIP Letters.
The National Archives of the UK (TNA): WO 315/64, Polish Army in USSR.
The National Archives of the UK (TNA): WO 315/67, PRC Disbandment, Rules, Leaflets.
The National Archives of the UK (TNA): WO 315/70, Procedure for Relegation.
The National Archives of the UK (TNA): WO 315/71, Documentations for the Relinquishing Commission.
The National Archives of the UK (TNA): WO 315/20, Polish Auxiliary Territorial Service, Polish Nursing Service.
The National Archives of the UK (TNA): WO AP/46, Operation Keynote.

Published material

Anders, Władysław, *Bez Ostatniego Rozdziału* (Warszawa: Bellona, 2007).
Anders, Władysław, *An Army in Exile* (Nashville: Battery Press, 1949).
Banulski, Zygmunt (ed.), *Wojsko Polskie w Drugiej Wojnie Światowej* (Warszawa: Bellona, 1994).

Bobińska, Anna, *Pomocnicza Wojskowa Służba Kobiet 2 Korpusu 1941–1945* (*Warszawa*: Krupski i S-ka, 1999).

Briggs, Susan, *Keep Smiling Through*, (London: Weidenfeld and Nicolson, 1975).

Brodecki, Bogusław, Wawer, Zbigniew and Kondracki, Tadeusz, *Polacy na Frontach II Wojny Światowej – Poles on the battlefronts of the Second World War* (Warszawa: Bellona, 2005).

Ciechanowski, Jan and Suchcitz, Andrzej (eds.), *General Władysław Sikorski: Poland's Wartime Leader* (London: Polish Institute and Sikorski Museum, 2007).

Cieślewicz, Stanisław, *Diary of a Carpathian Soldier 1939–1947 Dziennik Karpatczyka 1939–1947* (Self-published: Lulu 2009).

Conway, Martin and Gotovitch, José (eds.), *Europe in Exile: European Exile Communities in Britain 1940–45* (Oxford: Berghahn Books, 2001).

Davies, Norman, *Trail of Hope* (Oxford: Osprey Publishing, 2015)

Fenby, Jonathan, *Alliance* (London: Simon and Schuster, 2006).

Gallehawk, J, *Some Polish Contributions in the Second World War* (Report No 15 Bletchley Park Trust, 1999).

Hope, M, *Polish Deportees in the Soviet Union* (Dublin: Veritas, 2000).

Kisielewski, Tadeusz, *Po Zamachu* (Poznan: Rebis, 2012).

Kondracki, Tadeusz, *Historia Stowarzyszenia Polskich Kombatantów w Wielkiej Brytanii, (SPK)* (Londyn: Zarząd Głowny SPK w Wielkiej Brytanii,1996).

Malcher, G, *Blank Pages* (Woking: Pyrford Press, 1993).

Młotek, Mieczysław (ed.), *Trzecia Dywizja Strzelców Karpackich, 1942–1947, Tom I*, (London: Zarząd Główny Związku Karpatczyków, 1978).

Nanke Eryk, *Cena Bycia Innym* (Kraków: Biblioteka Centrum Dokumentacji Czynu Niepodległościowego, 2000).

Pietrzak, Jacek, *Polscy Uchodzcy na Bliskim Wschodzie* (Lódz: Wydawnictwo Uniwersytetu Lódzkiego, 2012).

Plokhy, S M. *Yalta, The Price of Peace* (Viking, New York 2010).

Prażmowska, A, *Britain and Poland, 1939–1943* (Cambridge: Cambridge University Press, 1995).

Pylat, J, Ciechanowski, J and Suchcitz, A (Eds.), *General Władisław Anders* (London: Polish University Abroad, 2008).

Radice, Giles (ed.), *What Needs to Change, New Visions for Britain* (London: Harper Collins, 1996).

Sebestyen, Victor, *1946: The Making of the Modern World* (London: Macmillan, 2014).

Stachura, P, (ed.), *The Poles in Britain 1940–2000* (London: Frank Cass, 2004).

Sword, Keith with Davies, Norman and Ciechanowski, Jan, *The Formation of the Polish Community in Great Britain 1939–1950* (London: School of Slavonic and East European Studies, University of London, 1989).

Suchcitz, Andrzej, *The Polish Ex-Combatant Association in Great Britain 1946–2003* (London: The Polish Ex-Combatant Association in Great Britain, 2003).

Sword, Keith, *Identity in Flux* (London: School of Slavonic and East European Studies, University of London, 1996).

Szczerbiński, M and Wolszy, T Z (eds.), *Z Dziejów Polski i Emigracji 1939–1989* (Gorzów: Instytut Kultury Fizycznej Poznański, AWF w Gorzowie 2003).

Williamson, David, *Poland Betrayed* (Barnsley: Pen and Sword Books, 2009).

Zaluski, Z, *Poles on the Fronts of the Second World War* (Warsaw: Interpress 1972).

Zamoyski, Adam, *Poland, A History* (London: Harper Press, 2009).
Zamoyski, Adam, *Warsaw 1920: Lenin's Failed Conquest of Europe* (London: Harper Press, 2008).

Index

2nd Polish Corps 94–95, 167

Acheson 36
Admiralty 75–76, 121
Aftermath Liaison Section 162, 164–165, 169, 171
Aliens Act 84, 181
Aliens Order 83, 158
Amalgamated Engineering Union 137, 139
Anders, General 31–32, 43, 45–46, 50, 54–57, 59–61, 63–64, 106, 115, 146, 164, 187
Anglo-Polish Alliance xii
Army Council 61
Army Education Scheme 64
Army Test 125
Arnhem 180
Assistance Allowance Board 67
Atlantic Charter 33, 38, 40, 188
Atlantic, Battle of the 20, 33, 38, 40, 166, 188
ATS 61, 75, 77, 79, 125, 157
Attlee, Clement xii, xiv, 40–41, 43
Austria 28, 34, 42, 94, 104

Baltic States 30, 33
BAOR 42, 167
Beck, Józef 19, 21
Belarus 42
Belgrade 60, 172
Berlin 20, 22, 25, 27, 30, 43, 116
Bevin, Ernest 43, 45–46, 49–50, 54–55, 58–65, 137–140, 143, 162
Blomfield, Major 168
Board of Education 64, 68
Bomber Command 33
Britain xii–xiii, 19–28, 30–35, 38–41, 43–47, 49–61, 63–68, 75, 78, 81, 83–84, 86–87, 93–94, 96–98, 101, 104–107, 111–113, 121, 124–126, 128, 135–137, 142–147, 149–150, 153, 162–163, 166–168, 170–173, 178, 180–182, 184, 188–190, 192, 196–200, 202–203
Britain, Battle of xii–xiii, 19–28, 30–35, 38–41, 43–47, 49–61, 63–68, 75, 78, 81, 83–84, 86–87, 93–94, 96–98, 101, 104–107, 111–113, 121, 124–126, 128, 135–137, 142–147, 149–150, 153, 162–163, 166–168, 170–173, 178, 180–182, 184, 188–190, 192, 196–200, 202–203
British 8th Army 32, 42
British Medical Council 68
British Safe Havens 32, 150, 173
Brown, William 39

Bucharest 23, 27, 34
Budapest 27, 34
Cambridge Proficiency Certificate in English 124
Camp, Service, Reception, Repatriation, Emigration, Families, Holding 46, 52, 80–84, 87–89, 94, 97, 104, 112, 118, 121–122, 126, 135, 158, 165–166, 169–170, 181–182, 187, 190–192
Canadian troops 80
Canadian Government 51
Carrot Scheme 134
Category E Personnel 57
Central Pool of Artists 98
Chamberlain, Neville 19, 111
Chile 51
Churchill's Pledge 41, 43, 46
Cicho Ciemni (Polish Special Forces) 66
Clayton, General 20–21
Cold War 34, 184
Command Structure 56–57, 63, 115, 118–120
Committee for the Education of Poles 124, 126, 136
Conditions of Service 56, 58, 63, 69, 71, 73, 75, 77–78
Czechoslovakia 34

Davidson, Lieutenant 20
D-Day 93
Dependants 49, 52, 57–59, 65–66, 82–84, 86–87, 121–123, 149, 173, 180–181, 188
Disabled Persons' Employment Corporation 180
discharge of Polish forces 162
Discharge 34, 65, 96, 106–107, 113, 133, 136, 157–164, 166, 169, 173–174
dispersal centres 157–158
Domański, Lieutenant 167
Dominican Republic 51
Dublin University 126
Dunkirk 27

Eastern Germany 34
Eastern Poland 22–23, 29, 31, 49, 77, 116
Education 64–65, 68, 86–87, 101, 115, 124, 126, 136, 181, 183–184, 191, 199
Education, Committee for the Education of Poles 64–65, 68, 86–87, 101, 115, 124, 126, 136, 181, 183–184, 191, 199
Egypt 46
El Alamein 28
Emigration 49–52, 54, 58, 82, 158, 162–163, 167, 197
Enigma Code 28

INDEX 209

Ergemont Duke Schomberg Temperance Orange Lodge No. 486 142
Estonia 22, 34

Fieldorf 113
Finland 22, 30, 33
First Armoured Division 42
Foreign Office 49–52, 54, 106, 137–142, 166–168
France 20–28, 33, 50, 53, 59, 66, 93–97, 106 112, 115–116, 167
Freedom and Independence organisation 145

Gdańsk 19
German Army 71
German Forces 20, 27, 36, 116
Germany xii, 19–23, 25, 28, 30, 32–34, 40, 42–43, 46–48, 54, 56, 63, 71, 78, 80, 84, 93–94, 100, 104–106, 143, 146, 197–198
Government of National Unity 39–40, 44, 48, 61, 166
Greece 34, 42
Guatemala 51
Guest, Dr, MP 38

His Majesty's Government xii, 32, 45–46, 54, 58 60, 66, 83, 131, 170, 172, 197
Hitler, Adolf 19, 22–23, 25, 27, 33, 111
Holland 50
Home Army 61, 77–78, 145–146
Home Commands 56, 63, 93, 98, 109, 122, 164, 170
Home Office 106, 144, 150, 167–168, 183, 186
Hostels 68, 83–86, 126, 173, 181, 184–185, 187, 191
Housing Estates 85–86, 181
Hungary 23, 26–27, 34

Independence and Democracy 146
India 32, 83, 181
Inter-Governmental Committee for Refugees 49–51
Interim Treasury Committee 44, 64, 121–122
Iron Curtain xiv, 34–35, 143, 172, 182, 197
Iżycki, Air Vice Marshal 54, 61

Japan 36, 198

Katski, Captain 168
Katyn 29
Kilmarnock Local Trades Council 140
Kirkcaldy Trade Council 138
Kopański, Lieutenant General 54, 66, 101, 115–116, 151, 164, 170
Korean War 181
Krasiński Museum 167
Kresowy Infantry Division 111
Labour xiii, 28–29, 39, 49–50, 58–60, 64, 68, 80, 84–85, 87, 95, 101, 103, 122, 124–125, 127, 130–131, 133–134, 136, 153, 158–159, 173–174, 180, 187, 197
Land Army 20, 78
Lane, Arthur Bliss 36
Latvia 22, 34
League of Nations 34
Lithuania 22–23, 34
Lloyd, Major 39–40
London Trades Council 139
Low Countries 20, 93
Lublin 40
Lwów 115
Lyne, Major General 55–57

Maczek, General 54, 164
Manchester and Salford Trades Council 138
Manningham-Buller 40 (has a hyphen)
Medical Companies 93
Mental Services 121
MI5 106, 144, 146, 148
MI6 148
Middle East 32, 46, 48, 54, 57, 66, 93–94, 126, 146, 167
Ministry of Defence 80, 87
Ministry of Health 68, 85, 122, 134, 169
Ministry of Labour and National Service 64, 68, 103, 130, 158–159, 180
Ministry of Labour 59, 64, 68, 85, 87, 95, 101, 103, 122, 124, 127, 130–131, 133–134, 158–159, 173–174, 180
Ministry of Pensions 122, 134, 150, 169, 180
Molotov, Vyacheslav 19, 22–23, 30
Molotov-Ribbentrop Agreement 22–23
Monte Cassino 95, 112
Morgan 39, 57
Moscow xii, 22–23, 25, 30–31, 35, 42, 148, 198
Munich Agreement 19

Naples 59, 94
National Armed Forces (NSZ) 145–146
National Assistance Board 85, 149–150, 157, 173, 180, 202
National Health Service 85, 123, 182
National Registration Identity Card 159
National Unity 39–40, 44, 48, 61, 166
Naval Wing 48, 75, 77, 118, 136
Nazi Germany xii, 22, 33, 100
News Chronicle 25
Nissen huts 80, 180, 187

Operation Barbarossa 30–31

Palestine 28, 32, 46, 95, 116
Parliament 21, 38–39, 105, 131
Petherick, Maurice, MP 40

Phoney War 23, 25, 33
Poland xii, xiv, 19–23, 25–36, 38–49, 51–52, 54–55, 58–61, 64, 75, 77–78, 82–83, 104, 115–116, 125, 136, 143–146, 150, 163, 166–168, 170–173, 181–182, 184, 186, 188–190, 196–198, 202
Poland, Invasion of xii, xiv, 19–23, 25–36, 38–49, 51–52, 54–55, 58–61, 64, 75, 77–78, 82–83, 104, 115–116, 125, 136, 143–146, 150, 163, 166–168, 170–173, 181–182, 184, 186, 188–190, 196–198, 202
Poles, Federation of xii, xiv, 19–21, 23, 25, 27–33, 35–41, 43–44, 46–52, 54, 57–60, 63–68, 78, 80–81, 83–85, 87, 104–105, 111–112, 121, 123–126, 128–130, 133–134, 136–137, 142–146, 153, 157, 159, 162, 167–168, 170–174, 178–182, 188–192, 196–199, 201–202
Polish 2nd Corps xiv, 32, 45–46, 54, 56, 59–60, 64, 77, 93–95, 166, 172
Polish Airforce 66, 192, 199, 201
Polish Allied Forces xiii–xiv, 28, 49, 58, 66, 68, 80, 98, 172, 188, 197
Polish Armed Forces 29, 48, 51, 64, 71, 77, 81, 113, 137, 140, 192
Polish Army Records 112
Polish cadet schools 64, 91, 124
Polish Corridor 19, 22
Polish Daily 84, 98, 184
Polish Ex-Combatants' Association 153
Polish Forces Official Committee 122
Polish Government of National Unity 44, 48, 61
Polish Government xii, 21–24, 26–27, 30–32, 35, 39–42, 44, 48, 57, 61, 78, 116, 121, 166–168, 170
Polish High Command 23, 32, 35, 37, 44–45, 54, 59–60, 66, 77, 115
Polish Land Forces 66, 69–70, 73, 93, 122–123, 167
Polish military hospitals 46, 121–122, 182
Polish Navy 24, 26, 75, 113, 122
Polish Records Office 102–104, 107, 112, 166
Polish Resettlement Act 65–68, 85, 122, 134, 149
Polish Resettlement Bill 62, 65
Polish Resettlement Corps xiii, xv, 44, 54, 61, 63–64, 66, 68–69, 71, 73, 75, 77–78, 81–84, 93, 95–96, 101–105, 107–110, 113–116, 118–119, 121–129, 131, 133–134, 136, 143–146, 148–151, 153, 157–160, 162, 164–165, 167–173, 180, 182, 187–189, 191–192, 196–197, 202–203
Polish Resettlement Trust 150, 152
Polish Saturday Schools 185
Polish Theatrical Bureau 185
Polish University Abroad 185
Polish Women's Auxiliary Service 60, 77, 95
post-traumatic stress disorder 149
Potsdam Conference 39, 42, 55
Prague 34
Price, Morgan Philips, MP xiv, 22, 30, 34, 39

Raczyński, Edward 21, 44
Radio Free Europe 184
RAF 20, 27, 53, 61, 66, 78, 93
Rawlings, Commander 20
Recalcitrant 84, 104–106, 169
Red Army xii, 19, 23, 29–37, 39, 42, 77, 181, 197–198
Regimental Paymaster 159
Remploy 133, 180
Repatriation 42, 46–49, 51–52, 58, 68, 78, 80–82, 105, 158, 162–163, 167, 172, 197–198
Resettlement in Britain 101, 173
Rhodesia 32, 83, 181
Riga 34
Romania 23, 26, 34, 116
Roosevelt, Franklin D 34, 36, 42
Royal Navy 27, 75, 80
Rudnicki, General 54, 164
Russian Army 36, 115

Savery, Professor 64
Second Polish Republic 23
Security Services 147
September Campaign 26, 28
Siberia 29
Sikorski Institute 112–113, 167–168
Sikorski, General xiii, 27, 30–32, 59, 112–113, 153–154, 167–168, 201
SOE 66, 78
Sofia 34
South Africa 32, 52
South America xiv, 51, 145, 197
Soviet Army xiii
Soviet Union xii, 19–20, 22, 25, 30–34, 39, 43, 55, 77, 116, 146, 172, 189, 197–198, 202
SPK 147, 171, 185, 192–196
St. Nicholas' Day 190
Stalin, Joseph xii, 19, 22–23, 25, 29–31, 33–34, 39, 42, 44, 60, 198
Świrski, Vice-Admiral 54, 60, 164

Teheran 33, 197
Tobruk 28, 32, 116
Trade Unions 58, 60, 124, 128, 130, 162
TUC 142

Ukraine 34, 42, 115
Unemployed Assistance Act 1934 68
Union of Polish Craftsman and Workers Association 185
United Nations 34, 54, 104, 144, 149, 172
United States xiv, 50, 53, 153, 170
Unseen and Unheard 66
untermensch 28
Vatican City 184
Victory Parade 202

Vilnius 34
Vocational Training 64, 124–126, 134, 169–170
War Office xiii, 45–47, 55–58, 61, 64, 66–67, 69, 71,
    75, 78, 80–81, 84–85, 87, 93, 95, 98, 101–107,
    112, 117–118, 121–122, 124, 127–129, 131,
    133–134, 136, 157, 159, 162–167, 169–171, 173,
    180, 182, 188
Warsaw Pact 42
Warsaw xii, 20–23, 25–28, 32, 34, 38, 42, 44, 48, 55,
    57, 61, 64, 104, 106, 113, 115, 144, 148, 166–168,
    170, 173, 181, 197
Washington 42, 50
West Germany 34, 42, 46–47
Willoughby de Eresby, Major Lord 39
Winston Churchill xii, 19, 27
Władysława Piechowska 77

Yalta xii, 33–35, 38–43, 144, 146, 150, 185, 197
YMCA 57, 153
Yugoslavia 60, 172
Yukon Huts 80

Zakrewski, Dr 122